THE REVE

Founder Editor, 195
General Editors: F. David H
and J. R.

BUSSY D'AMBOIS

Portrait of Chapman from *The Whole Works of Homer* (1616)

Bussy D'Ambois

GEORGE CHAPMAN

EDITED BY

NICHOLAS BROOKE

THE REVELS PLAYS

MANCHESTER
UNIVERSITY PRESS

This edition first published by Methuen & Co. 1964
Reprinted by Manchester University Press in paper covers 1979

Manchester University Press
Oxford Road, Manchester M13 9PL
ISBN 0 7190 1616 9

Printed in Great Britain by
Whitstable Litho Ltd., Whitstable, Kent

This edition of Chapman's play is dedicated

To PAMELA

and to our children,

who know now, as Hamlet never did,
that an Elizabethan ghost is nothing but a devil

General Editor's Preface

The Revels Plays began to appear in 1958, and in the General Editor's Preface included in the first few volumes the plan of the series was briefly sketched. All those concerned in the undertaking recognized that no rigid pattern could be proposed in advance: to some extent the collective experience of the editors would affect the series as it developed, and the textual situation was by no means uniform among the plays that we hoped to include. The need for flexibility is still recognized, and each editor indicates in his introduction the procedures that have seemed best in relation to his particular play.

Nevertheless, we were fairly convinced that in some matters our policy would remain constant, and no major change in any of these respects has been made. The introduction to each volume includes a discussion of the provenance of the text, the play's stage-history and reputation, its significance as a contribution to dramatic literature, and its place within the work of its author. The text is based on a fresh examination of the early editions. Modern spelling is used, archaic forms being preserved only when rhyme or metre demands them or when a modernized form would not give the required sense or would obscure a play upon words. The procedure adopted in punctuation varies to some extent according to the degree of authority which an editor can attribute to the punctuation of the copy-text, but in every instance it is intended that the punctuation used in a Revels volume should not obscure a dramatic or rhetorical suggestiveness which may be discerned in the copy. Editorial stage-directions are enclosed in square brackets. The collation aims at making clear the grounds for an editor's choice wherever the original or a frequently accepted modern reading has been departed from. Annotations attempt to explain difficult passages and to provide such comments and illustrations of usage as the editor considers desirable.

When the series was planned, it was intended that each volume should include a glossary. At an early stage, however, it was realized that this would mean either an arbitrary distribution of material between the glossary and the annotations or a duplication of material. It has therefore become our practice to dispense with a glossary but to include an index to the annotations, which avoids duplication and facilitates reference.

Act-divisions are employed if they appear in the copy-text or if the structure of the play clearly points to a five-act division. In other instances, only scene-numbers are inserted. All act- and scene-indications which do not derive from the copy-text are given unobtrusively in square brackets. In no instance is an editorial indication of locality introduced into a scene-heading. When an editor finds it necessary to comment on the location of a scene, this is done in the annotations.

The series continues to use the innovation in line-numbering that was introduced in the first volume. Stage-directions which occur on lines separate from the text are given the number of the immediately preceding line followed by a decimal point and 1, 2, 3, etc. Thus 163.5 indicates the fifth line of a stage-direction following line 163 of the scene. At the beginning of a scene the lines of a stage-direction are numbered 0.1, 0.2, etc.

The Revels Plays have begun with the re-editing of a number of the best-known tragedies and comedies of the later Elizabethan and Jacobean years, and there are many such plays to which the techniques of modern editing need to be applied. It is hoped, however, that the series will be able to include certain lesser-known plays which remain in general neglect despite the lively interest that an acquaintance with them can arouse.

It has always been in the forefront of attention that the plays included should be such as deserve and indeed demand performance. The editors have therefore given a record (necessarily incomplete) of modern productions; in the annotations there is, moreover, occasional conjecture on the way in which a scene or a piece of stage-business was done on the original stage. Perhaps, too, the absence of indications of locality and of editorial scene-headings will suggest the advantage of achieving in a modern theatre some approach to the characteristic fluidity of scene and the neutrality of acting-space that Shakespeare's fellows knew.

CLIFFORD LEECH

Toronto, 1963

Contents

Illustrations

Preface

The editorial matter for *Bussy D'Ambois* is bulkier than in previous Revels Plays, for two reasons. First, the existence of two distinct versions necessitates a very full collation; second, the complexities of Chapman's writing demand rather heavy commentary. I have tried to be as economical as possible, without failing to provide appropriate information. The textual problem also demands fairly full discussion in the Introduction, but here a convenient lack of information on source material helps to preserve the proportions, and so there is a fair space available for critical discussion of the play; though still less than I should like.

An editor must always owe much to his predecessors: thus I would acknowledge my large debts to Professors F. S. Boas and T. M. Parrott. I have also been particularly indebted to Parrott's editions of the other plays, to Phyllis Bartlett's edition of the poems, and to Allardyce Nicoll's edition of the Homeric translations. In the labour of consulting copies of the play in British libraries I was assisted by the Research Fund of the Durham Colleges in the University of Durham, and by the courtesy of the Librarians whose copies are listed in Appendix C. I should especially like to thank Mr Philip Grierson of Gonville and Caius College, Cambridge, who arranged for a copy to be at my disposal in Durham; and Mr Neville Collinge, of the Department of Classics at Durham, who did his best to save me from blunders in handling the Latin material in play and appendix. Professor Peter Ure of King's College, Newcastle, lent me valuable materials; the Introduction will show my debt to his published work on Chapman.

Mrs Barbara Rossiter very kindly sent me all that she could find of the late A. P. Rossiter's notes on Chapman: these include parts of a lecture course on his plays, notes for an extremely interesting lecture on the Machiavel figure in Jacobean drama, and fragments of a projected article on the *Bussy* texts. This last shows that, as he once told me, Rossiter had come to believe that the revision was Chapman's work, despite some aspects of the 1641 text which seemed to him comparable to 'bad quartos'. From this material I have drawn several valuable points which can only be generally acknowledged here. Others who, like myself, enjoyed the great delight of being a pupil of Rossiter's, will recognize his influence, however inadequately represented, throughout my Introduction: that is a debt which can never be adequately acknowledged.

The preparation of this edition has been held up for various reasons, and I have good cause to value the General Editor's patience; but he has also endured a steady fire of questions (some of them all too rhetorical), and I am warmly grateful for the care with which he has encouraged, scrutinized, and corrected every part of this volume, whilst leaving a large, possibly too large, discretion to me. Miss Newland Smith of the Broadwater Press has been most helpfully vigilant in detecting my errors.

I should also like to thank my wife, and our son James, for their help with the dull work of proof-correcting and indexing.

Eugene M. Waith's *The Herculean Hero in Marlowe, Chapman, Shakespeare and Dryden* (1962) unfortunately reached me too late to be made use of here.

NICHOLAS BROOKE

Norwich, 1963

Abbreviations

Abbott	E. A. Abbott, *A Shakespearian Grammar*, 1869.
Ferguson	A. S. Ferguson, 'The Plays of George Chapman', *M.L.R.* XIII, 1918, 1–22.
O.E.D.	*Oxford English Dictionary.*
Schoell	F. L. Schoell, *Etudes sur l'Humanisme Continental en Angleterre à la Fin de la Renaissance*, Paris, 1926.
Tilley	M. P. Tilley, *A Dictionary of the Proverbs in England in the Sixteenth and Seventeenth Centuries*, Ann Arbor, 1950.
Ure	Peter Ure, 'Chapman's "Tragedy of Bussy D'Ambois": Problems of the Revised Quarto', *M.L.R.* XLVIII, 1953, 257–69.
Wieler	J. W. Wieler, *George Chapman—The Effect of Stoicism upon his Tragedies*, New York, 1949.
Wing	D. Wing, *Short-title catalogue of books printed . . . 1641–1700*, New York, 1945–51.

PERIODICALS

ELH	*English Literary History.*
H.L.Q.	*Huntington Library Quarterly.*
J.E.G.P.	*Journal of English and Germanic Philology.*
M.L.Q.	*Modern Language Quarterly.*
M.L.R.	*Modern Language Review.*
M.P.	*Modern Philology.*
N. & Q.	*Notes and Queries.*

S.P.	*Studies in Philology.*
T.L.S.	*Times Literary Supplement.*

Quotations and line numbers for Chapman's works are from:

Tragedies, ed. T. M. Parrott, 1910.

Comedies, ed. T. M. Parrott, 1914.

Poems, ed. P. B. Bartlett, 1941.

Homer, ed. A. Nicoll, 1957, I *Iliads* (1616: earlier versions are referred to by date, e.g., 1598).
II *Odysses and the lesser Homerica.*

Abbreviations for Shakespeare's plays are those used in Onions, *A Shakespeare Glossary*; quotations and line-numbers are from the Oxford Shakespeare.

MODERN EDITIONS OF *BUSSY D'AMBOIS*

Dilke (D in collation)	C. W. Dilke, *Old English Plays*, 1814.
Pearson	*The Comedies and Tragedies of George Chapman*, vol. II, John Pearson, 1873.
Shepherd	R. H. Shepherd, *The Works of George Chapman*, vol. I: *Plays*, 1874.
Phelps	W. L. Phelps, The Mermaid Series, *George Chapman*, 1895.
Boas (Bo in collation)	F. S. Boas, The Belles-Lettres Series, *Bussy D'Ambois* and *The Revenge of Bussy D'Ambois*, 1905.
Neilson	W. A. Neilson, *The Chief Elizabethan Dramatists*, 1911.
Parrott (P in collation)	T. M. Parrott, *The Plays and Poems of George Chapman*, vol. I: *Tragedies*, 1910.
Brooke and Paradise (T in collation)	C. F. Tucker Brooke and N. B. Paradise, *English Drama 1580–1642*, Boston, 1933.

Spencer	Hazelton Spencer, *Elizabethan Plays*, 1934.
Baskervill etc.	C. R. Baskervill, V. B. Heltzel, A. H. Nethercot, *Elizabethan and Stuart Plays*, New York, 1934.
McIlwraith	A. K. McIlwraith, The World's Classics, *Five Stuart Tragedies*, 1953.
Jacquot	J. Jacquot, Collection Bilingue des Classiques Etrangers, *Bussy D'Amboise*, Paris, 1960.

Introduction

1. CHAPMAN'S CAREER, 1559–1634

Chapman is generally known today, if at all, as the translator of Homer whose work Keats looked into. Students who have been made aware that he was also an original poet and dramatist commonly think of him as a contorted and obscure writer of unquestioned, but also unattractive, elevation; and the obscurity seems wilful in the notoriously irascible defensiveness of his outbursts against his contemporaries (who took revenge, to his chagrin, by revealing that his Homer depended too heavily on Latin translations and glosses). It is unquestionably true that Chapman seldom underloads his work, whereas he often fails by overloading; yet he is one of those obviously difficult poets whose work really does repay attention. For the truth is that he was a fundamentally serious man of unquestionable talent and intelligence, who struggled throughout his work (including the Homer) to create a comprehensive image of the *quality* of human life. This consistent concern is manifest in almost all his writings, serious and trivial alike (juxtaposition of the two is characteristic of him), which are therefore unusually closely related to each other; much as the novels of D. H. Lawrence seem to grow each out of its predecessor, and for a similar reason. And like Lawrence, Chapman has seemed tedious and offensive to idle and prejudiced readers; humourless to lovers of triviality. Whereas in fact both authors frequently worked very successfully through comedy, and with Chapman one aspect of his complexity is an interfusion of the serious in the trivial, the profound in the absurd.

For the theatre, in fact, all Chapman's early work that survives is light comedy (Meres listed him in 1598 for tragedy, and Henslowe paid him in the same year for a tragedy 'on Benjamin's plot'; nothing survives of this). Six comedies apparently written between

1595 and 1605 survive, starting with the very successful (at least for Henslowe) farce *The Blind Beggar of Alexandria* and developing through the lightly moralized Plautine intrigues of *May Day* into the sophisticated amalgam of romance with 'humours' comedy in which Chapman has been claimed as Jonson's precursor. The priority is neither clear nor important, and a closer parallel is perhaps with *Twelfth Night*, though Chapman did not share Shakespeare's taste for transvestism. I do not think he ever achieved a complete success in this genre, but there is no question of the quality of some parts: in *The Gentleman Usher*, the romance is fully and impressively developed as an expression of the platonized sensuality of Chapman's early poems, linked to the idea of royal integrity in the 'natural man' which dominates the tragedies; but the humours are relatively weak. With *Monsieur D'Olive* the case is reversed: D'Olive himself is brilliantly presented as the type of courtly fop of ludicrous self-confidence that became a commonplace figure of Restoration comedy; but here the romance is perfunctory. *The Widow's Tears*, which may be slightly later in date, is a neatly sardonic handling of the Widow of Ephesus story, exposing the façade of conventional moral respectability and the sheer nastiness inherent in social ambition. Chapman also had a hand in *Eastward Ho!* (1605), written with Jonson and Marston; it seems strange enough that three such men should have collaborated at all, extraordinary that they should have turned out between them an excellent city comedy; but the final irony was that they were imprisoned for a merely commonplace libel on James I's Scottish entourage.

Neo-Platonism offered the late sixteenth century the best possibility of reconciling the complexities of experience, the conflicting demands of passion and reason, treating the mutability of sensual experience as symbolic of permanent realities; its presence is lightly felt in Chapman's comedies, but dominates the three important poems he produced in the 1590's. *The Shadow of Night* consists of two very different parts, *Hymnus in Noctem* and *Hymnus in Cynthiam.* The first is an extravagantly witty poem evolving its (semi-serious) ideas out of a series of paradoxes, of which the centre is the concept of Night as a oneness of perfection (symbolized in sexual love), a unity which is broken down into cold separateness by daylight. The same idea is pursued more seriously in the Hymn to Cynthia, a far more accomplished poem whose sexuality goes deep enough to explain the solemn perplexity with which it has usually been approached: the Platonic idea of intellectual contemplation which it promulgates (in the figure of Endymion) springs from the *pursuit* of sexual experience indefinitely prolonged, so as to preclude the supposed inadequacy of 'satisfaction'. The obscurity of the poem needs the defence which Chapman uttered most impressively in his letter *To Harriots* prefacing *Achilles' Shield* (1598), his first effort at translating Homer:

O had your perfect eye Organs to pierce
Into that Chaos whence this stiffled verse
By violence breakes: where Gloweworme like doth shine
In nights of sorrow, this hid soule of mine:
And how her genuine formes struggle for birth,
Vnder the clawes of this fowle Panther earth;
Then vnder all those formes you should discerne
My loue to you, in my desire to learne. (ll. 41–8)

Ovid's Banquet of Sense carried a similar defence, less movingly (and more arrogantly) expressed in the prose dedication to Matthew Roydon: 'Obscuritie in affection of words, & indigested concets, is pedanticall and childish; but where it shroudeth it selfe in the hart of his subiect, vtterd with fitnes of figure, and expressiue Epethites; with that darknes wil J still labour to be shadowed: rich Minerals are digd out of the bowels of the earth, not found in the superficies and dust of it' (ll. 29–34). The poem itself is far better controlled than *The Shadow of Night*, and far less obscure; it seems to me one of the finest in the Elizabethan erotic tradition. Ovidian irony balances Platonic mysticism, but the theme is not greatly different: Ovid climbs a wall to see Corinna preparing to bathe in her garden, and records a highly formalized sequence of experience through the responses of each sense in turn, leading towards the climax of Touch. As in the earlier poem, the coitus is deferred, but here there is no question of ultimate perversion in the witty conclusion:

Ouid well knew there was much more intended,
With whose omition none must be offended.

Harriots and Roydon were both associated with the group of free-thinkers to whom Raleigh (for whom Chapman wrote *De Guiana* in 1596) played host, and of whom Marlowe was the most distinguished and the most indiscreet member. It is clear that Marlowe was not only a friend of Chapman's, but a very potent influence on all his work from his early poems to his later tragedies; and even his classical translations may owe something to Marlowe's experiments with Ovid and Lucan. The association was closest in Chapman's completion of Marlowe's *Hero and Leander*; Chapman is both serious and witty, but Marlowe's extraordinary adroitness exposes any relative clumsiness in the sequel.

Chapman, like Spenser (in the Mutabilitie cantos) and Donne, seems gradually to have lost confidence in the Neo-Platonic synthesis: in *Bussy*, passion is still a central stress in the idea of a 'complete man'; but there is antithesis much more than synthesis. Subsequently, the dominant influence is rather the Latin Stoics: *Bussy* and *Byron* both contain translated passages from Plutarch's *Moralia* and Seneca's plays; *The Revenge of Bussy* (?1610–11) is heavily indebted to Epictetus, whose influence Chapman had already presented in the admirable poem, *The Teares of Peace* (1609) (see Schoell and Wieler[1]). The devotion to symbolic theory continued to influence his poetry, and emerges in the claims to visionary 'inspiration' with which he defended his Homer in *The Teares of Peace*. Inspiration is an embarrassing idea, but it provides for Chapman both a claim to the distinctive significance of all great poetry, and an explanation of his relative independence as a translator. He is capable (allowing for blunders) of good literal translation, but his epics are essentially a re-creation. Homer is interpreted and moralized in the texture of the verse, and so the evolution of the *Iliads* and *Odysses* lies intelligibly alongside the development of the tragedies from *Bussy* to *Chabot*. Achilles was Chapman's first heroic figure, a 'man of wrath' defying the pettiness of politicians with a heroic vaunt like Marlowe's Tamburlaine, and Chapman's own Bussy; like both of these he has strong affinities with the type-figure of Hercules. Chapman's admiration for the stature and god-like independence of the man is magnificently indicated, but it was

[1] For abbreviated references, see list of Abbreviations, pp. xv–xvii.

never unequivocal. In *To Harriots* (1598) he contrasts true Learning (a quality of the complete man) not only to 'formall Clearkes / Blowne for profession' (e.g., academic editors) but also to 'ignorants like *Hercules*'. The 'ignorance' of Achilles—his boorish stupidity—was always made plain, but increasingly plainer as the work progressed, especially in the final revisions for the complete *Iliads* of 1611. So finally a preference emerges for Odysseus, in whom Chapman stresses not so much Shakespeare's dog-fox as a quality of heroic endurance against the sustained attacks of the gods.

Thus in the tragedies, Bussy is explicitly associated with Hercules, and, like Achilles', his magnificent wrath is apt to boorishness; yet it was not until the much later sequel, *The Revenge of Bussy D'Ambois*, that he was explicitly accused of lacking Learning, and so contrasted with his (unhistorical) brother Clermont the Senecal man, the proponent of Stoic endurance who ultimately prefers suicide to submission to tyranny (like Cato in *Caesar and Pompey*). But Clermont is himself equivocally presented: he is not so obviously heroic as Odysseus, and Chapman's devotion to Stoicism still had to co-exist with the heroic quality of virtù: so the ghost of Bussy rises and prods Clermont to the revenge from which his reluctance is partly conscience and partly personal inadequacy.

'Learning', which has undergone a change of meaning between the two Bussy plays, is a key-word of Chapman's, developing with his idea of the 'complete man'. It relates, for him, to the whole experience of man and so is broader than Bacon's use in *The Advancement of Learning*, far broader than any modern use. In *Bussy*, v. iii. 38, it appears as one of the qualities of greatness: 'Young, learned, valiant, virtuous, and full mann'd'; but in *The Revenge* it is the central quality which includes others. In between, *The Teares of Peace* is largely concerned to expound the term. It grew out of the function commonly ascribed to Reason in the Renaissance:

> . . . this is Learning; To have skill to throwe
> Reignes on your bodies powres, that nothing knowe;
> And fill the soules powers, so with act, and art,
> That she can curbe the bodies angrie part . . . (ll. 504–7)

But whereas Reason is an innate faculty, Learning is acquired from experience of life, and only secondarily of books. Hence the man of learning is distinguished from 'active' (violently ambitious), 'passive' (self-indulgently useless), and 'intellective' men:

> And let a Scoller, all earths volumes carrie,
> He will be but a walking dictionarie:
> A meere articulate Clocke, that doth but speake
> By others arts; when wheeles weare, or springs breake,
> Or any fault is in him; hee can mend
> No more then clockes . . . (ll. 530–5)

Learning is a positive seen against all these negatives, and it is more than the sum of separate virtues; it represents a unity of indistinguishable parts. By this time, in short, it is used to define the final version of the 'complete man':

> . . . to direct
> Reason in such an Art, as that it can
> Turne blood to soule, and make both, one calme man.
> (ll. 557–9)

The association with valour has not disappeared, but the stress has shifted towards 'calm'.

In all Chapman's work he makes use of the Greek myth of a Golden Age of self-sufficient men from whom all subsequent history is a decline; the Achilles hero breaks through to some sparks of 'old humanity', and his defiant splendour seems always more attractive than the Stoic's sad acceptance of decline. But psychological realism plays an important part in Chapman's growing dissatisfaction with men of wrath, and the two-part play, *The Conspiracy and Tragedy of Byron* (1607–8), presents, very acutely, the capacity for almost lunatic deception by flatterers and self to which such a type is obviously prone. Thus the passionate search for an image of 'complete man', coupled with a recurrent recognition of his psychological impossibility, yields a series of conflicts of an essentially and profoundly dramatic nature, whose implication is clearly tragic. Some diminution of theatrical vitality in the later plays has often been remarked (and sometimes exaggerated), and most critics find *Bussy D'Ambois* Chapman's finest play. It stands, in the evolution I have sketched, at the richest point of his work, before the early Platonic belief in sensual experience had withered to insignificance (heroines cease to be important in the later plays, though I see no sign of the misogyny which Swinburne charged), and respect for Marlovian virtù had not finally succumbed to Stoic acknowledgement of its futility; the possibilities of life that Chapman observed are at their fullest tension, and the simplifying effects of the will to synthesize are least apparent here. The final point was probably *The Tragedy of Chabot*, though we have only a version prepared by Shirley (tactfully, I should guess): a noble elegy for the inevitable heart-break of a great man in a shabby world.

It is usually assumed that Chapman's work for the stage was done by 1614[1]; *The Whole Works of Homer* is dated 1616, and Chapman produced no major poems thereafter. During the 1620's he added only the apocryphal Homeric poems and some translations of Latin poetry. But his retirement does not seem to have been comfortable; his long friendship with Ben Jonson ended in vituperation, and an old bedevilment of debt continued. He defended himself successfully in a prolonged Chancery suit in 1619–22,[2] but the cause may have kept him in hiding for the previous five years (his patrons, Prince Henry and Somerset, had respectively died and been disgraced). To be sued for debt did not necessarily imply poverty, but he was contrasted with his older brother (who had inherited their father's house at Hitchin), who was found 'sufficient'. Chapman's financial failings seem always to have been compensated by his adroitness at law: he successfully sued in 1608 for return of bonds from an unpleasant character called Wolfall who protested that 'the saide Complainant, whoe att the first beinge a man of verry good parts and expectation, hath sethence verry unadvisedly spent the most parts of his tyme and his estate in ffrutlesse and vayne Poetry'![3] What, apart from borrowing money, Chapman did with the first thirty-five years of his life is no more certain than with Shakespeare. Hitchin was his base throughout his life, and there is enough evidence to make it likely that he served the Sadler family who had

[1] *Chabot* may have been later.

[2] See C. J. Sisson and R. Butman, 'George Chapman, 1612–22: Some New Facts', *M.L.R.* XLVI, 1951, 185–90. The best recent summary of Chapman's biography is in J. Jacquot, *George Chapman*, Paris, 1951.

[3] Cited in J. Robertson, 'The Early Life of George Chapman', *M.L.R.* XL, 1945, 157–65. See also Mark Eccles, 'Chapman's Early Years', *S.P.* XLIII, 1946, 176–93.

an estate there; if so, he *may* have engaged with them in military and diplomatic activity in the Netherlands and France. The title page of the *Homer* declares, round its magnificent engraving of Chapman, that he was aged fifty-seven in 1616, so he is assumed to have been born in or around 1559; he died in London in 1634.

2. *BUSSY D'AMBOIS* (?1604)

The two early versions of the play, printed in 1607 and 1641 respectively, differ considerably from one another; this edition departs from accepted practice in questioning Chapman's responsibility for much of the revision, and preferring (on the whole) the earlier version. The matter is fully discussed in Section 6 of this Introduction; for critical judgement, the difference is chiefly felt in the opening of Act II for the treatment of Tamyra and the theme of sexual passion, and in the sequence of events in Act V which bears on the significance of the dénouement.

(*a*) *The Dramatic Mode*

The play's reputation, at least since Swinburne,[1] has been for a heavy sententious manner, tricked out with Senecan rhetoric, ill-adapted to the theatre for which, we are often told, Chapman had little affection, and less talent. The adjective that has stuck is 'philosophical'; that *Bussy D'Ambois* was one of the most popular stage plays of its day is explained by its revenge formula, its spirits, ghost, trap-door, and so on. The impression given is of a rather quaint junction between sophisticated moralizing and crude melodrama. It is, oddly enough in the circumstances, treated almost invariably with high respect, but it is seldom made to sound attractive. But though this seems to be the commonest opinion, it is certainly not the only one: I review briefly some of the recent critical accounts in Section 3 of this Introduction, and they are bewilderingly varied. Chapman's work is philosophic, essentially undramatic; Chapman is no philosopher, essentially a dramatist; his verse is peculiarly opaque, or it is a transparently clear vehicle of his meaning; his moral position is orthodox Christian, or a Stoic response to the

[1] See p. lvi.

collapse of traditional Christianity. None of these positions is actually absurd, and I recite them here to insinuate the variety of qualities and attitudes that Chapman offers, and thus the nature of the critical problem as I see it: *Bussy D'Ambois* is an unusually complex play, in many respects (I think) a far more coherent achievement than has been realized, but not in any sense that can be reduced to a moral thesis; nevertheless, it is not perfectly integrated, and part of the difficulty of grasping it whole derives from Chapman's failure to bring all his complexities into clear focus. I shall go on to defend the play as brilliantly conceived in dramatic structure, as superbly organized in verse and prose that ranges from the energetically colloquial to the most impressively rhetorical, its flexibility (more or less) appropriately adjusted to the dramatic situation. I am convinced (with all an editor's notorious partiality) that this high praise is justified; yet it needs qualifying: the conflicts of experience and idea suggested are only some of them fully presented, some remain always undeveloped; the flexibility of Chapman's thought and language is often apt to disappear in an inflexibility of rhetorical rhythm—a mannerism which is yet in itself essential to the play's peculiar unity of tone.

I am assuming in this account that some adjustment is needed from the terms 'philosophy' and 'melodrama' as if they were tenor and vehicle. To treat them as such is to miss the development of both drama and dramatic criticism in this century which can best help us to grasp Chapman's achievement. It has become a commonplace that the original impulse to drama was not simply the interplay of individual human characters, but rather the personified presentation of religious and moral concepts, felt as conflicting. Behind Shakespeare's Tragedies, as more obviously behind his Histories, lie the traditions of the Morality play: but with a—very large—difference. *King Lear* explores through all superficies to the fundamental values of life, and to do this it ranges figures very simply distinguishable as 'good' and 'evil'; but there is no simple 'moral' to the play (despite all Edgar's efforts to find one) and the final dénouement is so firmly rooted in experience as opposed to abstraction, that a plot which is far more melodramatic than *Maria Martin* is universally acknowledged to be tragic.

It is hardly tactful to invoke Shakespeare before recommending Chapman: but we can only approach the unfamiliar from the familiar. It is apparent that in *Lear* Shakespeare achieves his universality of theme in part by reviving the structure of a Morality play more fully than in his other tragedies: Marlowe had done the same, even more obviously, in *Dr Faustus*; between the two, both in date (probably) and in structure, lies *Bussy D'Ambois*. This placing is firmly established in the opening scene where the two protagonists, Bussy and Monsieur, declare themselves and their moral functions in successive soliloquies obviously derived from the usage of Morality abstractions. The imitation does not end at the speech, it is carried into the emblematic significance of what we see: '*Enter Bussy D'Ambois, poor*' and '*Enter Monsieur with two Pages*'. The contrast of Poverty and Wealth is enforced in both their speeches:

Buss. Who is not poor, is monstrous; only Need
Gives form and worth to every human seed. (ll. 3–4)

Mons. There is no second place in numerous State
That holds more than a cipher: in a King
All places are contain'd. (ll. 34–6)

It is obvious that one familiar moral theme is being presented in the play, the opposition of humble virtue to corrupt ambition: Bussy ends his first speech:

We must to Virtue for her guide resort,
Or we shall shipwrack in our safest Port. (ll. 32–3)

And at l. 124 he can still say:

I am for honest actions, not for great:
If I may bring up a new fashion,
And rise in Court with virtue, speed his plough.

But by this time, one can no longer comment without remarking that the moral opposition has lost its simplicity: if Bussy is not for great actions, whence comes his impulse to 'rise in Court'? By the end of the speech he has arrived at Marlovian assertion, involving contempt for humility:

Many will say, that cannot rise at all,
Man's first hour's rise, is first step to his fall:

I'll venture that; men that fall low must die,
As well as men cast headlong from the sky. (ll. 136–9)

The familiar moral theme has yielded a no less familiar tragic implication; it is never fully discussed again, yet its presence is always felt, most obviously in Bussy's last solo appearance before his murder, in V. ii: '*Enter Bussy D'Ambois with two Pages*'. Unless we see the emblematic value of Chapman's staging, we shall miss this ironic inversion of the opening scene—Bussy in Monsieur's clothing; miss it because, after I. ii (where it is used to develop court comedy into a serious quarrel), it is scarcely referred to in words at all. This is, in short, an instance of the limited explicitness I have suggested as a criticism of Chapman: other, and more complex, concerns have developed to such proportions that this clearly planned structural theme, though still of vital importance, is given no final utterance at all. Its importance is vital because it insists that Bussy (as he deserts his given standard) is a figure to be criticized as well as admired; and more than that, because also the given standard—humble virtue—is itself questioned, so that in the Ghost's valediction it is Bussy's greatness *more* than his virtue which must cheer 'the aged sky' with 'new sparks of old humanity'. For all the Stoical ideas expressed in the play, the final stress is a positive one, however conscious we are made that it is a matter of sparks and not a steady flame.

Two points can well be made at once: first, that the play is a carefully planned whole; second, that the balance of interests develops in ways that sometimes distort and often obscure the simple evolution of the plan. There is no question of distinguishing between intention and accident (I certainly do not mean that Chapman ever set out to write a simple Morality), but of noting an often surprising difference between superficial simplicity of meaning and actual complexity, which calls for, and richly rewards, unusual alertness in the audience.

(*b*) *The Dramatic Poetry*

The characteristic just noted can be studied in the poetry of the very beginning of the play. Bussy's first speech appears superficially to be a high-flown piece of rhetoric boiling down in the end to no more than a recommendation of humble virtue. But in fact it wanders far from such a simple thought process, becoming more concerned with distinguishing true greatness from false, at the same time as asserting the doubtfulness of *any* true greatness. The initial abstractions indicate the fundamental reach of the play:

> Fortune, not Reason, rules the state of things.

This is the opposition which dominates the choric commentary on Bussy's murder in V. iii. 1–56, extended in the final speeches of Bussy and Friar Comolet. Here it gives an immediate sense of opposed values which is the impulse to dramatic exploration. The generality of this first statement ought to preclude the common idea that the play is 'about' the conflict of the individual and his society: that is felt mainly as a trivial reflection of the corruption of Nature.

The dominance of Fortune becomes immediately grotesque in

> Reward goes backwards, Honour on his head

and the concrete grotesquerie becomes explicit in the next line:

> Who is not poor, is monstrous.

As we arrive on that line we must still see poverty itself as monstrous (lacking Reward and Honour); but simultaneously another strong implication is that poor men are good men; and that is developed in

> only Need
> Gives form and worth to every human seed.

Need means 'poverty'; but a more abstract sense of 'necessity' as distinct from free will is needed to satisfy the sentence: the human seed grows healthily only under sustained discipline. This idea governs the abrupt switch to the other end of the scale which follows:

> As cedars beaten with incessant storms,
> So great men flourish.

Cedars resisting storms are defying circumstances (the necessity of submission) as much as 'great men' stand outside the restrictions of poverty, so that both senses of 'Need' inform these lines and condition the double sense of 'flourish': one may take it as healthy growth withstanding the storms; but it also had the pejorative sense of boastful gesturing, and it is that which is developed in the image of hollow statues which follows. This sort of ambivalence is sustained: poverty does not itself have 'form and worth'; but as soon as we look for richer growth we find only empty braggarts. Hence, in l. 18,

> Man is a torch borne in the wind,

the very opposite of a cedar; but 'torch' was also a common emblem of Reason, and we are immediately switched to contemplating the great seamen who use 'all their powers And skills' *successfully* to 'put a girdle round about the world'. That splendid image of human capacity is itself soon reduced to vulgar arrogance in l. 31:

> As if each private arm would sphere the world

and so we return to the final affirmation of humble virtue. Nothing else has ever been positively recommended; yet it would be absurd to claim that that is simply what the speech is 'about'. Latent throughout is the implication of a healthy development of human powers, whose reach should be almost infinite; this is seen to be bafflingly impossible, but also to be the positive drive without which nothing has value. So that, finally, we have been concerned with the other meaning of 'virtue', the Renaissance 'virtù' which gives greatness to man; and the imaginative stress veers continually between the two.

This imaginative complexity is explored through a remarkable sensitivity to words: the contrast between vulgar and high-flown, between nuances in two words of one meaning (e.g., 'seed' in l. 4 and 'spawn' in l. 13), between two meanings in one word (e.g., 'Need' and 'flourish'), and so on: language has for Chapman, as for many Elizabethans (pre-eminently Shakespeare), always this potential richness. Thus, despite its superficial formality, Chapman's poetry has a strong sense of spontaneous development in the words themselves: arriving on 'flourish' in one sense, he moves on without explanation from another; and even when some possible meanings are not explicitly involved, they still often seem to influence a subsequent development (which makes commentary clumsy).

There is, then, a sense of contrast between the outward rhetoric of Chapman's poetry and its inward sensitivity and complexity. All the notorious characteristics of the Senecan aura are present here: the epic similes, classical mythology, eruptions of Latinized vocabulary, syntactical tangles which sometimes defy unravelling. All these are immediately obvious; but their proportion to other, more sensitive, qualities is not nearly so overwhelming as has been claimed. *O.E.D.* rather overestimates the originality of Chapman's Latin vocabulary; but it also credits him with several first-recorded uses of colloquial words and phrases, and it is characteristic of him to juxtapose the two:

[who suppose] if they make him
Straddle enough, *strut*, and look big, and gape,
Their work is goodly: so our *tympanous* statists . . . (ll. 8–10)

Here the effect is mock-heroic, exposing the blown-up emptiness of great men; but it is also a link in a succession of grandiose touches which here and elsewhere sustain the pitch of the play, as it initiates a swelling rhythm in strong contrast to the broken movement of l. 9; events are at once trivial and splendid, high seriousness emerges even from trivial encounters, hostile or amorous. Thus Chapman is able to explore the Nature of Man, no less, in the context of nearly contemporaneous history, to bring Marlowe's heroic vision within the orbit of a daily world; and to sustain this range with an equivalent verbal and rhythmic variety.

The language of rhetoric is also sustained by a syntactic structure of logical sequence: 'as . . . so . . . yet . . . thus', and this powerful combination tends to direct attention away from the local richness into the apparently simple broad contention; tends in fact to construct a pattern at odds with the more spontaneous development I have tried to indicate. This implies a tension between poetry and syntax which can baffle analysis. In extreme cases, the syntax yields no satisfactory structure of 'meaning', functioning only as a rhetorical gesture to Reason. This was Boas's judgement on Bussy's dying speech, v. iii. 178–93, which is nevertheless impressive and, in general outline, not obscure. Bussy's proudly affirmed Stoicism has been confronted with the spectacle of Tamyra's bleeding body, and erupts into an overwhelming sense of disaster diminishing his achievement towards nonentity and poisoning all human life; for this the images of their bodies, the red sun, and erupting mountains all act simultaneously, all opposed to the endless snow which outlasts all melting. The inter-connections are rich and complex, both psychologically and symbolically, engaging a cosmic range of reference at the same time as a personal tragedy. 'My sun' is Tamyra as beloved, but also derives astronomical association from 'this prodigy'; its beams are red partly because of her blood, and even the mountains, Pindus and Ossa, still relate to her snowy breasts. But their destruction leaves Tamyra behind, and the continuing imagery of human bodies transfers to Bussy, whose organs throw up the mountainous oppression; but here the heroic image itself dissolves, as the mountains themselves 'melt' into the ocean of all human life, which Bussy enters bitterly, finding that his greatness, if it does not redeem nature, must destroy it. The violent bitterness subsides into resigned extinction in the new rhythm and image of Bussy's final words, ll. 188–93. Tamyra's wounds have been an emblem of the evil that Bussy has wrought outside himself, generalized to all human life. Though detailed analysis is difficult, the overall movement through a violent complexity of rhythm and image towards the steady dying fall would be likely to succeed far better in the theatre than in the study; not, as Dryden[1] supposed, as deceptive bombast, but as fully dramatic poetry.

(c) *The Dramatic Characters*

The opening speech has much of the nature of a Prologue to the play: it should be no surprise after this that Bussy's heroic battle is also seen as a vulgar murder, or that his heroic love is also a cheap adultery. The pursuit of 'virtù', however honest, ends inevitably in conflict with plain 'virtue'. Such a choric function Bussy's speech clearly has; but it is not therefore simply Chapman speaking through the actor (as Irving Ribner suggests[2]). The bland rhetorical surface is Bussy's grandiose justification of his own poverty; the complexity subsumed under that surface is not available to Bussy's

[1] See p. lv.

[2] 'Character and Theme in Chapman's *Bussy D'Ambois*', *ELH* XXVI, 1959, 482–96.

'consciousness'. To put this in terms of 'character' is to speak of Bussy's self-deception; and that is indeed indicated, and later developed to 'I'll venture that' in l. 138 when the concealed ambition becomes explicit. But the character aspect is only *part* of the effect: for what is revealed as beyond Bussy's self-knowledge *is* a full introduction to the themes of the play. Poetry, play, and character are all of a piece in this way: the simultaneous development of abstract and concrete in the verse is akin to the tradition of allegorical poetry, and the figures who act and speak do so simultaneously as persons and as principles, in the way of Morality drama, not of Greek choruses. For this 'choric' utterance develops a debate which is dramatic precisely because the principles are in conflict and *not* a single reconciled 'view' of the author's. Bussy himself is certainly no *mere* abstraction, but in him is explored precisely the conflict of the two meanings of 'virtue' which come out in his opening speech: his moral effort is to achieve the harmony of goodness and greatness, which from the beginning he indicates as impossible. That is his abstract function; it is concretely presented in a particular character—of a 'man of spirit', and in that too Chapman offers an essential doubleness. Such a man as Bussy is capable of unusual independence and achievement, but the particular nature that makes that possible has also a tendency to brashness, arrogance, and bullying. When Monsieur and Bussy engage in 'flyting' at the end of III. ii, the mud they fling at each other sticks to Bussy as well as Monsieur:

I think thee then a man,
That dares as much as a wild horse or tiger;
As headstrong and as bloody. (ll. 336–8)

The doubleness apparent in the moral values Bussy represents thus emerges also in the kind of man he is felt to be. Chapman's figures are not, what Coleridge called Shakespeare's, 'genera intensely individualized', but they have a strongly felt human aspect as well as a moral function; they are part of the play, very much alive as dramatic protagonists, as parts for actors to play, but not with the kind of life that moves far out of its context or is ever in danger of distorting the dramatic structure. The only possible exception, I think, is the extraordinarily moving awareness of the suffering of

Montsurry and Tamyra after Bussy is dead; but this is felt about their situation rather than themselves; it is again more generic than individual, and it is developed as a condition of the play's last statement, Comolet's recognition that adequate judgement of men is impossible to man:

> My terrors are struck inward, and no more
> My penance will allow they shall enforce
> Earthly afflictions but upon myself. (v. iii. 265–7; not in *1641*)

(d) The Structural Outline

The action of the play is, for its period, unusually firmly organized: the five acts are essential structural units, and no mere gesture to classical precedent; between each of the first four a significant action is placed whose fulfilment seems to presuppose a brief interval, but which is also used to link the acts together and to assert the closeness of the sequence of events. Between I and II Bussy fights the duel which is arranged in I. ii and described in II. i; between II and III Bussy and Tamyra achieve the sexual intercourse to which they exit from II. ii, and from which they return in III. i; at the end of III. ii Bussy and Monsieur exit to the King's banquet, and IV. i opens with the court emerging from the feast. Between IV and V there is no such event, but a structural break is still clear: in IV. ii we have seen simultaneously the two conferences, of Bussy, Tamyra, and Comolet on the one hand, and of Monsieur, Guise, and Montsurry on the other; at the beginning of V. i the immediate consequence is shown as Montsurry confronts Tamyra with his knowledge of her adultery.

The same kind of careful planning is felt within the acts: each is divided into two (not always equal) parts. In I. i Bussy accepts Monsieur's offer of patronage, but loses his dignity in receiving the cash from the pompous comic steward, Maffé; a comic medium is used again in I. ii to present Bussy's arrival at court, his incongruity there, and the consequent quarrel with Barrisor and his friends. II. i shifts the plane from comedy to heroic splendour in the Nuncius' description of the duel, which leads to Bussy's pardon and his consequently enhanced status; II. ii opens (in the original version only) with a discussion overlapping in time with the previous scene, as to what Bussy's fate will be, with comments on his behaviour in I. ii, and contrasting Monsieur and Bussy as wooers for Tamyra, on whom the scene concentrates. II. i and II. ii are in fact balancing the two passions of Valour and Sex. Act III is rather less clearly divided; though it has two scenes, i is short, and ii both long and involving a succession of more or less distinct episodes. III. i presents the satisfied love and its danger, III. ii. 1–130 shows Bussy equally successful at the King's elbow, provoking the Guise's anger and Henry's protective gesture of reconciliation; ll. 131–285 present the new alliance of Monsieur, Guise, and Montsurry, and their discovery (in bawdy comedy), from the maids, of Bussy's affaire; finally ll. 286–412 bring Monsieur and Bussy together again in an atmosphere of fear, distrust, and hatred subsumed under a veneer of intimate friendship. Overall then, Act III has a (Shakespeare-like) combination of the Hero in triumph coupled with a rapid development towards disaster, and for this the structural break is rather after the King's exit (III. ii. 130) than between the so-called scenes. IV. i leads from the uneasy banquet to Montsurry's first confrontation of Tamyra; it is (rather strangely) divided from IV. ii by music while Tamyra writes a fatal letter; she then re-enters to Bussy and Comolet to invoke Behemoth and the vision of their enemies, which provides them with knowledge which is yet useless to save them: a change of dramatic pitch for which the music may be intended as an operatic prelude. Act V has technically three scenes, but in fact two major parts divided by a choric dialogue between Guise and Monsieur (V. iii. 1–56); V. i and V. ii show us Tamyra and Bussy separately before the complicated plot re-unites them in V. iii for Bussy's murder and the final judgements of the play.

This carefulness of dramatic structure can well be compared to the surface rhetoric and assertive syntax I noticed in the verse: it is in fact a kind of dramatic rhetoric asserting a clear movement from obscurity to success in Love and State, to betrayal and death. And, like the verse rhetoric, it covers a more subtle and diverse movement in the play's detail, on the one hand providing a valuable organization, and on the other (once again) a kind of mask which sometimes draws too much attention to itself, so that the material it controls is obscured. That is why the play can seem mere melodrama: the strongly rhetorical verse and the strong dramatic structure can become opaque; the life of Chapman's tragedy lies within them. Finally, the allegorical juxtaposition of abstract and concrete in the verse is reflected in the morality-play characteristics I remarked in the structure, as well as in the emblematic suggestions of Chapman's staging.

(*e*) *The Development of the Play*

Bussy's opening speech serves the double function of self-introduction and prologue: we are directed at once to a concern with the 'state of things', seen as unstably balanced between Fortune and Reason, a context where the actions of men must likewise be balanced between assertive Will ('using all their powers / And skills') and submission to Need—a balance which the speech both states to be impossible and yet strongly suggests as the only valid ambition. So that it also enlarges on two contrasting forms of 'great men': the colossic statues and the successful seamen. Monsieur's soliloquy is a more simply personal statement, but it extends the prologue by adding a third response to the unstable world, that of the Machiavel: Monsieur is fully as ambitious—

> There's but a thread betwixt me and a Crown (l. 41)

—but he is in no sense an empty strutter; nor on the other hand is he a 'great seaman': he has, in full measure, 'powers and skills', but they are not at all related to Virtue, except by patently false profession:

> I would not wish it [the thread] cut, unless by Nature;
> Yet to prepare me for that likely fortune . . . (ll. 42–3)

The irony is obvious: Monsieur's submission to patience is based, not on the virtue he professes, but on the calculation that Fortune is likely to support him. As a person, Monsieur has the characteristic of perfectly clear-headed hypocrisy; but, again, the person is immediately felt as the reflection of an attitude. Monsieur accepts without regret the rule of Fortune, and is blind to any other scale of values. It is a blindness whose compensation is exceptionally clear sight within the limits of total cynicism. Hence, though Chapman does not distinguish the utterance of his figures in anything like the way that Shakespeare does, there is a difference between Monsieur's speech and Bussy's: where Bussy's was both confused and exploratory, Monsieur's is perfectly clear and definitive, without any interest in fundamental problems, only a concern with limited practical objectives—here the diagnosis of Bussy's condition:

> A man of spirit beyond the reach of fear,
> Who (discontent with his neglected worth) . . . (ll. 46–7)

In other words, a malcontent, easily accessible to bribery:

> None loathes the world so much, nor loves to scoff it,
> But gold and grace will make him surfeit of it. (ll. 52–3)

The quality of the scene that follows is in its presentation of the rightness and the wrongness of this diagnosis. Bussy's analysis of the Court (ll. 84–104) has all the malcontent's extravagance, against Monsieur's deployment of classical precedents and sound moral doctrine (ll. 76–81); in short, Bussy behaves exactly as predicted—scoffs the world and accepts the gold. The result is the brilliant amalgam of self-deception and positive values which I discussed in Bussy's soliloquy after Monsieur's exit: Bussy claims that

> a smooth plain ground
> Will never nourish any politic seed, (ll. 122–3)

but accepts from Monsieur the notion that Fortune's gifts must be swiftly taken. In so far as this is felt to be equivocation, Monsieur is vindicated; but if Bussy repeats Monsieur's image of Fortune (such repetition of idea in changed context is a device to be noted elsewhere), he also recalls his own image of the healthy seed; and however much he now admits his ambition to rise, he yet retains his devotion to virtue—'I'll venture that' is equally compounded of braggadocio and courageous challenge to Monsieur's cynicism. The pattern of the play is fully suggested in this prologue: the victories will be Monsieur's, but they must be Pyrrhic, for the values he excludes transcend his politic schemes.

But never easily: Monsieur is obviously sinister to Bussy, as later he is repulsive to Tamyra; but he is a strong antagonist and Chapman never undervalues his position. The rest of this scene deflates both the mighty opposites: Monsieur's miscalculation is evident when he sends his stupid, arrogant steward to pay Bussy—a dangerous insult; in face of it, Bussy loses his virtue in either sense, reduced to a merely vulgar violence: the vaunting hero is comically revealed as blustering bully (albeit provoked).

The first scene, then, starts firmly with the individual protagonists, and establishes the contrasts and limitations of the attitudes and values they stand for. Scene ii provides the contrast of the full court, and uses it to present and comment on the society they must inhabit, as an epitome of the contemporary world. The French King eulogizing Elizabeth's English court in retort against Guise's mockery of the cult of the old Queen, is a charmingly oblique way of criticizing James I; but its obliquity has the further use that what Henry really achieves is a contrast of ideal and real detached from any particular locality:

> Courts should be th' abstracts of their Kingdoms,
> In all the Beauty, State, and Worth they hold . . . (ll. 21–2)

> . . . our French Court
> Is a mere mirror of confusion to it:
> The King and subject, Lord and every slave
> Dance a continual Hay . . . (ll. 26–9)

Hence the image of Society to which the ideal Individual must be matched is the orthodox one of an orderly dance (unlike the Hay): it does not correspond to the fact as given in the prose half of the scene, nor is it obviously a context for the exercise of Bussy's venturing spirit. It comes to represent, in Acts II and III, another force against which Bussy must prove himself; so for the rest of this scene we are shown the 'continual Hay', the trivial empty round of meaningless flirtations and quarrels. The deflation of heroic vision matches Maffé's part in Scene i, but here the counterpoint is more elaborately sustained: Bussy's impertinent bawdry with the Duchess angers the chess-playing Guise, whose literalness is at once jealousy and an arrogantly simple defence of the hierarchy Henry has defined; the Guise's sense of Order has none of the flexibility of a dance. The quarrel is ridiculous, but serious; its triviality is pointed in one way by Monsieur's aside in heroic verse (ll. 138–46), interpreting Bussy's independence as evidence of the great spirit so conspicuously absent in the cheap prose; it is a useful reminder before the bear-baiting which follows, insisting on the sense of Bussy as a man out of place, ill at ease, and absurd because of it; his discomfiture ultimately condemning his tormentors.

I have ascribed a function to Monsieur's speech, and I believe it to be correct: but here is a case of the limited explicitness of Chapman's writing. I cannot point to the text for justification of the ironic effect I claim, and it may well be felt that all Chapman is doing—very clumsily—is to try to persuade us that a boor is a great man. The difficulty arises because there is no irony in the language, it inheres only in the juxtaposition of unlike utterances, of opposite valuations; if it is not positively clumsy, it certainly lacks finesse, but as a reminder of the ambivalence with which Bussy is to be regarded it is very necessary at this stage. It is necessary, too, as an anticipation of the far larger revaluation of Bussy's part in the duel which takes place in II. i. Henry's opening emblem of Envy as a monstrous bird of prey addicted to physical corruption ('That passes all the body's soundest parts, / And dwells upon the sores') is the first appearance of a recurrent motif, the strong sense of nausea and perverse appetite identifying Bussy's opponents; it emerges later in Tamyra's revulsion from Monsieur, and in Montsurry's degeneration in jealousy, as well as in the language Monsieur and Bussy use to each other at the end of III. ii. The stench of corruption is so powerfully suggested that the complexities of judgement proper to Bussy's case can easily be suspended in the awareness that he is, at least, healthy. It needs all of that to suspend our disbelief in what follows: the Nuncius' speech breaks abruptly into the highest epic pitch:

> What Atlas, or Olympus lifts his head
> So far past covert, that with air enough
> My words may be inform'd? (ll. 25–7)

The 'air' seems to be dangerously windy. The speech is not apparently a direct translation from anything in Seneca, but Bussy, as the Nuncius gives him here, is unquestionably Hercules. In II. i. 2,

Henry spoke of D'Ambois' 'sudden bravery, and great spirit': if we saw largely the bravery (=brashness) in I. ii, we have here more than all the great spirit. 'More than all' remains true, I think, though this sense of Bussy's capacity for heroic action is certainly to be taken seriously; we cannot easily forget its disproportion to the vulgarity of the quarrel; and just as Monsieur in I. ii had to remind us of the great spirit amidst the mere bravery, so here, vice versa, the Guise voices a discordant view in l. 105:

O piteous and horrid murder!

The Nuncius' inflated rhetoric is thus known for what it is: a partial, selective statement, a way of bringing out an aspect of the truth, with no pretence that it is the whole (though great insistence on its importance). The device is not altogether satisfactory, and Chapman himself parodied it in *The Widow's Tears*, IV. i. 49–100. None the less, with all its defects, it is an impressive assertion of the potential greatness of man in distinction from the littleness of the normal vision; and, as such, an essential prelude to the wholly serious debate on Nature which ensues.

The Nuncius called the duel heroic labour; Guise called it horrid murder. It does not require any factitious defence of duelling to see that it was not quite either of those things. That is the burthen of Monsieur's defence: if the heroic justification of Bussy is to succeed, the idea of Society as rigidly based on Order must be modified. The balance to be struck between individual and society is an extremely difficult one, perhaps impossible; hence the debate is carried at once to fundamentals, yet remains essentially dramatic in its indecisiveness. Monsieur intrudes Nature first in the simple form of an appeal to brotherly love; to this Henry's retort is sharply Guise-like:

these wilful murders
Are ever past our pardon. (ll. 149–50)

Monsieur proceeds to distinguish justice from law, and to assert the 'free man's' right to supply the particular deficiencies of law, and Henry once more objects that this becomes a licence for butchery. The interesting point is that all this is put into Monsieur's mouth; he invokes the principles only to support the particular case. Hence Henry, granting Bussy's life, dismisses the arguments with a bare 'Well brother...' Bussy's speech (ll. 185–204) reverses this order and begs, not for his life, but for acknowledgement of his *right* to live:

> That I may so make good what God and Nature
> Have given me for my good: since I am free
> (Offending no just law), let no law make
> By any wrong it does, my life her slave . . . (ll. 193–6)
>
> Let me be King myself (as man was made) . . . (l. 198)

The appeal is to the Greek (and Renaissance) concept of an original Golden World from which the present is a decline; a sophisticated relation of the myth of the Fall in Genesis. Bussy has no idea of challenging the King's authority: the final assertion is, that there is no conflict:

> Who to himself is law, no law doth need,
> Offends no King, and is a King indeed. (ll. 203–4)

Bussy's insistence on the question of values is in marked contrast to Monsieur's politic argument; the final rhyming responses endorse the different attitudes. But whereas the Guise's bluntness had before the salutary effect of calling a spade a spade, it has now the narrow hostility of an inflexible mind making no response at all to the imaginative appeal of 'free men', or the argument for a justice transcending law. It is an instance of the dramatic economy of which Chapman is capable amidst his more obvious prolixity: Guise speaks only two lines in the scene, and they are nearly identical; in them his quality and his limitation are fully defined. The strict legal orthodoxy is shifted from Henry on to Guise, and of that he remains the protagonist to the end; his military taciturnity is psychologically appropriate to his attitude.

The stress in II. i, then, is on the heroic freedom of which man is capable; II. ii reverses that, to revive the concept of necessary limitation on freedom. The opening takes us back rapidly to the lighter tone of I. ii, in the form of a critique of both Bussy and her Duchess-ship; Guise announces D'Ambois' pardon in characteristic language—'where's a King? Where law?'—and is allowed his fullest verse so far, though still not very full: he is now (in the 1607 text only) fully established as one of the major figures, even if the least of them. With his departure an undercurrent from the previous dialogue—Tamyra protesting too much—comes out into full exposition of the theme of Passion (ll. 32–49). The fact is expected, but the particular terms of it are of vital importance, so that its omission in the revised play seems to me disastrous. The whole speech is made of a single simile, worked out in closer relevance of detail than usual: Tamyra's passion is compared to volcanic eruption of a fume in 'the womb of Earth':

> The more it is compress'd, the more it rageth. (l. 38)

The condition is put very clearly beyond the reach of 'self-control': the explosion is inevitable, *because* of Tamyra's resistance to it; and when it comes it inverts all the values by which she lives:

> All bars made engines to his insolent fury. (l. 41)

Just so must all the appearances of Tamyra's happy marriage, for which she is known, be used as cover for her adulterous satisfaction; and the emblem of this is her use of her Friar-confessor as pandar, a bar made engine:

> and that holy man
> That from my cradle counsell'd for my soul,
> I now must make an agent for my blood. (ll. 47–9)

This I think explains, what has puzzled some critics, why Chapman gives such a function to a Friar. This presentation of passion as more than irresistible, as the more dangerous precisely because it *is* resisted, precludes the crudities of moral indignation that have been urged against Tamyra (hardly tolerable anyhow when Freud is every man's familiar), and makes of her position an extraordinarily powerful instance of an unavoidable necessity radically opposed to the human freedom Bussy has been claiming (she later refers to it as 'urgent destiny'). This does not mean that Tamyra's subsequent behaviour is uncriticized (any more than Bussy's): her 'bars made engines' are fully, and ironically, exposed. To the Monsieur's proposition she can still return an answer which, hitherto, had been honest, taking her stand on her honour and her 'firm husband'. Monsieur cannot believe in such values: for him, the only explanation is hypocrisy. The point—that the values are real, and that Tamyra has lived by them—is brilliantly made simultaneously with the revelation that she must *now* fulfil Monsieur's expectation and be the common courtly hypocrite (even in front of her lover).

By the end of Act II, then, Bussy's freedom is submitted to Tamyra's necessity; when we see them again in III. i their passion is felt as something much more positive. But its power is of a kind which precludes any simple judgement of good or evil: they are placed, and know it, outside the shelter of the moral order. To Tamyra, the knowledge is terrifying:

> So confident a spotless conscience is;
> So weak a guilty . . . (ll. 8–9)

to Bussy, it is exhilarating:

> Sin is a coward Madam, and insults
> But on our weakness . . . (ll. 18–19)

The tone of his speech is, again, a compound of courage and defiance; its argument deals narrowly with the (improbable) safety of their secret between the three who know it; but the terms in which it is developed indicate Bussy's confidence in a completeness of satisfaction he has not felt before: his relationship with Tamyra is the embodiment of all that's opposite to 'the witch Policy' and 'Goddess Money'; but for Tamyra it is the negation of her moral life:

> What shall weak Dames do, when th' whole work of Nature
> Hath a strong finger in each one of us?
> Needs must that sweep away the silly cobweb
> Of our still-undone labours. (ll. 47–50)

The vapours that seem 'golden' to Bussy are for Tamyra 'thick and black'.

The recognition that these judgements cannot be reconciled, nor one preferred to the other, is achieved in this scene, and sustained to the end of the play. The painful truth of Tamyra's loss of integrity is immediately felt in the hypocrisy she must oppose to Montsurry's confidence of their love and desire for coitus on his return home.

That Bussy's triumph here has no stability is abundantly demonstrated; that the same is true of his pre-eminence at Court is a main theme of III. ii. Bussy is established at the King's elbow, as his Eagle, the champion of Truth. The conventional satiric targets involved, despite the concrete vitality of language with which Chapman animates them, make this one of the play's dullest passages. Yet effective placing justifies its presence: it is a formal flyting, and gives point to the more precisely aimed speeches of Monsieur and Bussy which match it at the end of this long scene; it is also used as a trap to catch the Guise. 'If the cap fits, wear it'—he finds his own particular image amongst Bussy's generalized figures, and re-opens their quarrel at a singularly cheap level. Henry is obliged to make peace: and doing it, commits himself to a full endorsement of the values Bussy had claimed in II. i. Bussy's Virtue is that of a man of the Golden Age:

> No envy, no disjunction, had dissolv'd
> Or pluck'd out one stick of the golden faggot
> In which the world of Saturn was compris'd,
> Had all been held together with the nerves,
> The genius and th' ingenuous soul of D'Ambois. (ll. 103–7)

This is the height of Bussy's ascendance, the fullest statement of the value at which he aims; it is immediately followed by every sign of envy and disjunction: Monsieur and Guise plotting with Montsurry, and extracting knowledge of the adultery in a scene of nicely judged trivial prose. The vulgarity of their flirtation with the maids reaffirms the vulgarity of the whole court, and the command of the maids over these circumstances, cheap as it is (Pero is as much moved by envy as Monsieur is), yet makes the prancing lords look cheaper.

The prose has (as usual) a significant undercurrent: that Tamyra is Bussy's mistress is a real shock to Monsieur. He had taken (rightly, as I noted) her rejection of him in II. ii to be honest—had been forced to recognize the power of values his cynicism would not acknowledge. Now that his original diagnosis is confirmed, his assurance is shaken; this is given in prose in ll. 199–209, but its full development is the strange verse soliloquy, ll. 286–302: if Tamyra exceeds his rational comprehension, so does Bussy:

> I fear him strangely,
> And may resemble his advanced valour
> Unto a spirit rais'd without a circle . . . (ll. 298–300)

The subsequent dialogue is conditioned by this fear; and in its echo of the opening of the scene offers an analysis of Bussy—as braggart bully—opposite to Henry's encomium, but not much less accurate: it involves Bussy in the language of corruption and putrefaction which attends Monsieur's influence.

The Court scene which opens IV. i seems to me one of the most difficult things in the play: the counterpoint is too ambitious to be fully grasped. An elegant courtly argument on the lack of gaiety at the feast is sustained in high philosophical terms which are themselves at once a part of the courtly game, and also a fully serious evaluation (by Bussy) of the relations of men and women and the significance of passion. And the evaluation—the play's only direct attempt at this question—is itself equivocal, like the moon to which Bussy compares women. It is the image of Elizabeth, of beauty, and of influence; but also of changeability, and of lunacy. The passions of men are influenced by women; without them there is no beauty, but over them masculine valour has no power except by corruption. The tension in the scene is therefore a product of the excitement Bussy and Tamyra feel (Henry notes a new maturity in her, ll. 62–5), together with Monsieur's hinted knowledge. When he hints, Bussy explodes into violent rant, and Monsieur in reply sinks to fawning flattery; but the insinuation—that nature has no proportioned end for the hero soul—sustains the play's main theme, and anticipates the final debate in V. iii. It is therefore appropriate for Henry to conclude the scene with a direct anticipation of Tragedy. All this in little over 100 lines is an extraordinary feat of compression, and much of it is brilliant; but there is too much for all of it to be clear. The rest of the scene has no difficulties: Montsurry's peace of mind is destroyed by the crude hints of Monsieur, and he is brought to recognize the vulnerability of his love, the violence of jealousy to which he is prone. His honesty is sharply contrasted with Tamyra's rhetorical hypocrisy; the moon's beauty is changeable indeed.

If IV. i, whatever its degree of success, shows Chapman's writing for the stage at its most complex (its tensions ought to be very effective in the theatre), IV. ii falls to his crudest. Almost all that matters in the scene is the spectacular effect of conjuring spirits and visions, and the rhetoric which goes before it seems to have no function but to prepare the atmosphere. Bussy's turgid outburst at Tamyra's cry of fear (ll. 9–17) is merely absurd, the worst speech in the play (scarcely improved in the revision). The critical question is therefore of the value, to the play, of this spirit spectacle. James Smith[1] thought it merely a theatrical 'intrusion', and many other critics imply a similar judgement—factitious excitement to eke out Chapman's untheatrical talents. But Chapman's talents seem to me eminently theatrical, and once past the embarrassing preliminaries he handles the scene with obvious skill. He takes a hint from *Dr Faustus*, and stresses the ironic impotence of devils in Behemoth's petulant:

> This is your slackness, not t' invoke our powers
> When first your acts set forth to their effects. (ll. 76–7)

The responsibility remains with man. The cumulative effect of points like this, together with the oracular futility of the foreknowledge Behemoth *does* provide, gives the scene a central place as an image of necessity: the devil's foreknowledge makes man's will anything but free, whilst the devil's own impotence makes his foreknowledge ridiculous. Monsieur and Co., plotting in a vision seen by the enemies that cannot touch them, have the diminutive absurdity of puppets.

These ideas are latent in the scene as well as the sheer sense of horror which yields the powerful image of hell in Bussy's final speech. But my reference to *Faustus* points the weakness: Behemoth has nothing like the words Marlowe gives to Mephistophilis; Chapman has valid uses for his spectacle, but he barely succeeds in making them explicit.

The recovery of full verbal control in V. i is very striking. Comolet's part-powerful, part-feeble effort to restrain Montsurry's violence degenerates into cowardly flight from his responsibility as pandar. When Tamyra repeats the appeal to forbear

[1] 'Revaluations (VII): George Chapman', *Scrutiny* IV, 45.

In wreak of great sins, to engender greater,
And make my love's corruption generate murder (ll. 88–9)

Montsurry can reply:

It follows needfully as child and parent;
The chain-shot of thy lust is yet aloft,
And it must murder. (ll. 90–2)

The definition of 'necessity' as an inevitability of passion is justified by the outstanding quality of the long speech, ll. 55–87: the action of jealousy on Montsurry turns to a nausea which develops its own imaginative rhythm into a lyric of sexual disgust:

Come Siren, sing, and dash against my rocks
Thy ruffi'n Galley, laden for thy lust . . . (ll. 60–1)

Sing (that is, write), and then take from mine eyes
The mists that hide the most inscrutable Pandar
That ever lapp'd up an adulterous vomit. (ll. 68–70)

It is obviously irrelevant to question whether Montsurry was too trusting, too uxorious, or whatever, as moral explanation of this poetry: its psychological rightness is quite obvious, and it makes utterly convincing the sadistic satisfaction Montsurry derives from stabbing and torturing his wife. But it is also felt as the consummation of the unhealthy poetry which we have seen recurring round Monsieur's suppurating mind, and Montsurry has caught the disease from Monsieur. A main theme of the play thus emerges from the particular psychological observation, and when Montsurry stabs his wife, he carves her as an emblem of Adultery (ll. 132 ff.): the abstract is as strongly present in the concrete as ever.

This becomes increasingly felt in V. ii after Bussy recalls Behemoth (in very different verse from IV. ii: the oppositions of light and dark amount to something here, as Lamb noticed), in their strikingly terse interchange:

Buss. Who lets thee?
Beh. Fate.
Buss. Who are Fate's ministers?
Beh. The Guise and Monsieur.
Buss. A fit pair of shears
To cut the threads of Kings, and kingly spirits. (ll. 61–3)

Bussy recovers his normal rhythm; but he returns to the same bare utterance of fundamentals after the devil's exit:

> though I die . . .
> Should not my powers obey when she commands,
> My motion must be rebel to my will:
> My will, to life . . . (ll. 68–72)

The positive force of 'life' given here is opposed, not to death, but to Fate. In this verse, backed by the suggestiveness of a supernatural presence, the opposition of Bussy to Guise and Monsieur becomes the opposition of positive life to the negations of fate; all the oppositions I have noted—of health to disease, of freedom to servitude, and so on—are thus associated at the climax in this fundamental sense.

Thus when Guise and Monsieur enter to open the final scene (v. iii) they have lost their specific identity as conspirators (in Act v that rôle is entirely carried by Montsurry) and taken on, via the movement I have noted in v. ii, the abstract quality of choric voices, and this is emphasized by their appearance 'above', presumably on a balcony, as spectators rather than participants in the final action. In that rôle they explicate the debate on Nature, on the purpose or purposelessness of creation: to Monsieur,

> Nature hath no end
> In her great works, responsive to their worths. (ll. 1–2)

To the Guise, this is a superficial pragmatism: 'like a worldly man . . . by th' events / Values the worth of things'; Nature cannot

> give a whole man valour, virtue, learning,
> Without an end more excellent than those
> On whom she no such worthy part bestows. (ll. 34–6)

Monsieur sees just this as the significance of the murder to be done:

> Young, learned, valiant, virtuous, and full mann'd;
> . . . this full creature now shall reel and fall (ll. 38, 46)

and his speech revives the images and concepts of I. i:

> as the winds sing through a hollow tree . . .
> But a tree solid . . . they rend up by th' root . . . (ll. 42–5)

and the final Senecan simile of the sea leads to

As Fortune swings about the restless state
Of Virtue, now thrown into all men's hate. (ll. 55–6)

The play has returned to the questions with which it began: the death of Bussy is to judge the values that his life has explored. This choric interlude is effective as pause between Montsurry's preparation of his plot (with Tamyra in v. i and with Bussy in v. ii) and its execution in v. iii; its achievement is, by recapitulation, to focus attention clearly on the *significance* of the final action, to ensure, by indicating the universal concerns involved, that we shall respond to the catastrophe as tragedy, and not as melodrama. It has puzzled critics, partly because all modern editions follow the revised placing between v. i and ii which deprives it of preparation in v. ii as well as its immediate bearing on the last scene.[1] But even more perhaps, the objection arose from the presuppositions of the naturalistic tradition of later drama. The process of Chapman's drama as I have tried to present it should evaporate the strangeness: the continual interfusion of abstract and concrete in the poetry, the emblematic staging, and the deliberate use of conventions from Morality plays all tend towards this kind of development. Nor does it involve inconsistency in the kind of 'character' such a drama presents: Monsieur and Guise speak for the attitudes they have represented. The cynical Monsieur believes only in capricious Fortune; the rigid legalist Guise asserts an orthodox teleological argument for Nature's orderliness; but these attitudes cannot simply be confined to the men who utter them.

Monsieur and Guise do not leave the stage: they remain above as detached spectators of all the rest; silent, brooding Fates, reminiscent of the devils who watch Faustus torn to pieces at the end of Marlowe's play (in the text of 1616). It is against this setting, summing up the whole play, that we must see Bussy's successive valuations of his own death, wherein, as Eliot put it, he expires in an odour of Seneca. This is more than superficially true: there are only 70 lines between the pistol shots and the direction '*moritur*'; nine of them (ll. 147–55) are almost literally translated from Hercules' speeches on his pyre, and most of the rest sustains the same tone,

[1] See p. lxix.

and the same ideas. Bussy's first reaction is to recognize the treachery of Fate:

> 'tis enough for me
> That Guise and Monsieur, Death and Destiny
> Come behind D'Ambois. (ll. 123–5)

His body, mind, and soul have not fulfilled their apparent worth: there are no ultimate values more significant than the triviality of the Court:

> let my death
> Define life nothing but a Courtier's breath. (ll. 131–2)

The 'abstract' of all things is (as in I. i. 18–19) 'a dream but of a shade'. But Bussy can restore his confidence by a Stoical death:

> I'll not complain to earth yet, but to heaven . . . (l. 135)

> . . . I am up
> Here like a Roman statue; I will stand
> Till death hath made me marble. (ll. 143–5)

The Stoical fortitude suggests Seneca; the complaint to heaven, Hercules: hence the translated lines. Bussy, whose initial despair led to belief in Monsieur's chance-ruled life, has come to see himself as a successful hero in Guise's terms—a noble death is the end for which Nature designed him. In the complacence this engenders he proceeds to forgive his murderers and to ordain the reconciliation of Montsurry and Tamyra. The gesture is splendid in itself, but it would be patently false to the complexity of the play. Bussy has so far, as Eliot said of Othello, been cheering himself up. In the egotism of his noble death he ignores the suffering of the lives for which he has become responsible. He has propped himself up as a visible and audible emblem of the dying Hero; but Chapman matches him with another visible emblem, Tamyra baring her bleeding arms and breasts. The shock brings Bussy to a final despair, endorsing Monsieur's prediction:

> O frail condition of strength, valour, virtue . . .
> Made to express it like a falling star
> Silently glanc'd—that like a thunderbolt
> Look'd to have stuck, and shook the firmament. *He dies.*
> (ll. 188, 191–3)

This is not the odour of Seneca: in fact, it is directly opposed to Hercules' contempt for Dejanira. But neither is it the play's last word. Comolet's ghost proceeds to judgement, demanding Christian reconcilement of Montsurry and his wife, under threat of eternal 'haunt and horror'. The subsequent dialogue between them is one of the finest things in the play, and it serves here to restore the complex awareness that Bussy tried vainly to simplify. Tamyra's conflict of love and conscience yields the discovery that '(shunning all) I strike on all offence', and she condemns herself to an emblematic fate:

to the open deserts
(Like to hunted tigers) I will fly . . . (ll. 243–4)

Montsurry's conflict is no less moving, and very much of a piece with the psychological validity of his language in v. i: his feeling for Tamyra is a love he can neither diminish nor satisfy. They can forgive, but not be reconciled, and so must move apart:

so let our love
Now turn from me, as here I turn from thee,
And may both points of heaven's straight axletree
Conjoin in one, before thyself and me. (ll. 261–4)

Judgement, on the recognition of experience like this, is impossible, even for Comolet:

My terrors are struck inward, and no more
My penance will allow they shall enforce
Earthly afflictions but upon myself. (ll. 265–7)

This is the more impressive, because the Friar has not only the sanction of the priesthood, but also (being now a ghost) of the supernatural. The smug assurance with which he opened the scene, replying to Tamyra's

all his [Man's] power to live
Is given to no end, but t' have power to grieve

with

'Tis the just curse of our abus'd creation (ll. 67–9)

—this is abandoned, along with his demand for 'Christian reconcilement' of the irreconcileable. When this has been grasped, and not before, it becomes possible to forgive Bussy, and to grant him after all some part of the stature of Hercules:

> Join flames with Hercules . . . and th' aged sky,
> Cheer with new sparks of old humanity. (ll. 270–4)

It is, finally, not as a shooting star nor as a thunderbolt that Bussy's 'power to live' can be approved, but as new sparks of old humanity that can transcend the abuses of creation.

The extraordinary quality of this ending is that it does succeed in maintaining this (however modified) positive stress without betraying either the ambivalence with which Bussy has always been regarded, or the profoundly disturbing knowledge of human experience that the play has given us. The conclusion is, in fact, fully adequate to the play; and it has, issuing from the complex and very closely worked process I have tried to show in development, precisely the quality of 'inevitability' which Smith claimed for it. And, as he noted, there are very few English plays for which we can make such a claim. Shakespeare apart, Chapman's achievement is, I think, unique. And even in Shakespeare, this particular quality is rare: *Hamlet*, which constantly displays a range of genius beyond Chapman's, is deficient in this respect; its ending fails to take account of half the play. The sweet Prince whom choirs of angels must hymn to his rest was no more consistently sweet than Bussy is consistently noble, yet Shakespeare's last lines sound the panegyric without apology.

Comparison with Shakespeare cannot be pressed, of course. The resemblance to Ben Jonson's tragedies is much closer; and the superiority is clearly Chapman's. When the psychology of the hero was regarded as the be-all and end-all of drama, in the nineteenth century, Chapman's use of abstraction in structure and language seemed rebarbative; but audiences accustomed to Brecht or Beckett might well appreciate the range of his drama without having to overlook the vividness and acuteness of his psychological perception: his quality is essentially as poetic dramatist, not philosopher. The human predicament as he explores it, and the power to live that he endorses, have not lost their relevance. His work would make severe demands on modern actors; but he provides dramatic material that could reward a sufficient cast: if a National Theatre ever does rise from the dust of the South Bank, he should have an early claim to its consideration.

3. STAGE AND CRITICAL HISTORY

Bussy D'Ambois was a persistent success on the Jacobean and Caroline stage.[1] It was printed in 1607 'as it hath been often presented at Paules', but since Chapman wrote most of his plays at that time for the rival boys' company, the Queen's Revels, Parrott conjectured that *Bussy* had also been theirs, perhaps taken over to Paul's by the manager, Kirkham, who transferred in 1605–6. The play was later associated with the heroic actor Nathan Field, who probably revived it when he staged its sequel,[2] *The Revenge of Bussy D'Ambois*, during his management of the Queen's Revels 1610–16, and then took it with him to the King's Men for whom he played till his death in 1619. A Prologue for the King's Men, printed in 1641 (Appendix A), shows that they regarded it as their property and were reasserting their claims against the success of a rival company. Field, then dead, is said to have first given it name, and his successor had become too old for the part; so a new actor is taking over the rôle. Field could have been literally the first Bussy, but this is not proven; his successor is unknown, but the third man was probably Eliard Swanston[3] who played leads in the 1630's, when *Bussy* was twice performed at Court.[4]

Webster, in his preface to *The White Devil* (1612), put Chapman first among contemporary dramatists, and similar references are quite common; allusions to *Bussy* indicate its popularity, and it seems probable that the whole idea of Tourneur's *The Atheist's Tragedy* grows from Christian reaction to both the *Bussy* plays, the atheist D'Amville echoing D'Ambois, and the Christian Charle-

[1] Details on stage history in the seventeenth century are drawn from G. E. Bentley, *The Jacobean and Caroline Stage*, Oxford, 1941–56.

[2] See T. M. Parrott, 'The Date of Chapman's Bussy D'Ambois', *M.L.R.* III, 1908, 126–40, supported by P. Ure, 'The Date of the Revision of Chapman's "The Tragedy of Bussy D'Ambois"', *N. & Q.* CXCVII, 1952, 1–2.

[3] Gayton, *Pleasant Notes on Don Quixote* (1654), refers to Swanston as Bussy; Bentley, *op. cit.*, II. 597.

[4] 7 April 1634 and 27 March 1638.

mont 'improving' the moral ideas of Clermont in *The Revenge*.[1]

Bussy was quickly revived after the Restoration: Thomas Jordan, in *A Prologue to the King, August 16, 1660*, refers to it as being performed at the Red Bull, and we know that Dryden and D'Urfey both saw Charles Hart in the rôle. Dryden's comments in 1681[2] are well known:

> I have sometimes wondered, in the reading, what was become of those glaring colours which amazed me in *Bussy D'Amboys* upon the theatre; but when I had taken up what I supposed a fallen star, I found I had been cozened with a jelly; nothing but a cold, dull mass, which glittered no longer than it was shooting; a dwarfish thought, dressed up in gigantic words, repetition in abundance, looseness of expression, and gross hyperboles; the sense of one line expanded prodigiously into ten; and, to sum up all, uncorrect English, and a hideous mingle of false poetry, and true nonsense; or, at best, a scantling of wit, which lay gasping for life, and groaning beneath a heap of rubbish. A famous modern poet used to sacrifice every year a Statius to Virgil's *Manes*; and I have indignation enough to burn a *D'Amboys* annually, to the memory of Jonson.

This does at least indicate how successful Chapman's verse could be on the stage. Langbaine,[3] in 1691, suggested that Dryden had gone too far in indignation; and Thomas D'Urfey, in the same year, printed his 'improved' version, sub-titled *The Husband's Revenge*. The dedication explains that he had seen Hart some sixteen years earlier, and that despite 'obsolete phrases and intolerable Fustian' it had 'some extraordinary Beauties' which 'so attracted not only me, but the town in general, that they were obliged to pass by and excuse the gross Errors in the Writing, and allow it amongst the Rank of the Topping Tragedies of that Time'. The play had died with Hart, and D'Urfey attempted a purging of the fustian, with some revision of the plot, chiefly for Tamyra's sake, 'whom Mr. Chapman had drawn quite otherwise, he making her lewd, onely for the sake of lewdness'. A great deal of Chapman's verse survives

[1] See C. Leech, 'The Atheist's Tragedy as a Dramatic Comment on Chapman's Bussy Plays', *J.E.G.P.* LII, 1953, 525–30.

[2] Dedication of *The Spanish Friar*, in *Essays of John Dryden*, ed. W. P. Ker, Oxford, 1926, I. 246.

[3] *An Account of the English Dramatic Poets*, Oxford, 1691.

only slightly modified, together with the new, or more heavily revised, material. The Friar's part is largely given to Tamyra's confidante, obviously imitated from Juliet's Nurse, and the moral problem is 'solved' by providing a pre-contract for Tamyra and Bussy 'which gives some Excuse for her Love afterwards' when he unexpectedly confronts her at Court.

D'Urfey says he had some difficulty in getting it acted, but eventually Mountfort played Bussy to Mrs Bracegirdle's Tamyra; they 'had that Applause from the Audience, which declared their Satisfaction'—but there is no evidence it was ever repeated. Indeed, I know of no professional performance since that date, though in this century the play has occasionally been done in universities in England and America.

In the eighteenth century, criticism was equally thin, and revival of interest was relatively slow. Lamb printed the Nuncius scene from II. i and a few other brief passages in his *Specimens* (1808); and in 1827 he added some of the poetry of light and darkness, notably Bussy's invocation from V. ii, with the comment 'This . . . is tremendous, to the curdling of the blood. I know nothing in poetry like it.' Dilke edited the play in 1814, but the most important event was the publication in 1875 of Shepherd's edition of all Chapman's works, with a long and characteristically enthusiastic essay by Swinburne prefacing Volume II. The new interest generated is witnessed by the fairly numerous editions in the twentieth century, and was endorsed for a new generation by T. S. Eliot's essay, 'Four Elizabethan Dramatists',[1] in 1924. Eliot placed Chapman with Tourneur, Webster, and Middleton, concluding his case for convention rather than realism with the judgement:

> Chapman appears to have been potentially perhaps the greatest artist of all these men: his was the mind which was the most classical, his was the drama which is the most independent in its tendency toward a dramatic form—although it may seem the most formless and the most indifferent to dramatic necessities.

A hint which seems to me very relevant to Chapman's use of morality-play formulae, as well as his conscious rhetoric.

[1] Reprinted in *Selected Essays*, 1932.

Yet, although Hardin Craig[1] thought Chapman pre-eminently a psychological dramatist, criticism has largely concentrated on his more abstract ideas. Ennis Rees[2] found orthodox Christianity where R. H. Perkinson[3] saw a failure to grasp the idea of Providence; J. W. Wieler[4] saw Bussy as a Stoic hero flawed by passion, whereas E. Schwartz[5] found the fault only in Nature's fortuitousness; for Rees, Bussy is a wholly bad man, for Schwartz a wholly good one. Small wonder Robert Ornstein[6] found mere confusion, and mocked the play, using it as a stalking-horse to his praise of *Byron's Tragedy*.[7] The fact is that the ethical ideas can only be approached through the dramatic structure such variety of opinion implies. James Smith[8] made this point strongly in 1935, finding the poetry 'essentially dramatic'; and the most recent studies, by Irving Ribner[9] and Peter Ure,[10] explore this aspect further; Ribner still finds choric utterance psychologically implausible; Ure sees that all utterances have to be referred to the speaker and the context, but denies the ambivalence which I have claimed.

4. DATE

Parrott's[11] contention for a date in or around 1604 has been widely, but not universally, accepted. It is based almost entirely on topical allusions in I. ii: (*a*) 'their old Queen' (l. 12) refers to Elizabeth, and would not have been tactful during her lifetime; (*b*) ''Tis leap-year, Lady' (l. 79) is a bawdy joke which need have no reference to

[1] *The Enchanted Glass*, Oxford, 1950.

[2] *The Tragedies of George Chapman*, Cambridge, Mass., 1954.

[3] 'Nature and the Tragic Hero in Chapman's Bussy Plays', *M.L.Q.* III, 1957, 163–71.

[4] *Op. cit.*

[5] 'Seneca, Homer, and Chapman's Bussy D'Ambois', *J.E.G.P.* LVI, 1957, 163–71.

[6] *The Moral Vision of Jacobean Tragedy*, Madison, 1960, pp. 47–60.

[7] His assertion that Bussy 'dies triumphant, certain that he has achieved immortal fame in his fight against evil' is a very strange interpretation of V. iii. 178–93; it may be that Ornstein's general contempt for Act V is in part the result of the maladroit revision in the later text (see p. lxix).

[8] *Scrutiny* III, 1935, 339–50 and IV, 45–61.

[9] *Loc. cit.*

[10] 'Chapman's Tragedies' in *Stratford-upon-Avon Studies*, ed. J. R. Brown and B. Harris, I, *Jacobean Theatre*, 1960.

[11] *Loc. cit.*, *M.L.R.* III, 1908.

date, but 1604 was a leap-year; (*c*) 'Knight of the new edition' (l. 111) and (*d*) 'new-denizened Lord' (l. 154) both refer to the lavish distribution of honours in Jacobean politics, much like the lines in *Eastward Ho!* for which Chapman was imprisoned in 1605; there are none such in his later plays, so this suggests a date between 1603 and 1605, and 1604 becomes acceptable.

If *Bussy* was actually written earlier, there must have been (as Boas[1] supposed) a revision at this time. The only serious evidence for an earlier date is an allusion in Dekker's *Satiromastix*[2] (1601), IV. i. 138–40:

> *Tucca.* Goe not out Farding Candle, goe not out, for trusty *Damboys* now the deed is done, Ile pledge this Epigram in wine, Ile swallow it, I, yes.

Tucca (as Parrott noted) is an imitation of Pistol: his speeches echo well-known lines, and nothing in *Bussy* explains this particular phrase. W. J. Lawrence[3] claimed the candle as an echo of V. iii. 252–61; but there is no verbal similarity, and the image was commonplace. When Tucca goes on to discuss conjuring devils, there is no likeness at all to *Bussy*. E. Schwartz,[4] dating all Chapman's tragedies much earlier than Parrott, has revived Henslowe's payment in 1598 for 'Perowe's sewt wh. wm. Sley were', although, as Parrott pointed out, Sly must have been too old for this Pero in 1598. Schwartz ignores the allusions in I. ii, and altogether his case is very flimsy; he wants to retain the traditional sequence of tragedies because most critics have found it appropriate; but most critics have also found a Jacobean date for *Bussy* appropriate. The concentration of all internal evidence in one scene might be suspicious, but the satiric nature of the scene explains it. Dekker's allusion may well be to one of the lost plays on French history which we know to have existed (e.g., his and Drayton's *Civil Wars of France*). I

[1] *Ed. cit.*, Introduction, p. xii n.

[2] Ed. Fredson Bowers, *The Dramatic Works of Thomas Dekker*, I, Cambridge, 1953.

[3] 'Dekker's Theatrical Allusiveness', *T.L.S.*, 30 January 1937, p. 72; supported by R. G. Howarth, 'The Date of Bussy D'Ambois', *N. & Q.* CLXXVII, 1939, 25.

[4] 'The Dates and Order of Chapman's Tragedies', *M.P.* LVII, 1959–60, 80–2.

think we must accept that the tragedy or tragedies to which Meres referred in *Palladis Tamia* (1598) are lost, and take *c.* 1604 as the probable, though not certain, date for *Bussy*.

5. SOURCES

No known account of Bussy's career is early enough for Chapman's use; the earliest, De Thou's *Historiae Sui Temporis*, was not printed till 1609. Mme. C.-E. Engel[1] listed all the scraps of earlier French material, and believed them sufficient basis for the play, which seems to me highly unlikely. Jacquot[2] repeats her contention that Chapman had read Dampmartin's *Du Bonheur de la Cour* (1592), a moral disputation with Bussy as interlocutor, but even here the evidence is not very convincing. For the *Byron* plays Chapman relied heavily on *The General Inventorie of the History of France* (1607) by his friend (and distant relative) Edward Grimestone, whose family had been diplomats in Paris during the second half of the sixteenth century.[3] The likeliest explanation would seem to be that Chapman had details of Bussy's story from Grimestone, either in manuscript or by word of mouth.

Bussy was not, historically, a man of outstanding significance: to historians,[4] he has never been worth more than a short reference in the general account of Henry III's relations with his brother Alençon, the Monsieur. Bussy was never poor; born about 1550, he was brought up at court; his transference of loyalty was from the King to Monsieur in 1574; the height of his career was a provincial governorship in Anjou, where he achieved only the hatred of his subjects. His only serious involvement with the Guise seems to have been in the St Bartholomew massacre, when he took the opportunity to murder his own cousin. He seems to have been known for personal courage, violent temper, sexual intrigue, and duelling. How these were estimated depends on the politics and religion of the reporter, but no one gave him heroic status. If he had merited

[1] 'Les Sources du "Bussy D'Amboise" de Chapman', *Revue de Littérature Comparée* XII, 1932, 587–95.

[2] *Ed. cit.*, Introduction, pp. l–lviii.

[3] See M. Eccles, *loc. cit.*

[4] A brief, and hostile, account is provided in *Dictionnaire de Biographie Française*, ed. Prevost and D'Amat, vol. VII, Paris 1956, columns 724–5. Jacquot, *ed. cit.*, pp. xxii–lviii, examines the early sources fully.

that, he would no doubt have been suppressed earlier; as it was, he was murdered when barely thirty, probably with the complicity of both the King and Monsieur (who was in England at the time). There are conflicting accounts of how Montsoreau revenged his wife's affaire, some of which correspond closely enough with Chapman's. The facts of Bussy's career may not appear inspiring, but he does seem to have acquired some legendary status in France again in a minor degree, as 'scholar and poet', defiant in defence of love. Hence his presence in Dampmartin's dialogue, and also as the hero, Lysis, of a romance about his death by François de Rosset, printed in 1619. Extant letters and verses justify such a reputation rather as striven for than earned; but his death did produce a crop of adulatory poems from his friends. If the *Satiromastix* reference is not to Chapman's play, Bussy must have already appeared on the English stage, and an English legend (perhaps as the supremely French lover ?) may also have influenced Chapman's view.

We simply have not the necessary information to discuss the transformation of historical Bussy into dramatic hero. A sense of recent history clearly mattered for Chapman's purpose; but he was not so much interpreting the man as recreating him for a moral and dramatic function, as he explained later in the preface to *The Revenge of Bussy*:

> And for the autentical truth of either person or action, who (worth the respecting) will expect it in a poem, whose subject is not truth, but things like truth? Poor envious souls they are that cavil at truth's want in these natural fictions; material instruction, elegant and sententious excitation to virtue, and deflection from her contrary, being the soul, limbs, and limits of an autentical tragedy.

The sources of Chapman's dramatic and moral ideas in Seneca's *Hercules on Oeta* and Plutarch's *Moralia* are touched on in Section 2 of the Introduction, and the most relevant passages presented and discussed in Appendix B.

6. THE TEXT

The play was twice printed in the seventeenth century, in 1607–8[1]

[1] The date was apparently changed during the printing of the title page; see W. W. Greg, *A Bibliography of the English Printed Drama to the Restoration*, 1939, I. 377.

and in 1641.[1] The 1607 title-page offers the play '*As it hath been often presented at Paules*', whereas *1641* reads 'As it hath been often Acted with great Applause. *Being much corrected and amended by the Author before his death*'. Chapman's name does not appear on a title-page until 1657, but his authorship of at least the original version has never been questioned. The 1641 title-page is certainly right in claiming much correction and amendment, but whether it is right to ascribe this work to the original author is more difficult to decide. Editors have accepted this statement, and based their editions on the later text. I have found this hard to accept, and have finally decided to follow 1607–8. To explain why, I must first establish as clearly as possible the nature of the copy used by each printer, and then consider the source or sources of the corrections and additions.

1607–8, which I shall call 'A', is well and tidily printed and reasonably free from obvious misprints. It has several of the characteristics of a text printed from author's manuscript rather than from a theatre prompt-book: stage-directions are few and inadequate; speech-prefixes vary very considerably (e.g. for Bussy: *Buss.*, *Bus.*, *Buc.*, *D'Amb.*) in a way which cannot be blamed on the compositor(s);[2] there is a redundant prefix, *Bus.*, at v. iii. 166, when Bussy is already speaking; the initial directions for scenes consist only of lists of characters, and extras (attendants and so on) and properties are usually omitted. On two occasions these directions include characters who must in fact have entered later (Nuncius at II. i, and Montsurry and Tamyra at III. ii): this might imply a prompter's list, but it seems to me equally likely to be the author setting out the main figures for his scene. These inadequacies are confined to incidentals, the text itself is coherent and (though it often needs explaining) very seldom needs emendation. It therefore seems to me probable that A was a relatively faithful rendering of the manuscript which Chapman supplied to the theatre, and from which the prompt-book had been copied. (It is just possible that the book-

[1] The sheets of this edition were re-issued with altered titles in 1641 again, 1646, and 1657. For a full bibliographical description of both editions, see Greg, *op. cit.*, pp. 377–9.

[2] I have not been able to discover clear evidence of more than one compositor engaged on either printing.

keeper had made preliminary notes: the occasional conflation of Latin and English in the directions,[1] and the cast-lists before scenes, may be his work; but they need not be.)

1641, called 'B', on the other hand, for all its extensive differences, is not derived direct from a manuscript, but from a corrected copy of A. The typographical similarity is obvious on every page: although there are some fairly consistent differences of practice, spelling and capitalization are followed in detail; punctuation is usually identical, only occasionally modified to help the sense; prose printed as verse in I. ii and III. ii is so printed again in B; the stage direction at I. ii. 107.1 is moved back some twenty lines, but the misprint '*Pyrlot*' is repeated; the music which in A strangely covered a brief interval before IV. ii while Tamyra wrote her letter is replaced in B by dialogue, but the direction still calls for music; and so on. Clearly then, a copy of A was corrected, sometimes heavily, by reference to a manuscript.

The printing is untidy, and there are more misprints than in A, though not very many more as far as printed copy was used: in two places, however, in Act V, V. iii. 18–22 and V. iii. 268–74, the misprints increase considerably. The latter includes the words '*Jove* flames with her rules' where A reads 'Joine flames with Hercules': a curious error, for B's blunders could only (and easily) have been made from misreading manuscript, although there was in fact printed copy available. This must have happened, I think, because the speech in which these lines occur was shifted to an earlier position (after V. iii. 193); and the corrector, finding them in his manuscript, did not know that they were overleaf in his printed copy, and so wrote them out as an addition. The same explanation seems to me likely for the strange nonsense which B makes of V. iii. 18–22, which again was shifted to a much earlier position (before V. ii), though here the errors do not necessarily depend on misreading manuscript. These are the only places[2] at which we can try to judge the quality of the transmission of manuscript material into print in B: and they are very discouraging. The fault may lie with an earlier

[1] *Ascendit Bussy with Comolet*, IV. ii. 7; *Intrat vmbra, Comolet to the Countesse, wrapt in a Canapie*, V. iii. 56.1–2.

[2] See also note on III. ii. 303.

Bussy D'Ambois:

A TRAGEDIE:

As it hath been often Acted with great Applause.

Being much corrected and amended by the Author before his death.

LONDON:
Printed by *A. N.* for *Robert Lunne.*
1641.

copyist, or with the 'corrector' of the printed copy, or with the compositor; on the whole the last seems the most probable.

If that is so, the compositor found the corrector's hand hard to read, and all passages peculiar to B are open to suspicion. The corrector's own work is harder to judge: he made a double blunder in the direction at IV. ii; and there are a few other places where either he bungled the correction, or the compositor misinterpreted his instructions (e.g. II. i. 0.1; IV. i. 69–73; IV. i. 145–6; V. i. 31, 39); on the other hand he was thorough in eliminating Comolet's name: the prefix *Com.* stands in only two places, one of which was corrected during the printing. It appears from the rare but significant changes he made in punctuation that he was not a mere hack, but a man capable of some editorial discretion. He sometimes seems to supply the correct word where A misprints, possibly by guesswork (and at IV. ii. 131–2 I suspect a false emendation). On the whole, since he cannot be much faulted, one must suppose that he was a fairly conscientious worker, and that is borne out by the number of trifling changes he bothered to make; but it is not likely that his collation was unduly thorough, and the copy which resulted cannot have been a wholly accurate rendering of the manuscript he was using.

That manuscript seems to have been a prompt-book which had been used in the theatre in the 1630's: it contains one obvious prompter's note—*Table Chesbord & Tapers behind the Arras* at I. i. 149–51 for use at the beginning of I. ii;[1] its stage-directions are sufficiently comprehensive (though curiously often in Latin: see below); in some places properties required on the stage have been added to the directions, e.g. *with a book* (II. ii), *with a Chaine of Pearle* (III. i), *with a letter* (IV. i), *with tapers* (V. ii); a Prologue and Epilogue are added, wholly concerned with the actors and not at all with the play, apparently written in the 1630's.[2] Between this late prompt-book and the original manuscript of the revised version we must suppose the passage of at least twenty years,[3] during which (as the Prologue attests) the play was regularly revived; so

[1] *Pistols shot within*, V. iii. 118 (for 120), may be another.
[2] Printed here in Appendix A; see Section 3 of the Introduction.
[3] See p. liv and n. 2.

the prompt-book may very possibly have been replaced one or more times. Between the reviser's manuscript and the final prompt-book, then, stands at least one copyist; between that and the printer's copy stands the corrector; and between his work and the printed edition stands the compositor with an apparent talent for misreading the corrector's handwriting. The chance of error in this process of transmission stands uncomfortably high.

On bibliographical grounds, then, A is very much to be preferred. But the revisions themselves may still be Chapman's work (as the title-page presumably implies); if so, they represent (however inadequately) his latest thoughts on the play, and it is normal editorial practice to respect the author's latest decisions. Boas and Parrott both believed that the bulk of the revision was Chapman's work, though Boas was sufficiently uncertain of B's authority to allow himself some editorial discretion, and so in a few cases of marked superiority (most notably II. ii. 1–50) he followed A. Parrott was more rigorously consistent; but he admitted to doubts about some passages (e.g. V. iii. 69a–f) which he thought looked more like the work of a theatre hack than Chapman. More recently Miss Sturman[1] has argued that on the contrary the revisions are altogether second-rate; she notes that B was apparently the only complete 'book' (as distinct from pamphlet) to come from the press of 'A.N.' or the publisher Robert Lunne, and that they produced it in the year in which William Aspley, the publisher of A (who had been Master of the Stationers' Company in 1640), died: this information is useful, but it does not establish the falsity of their claim that the revisions were authorial. Miss Sturman points out that such a claim was good advertisement; this is true, but I find it hard to believe that such an elaborate correction of printed copy would have been undertaken except in good faith. She also asserts that there are no 'new' words in the additions, although such coinages are usual in Chapman's work, and this may have some significance, though I question whether a statistician would be impressed. Her other points are much less convincing, and Ure[2] had no difficulty in dis-

[1] Berta Sturman, 'The 1641 Edition of Chapman's *Bussy D'Ambois*', *H.L.Q.* XIV, 1950–1, 171–201.

[2] See list of Abbreviations.

posing of her rashly generalized contention. It cannot, I think, be denied that some lines peculiar to B are very good indeed, and also very like Chapman's distinctive manner (e.g. III. ii. 152–6, V. iii. 137–40); that, in other words, since we lack any conclusive external evidence on the matter, we *must* accept some of the revision as Chapman's work. If Miss Sturman is right at all then, we shall have to believe that the revision was the work of more than one hand. Parrott, in fact, assumed at least two hands: 'God' is in all places reduced to 'heaven', no doubt because of the 'Blasphemy' Act of 1606, and that is hardly a labour demanding the author's attention; furthermore (as I have noted) Parrott had some misgivings that the work had been re-touched in the theatre here and there. To some extent he covered that suspicion by suggesting that Chapman revised his play under advice from the actor Nathan Field, and he believed that the prime motive for the revision was theatrical need or convenience (e.g. the new beginning for IV. ii).

Parrott and Miss Sturman both argue as though it were possible to assign *some* motive for almost all the changes made; Ure stressed a most important point about the revision: 'it can be defined neatly by saying that about half the reviser's busy activity seems to have been totally wasted... [he] has altered word, or phrase, or line, and has neither weakened nor strengthened his original; he fidgets with the text...'[1] That is my impression too; and even when Ure is prepared to allow some preference one way or the other, I often feel it to be a trivial or (as he admits) controversial one. But I am not sure that Ure's conclusion follows: 'this reviser went through the text carefully pen in hand and in an anxious mood... That it was Chapman himself... seems much the easiest explanation...'[2] This argument assumes that most of these numerous neither-better-nor-worse changes were deliberately made. If they were, then I agree that only Chapman himself could have bothered; but I am inclined to believe that a great many are so casual as to be accidental, and if that is so they do not necessarily point to Chapman at all. In fact, a considerable group of these changes involve only the substitution of synonymous words or phrases (e.g. boast—vaunt, 'Tis fit I get—'Tis good I get); the kind of thing that copyists and even composi-

[1] Ure, p. 257. [2] Ure, p. 264.

tors are commonly blamed for. The transmission of the text, as I have presented it, makes several such figures inevitable.

If, then, one were trying to classify changes under heads attributable to different sources, one could assert a number where the poetic quality is unmistakably Chapman; a number where the motive is obviously 'theatrical' and without poetic merit; and a number which could easily be due to copyists. And in each of these groups there are extreme cases which I find it hard to attribute to either of the other sources. But yet, on the other hand, I find it quite impossible to go right through the revisions assigning each one to its distinct source: the cases shade through every gradation; each source seems inextricably linked with another, as if, after all, one hand *was* responsible for all. In other words, looked at in this way, I find the problem yielding contradictory answers: it is almost equally hard to believe in one hand, and in several hands.

Something can be done to simplify the picture, if one imagines the deliberate reviser to have been responsible for a number of accidental slips: whether or not he was Chapman himself, the extent of his work shows that he took on himself the rôle of author; and if, as I am inclined to think, he madehis revision by copying the whole play out, he could well have been freer than the most careless copyist over the changing of unimportant words—sometimes through sheer inadvertence, sometimes because a slight preference struck him as he wrote.

Clearly the best candidate for treating the text in such a proprietary manner is Chapman himself. Thus the question narrows to whether the 'good' and the 'theatrical' (and sometimes bad) groups of changes can be reconciled as all his own work. Parrott, as I have said, tried to achieve this by suggesting Field as a theatrical adviser. Yet there are difficulties. The usual view of Chapman's development after *Bussy* is of a philosophical preoccupation which leads him away from theatrical excitement. I think this has been overstressed; but Parrott's theory assumes the revision of this play to have been close to the writing of its sequel—and *The Revenge of Bussy D'Ambois* certainly makes less concession to the theatre than even the original version of the *Tragedy*. So that one is asked to believe that Chapman made his new play less theatrical at nearly the same time as he re-made his old one more so. It could have happened, but I doubt if it did.

A more serious objection to Chapman as reviser lies in the nature of these 'theatrical' changes. 'Theatrical' is a word of various implications: Parrott obviously intends it to convey convenience of production in the theatre; Ure is rather more precise, and speaks of 'useful explanatory dialogue', 'clarification of the action', and so on. Sometimes the changes are of that kind; but more commonly they seem to me 'theatrical' in another and less commendable sense: theatrical in taste rather than necessity, stressing the trappings of melodrama (ghosts, secret passages, etc.) and not the main action of the play. The added lines at III. ii. 130 do, I think, have the value Parrott was suggesting, of providing useful exit lines for Tamyra and the Duchess, who have been silent too long. Similarly the entry for Bussy and the Friar added at the beginning of IV. ii is clearly intended to dispense with the musical interlude which Chapman put there; but the actual words provided are peculiar: Bussy is made to guess that Monsieur knows of his affair with Tamyra, which is clumsy since we have seen Monsieur hinting his knowledge already; and there follows a superfluous addition for Tamyra:

> Our love is knowne,
> Your Monsieur hath a paper where is writ
> Some secret tokens that decipher it.

This perfunctory couplet tells *us* what we know already from IV. i, and explains to Bussy what he has just guessed. The result is to belabour the explanation of what is quite clear, in such a way as to make us see possible lacunae in the plot we would never otherwise have noticed (e.g. what paper, written by whom ?). It derives, I suspect, rather from a preoccupation with the details of plotting and intrigue than from any real theatrical necessity.

Theatrical convenience can certainly be argued for the additions at V. i. 1 and 37; but later in Act V there are again signs of a wish to explain what is not obscure, and by explaining to focus attention on the complications of the plot. So for instance the revision at V. ii. 83–8 (which is quite well written) harps on the effects of disguise and prediction; and at V. iii. 69–74 (as Parrott noted) a passage of characteristic Chapman 'philosophy' is deleted in favour of a rather fatuous statement on the limited powers of ghosts.

This tendency to be 'theatrical' in a bad sense is most striking in the revised sequence of events in Act v. I have discussed in Section 2 of the Introduction (pp. xlix–l) how in A Monsieur and Guise are detached from the action and turned into first choric figures and then silent Fates. All this is changed in B; the duologue is brought forward and on to the main stage, so that the new rôle of the speakers is obscured; it is followed by a brief addition which revives Monsieur's and Guise's activity as plotters; when before Scene iii they re-enter (on the upper stage now), they are twice made to enter the dialogue—once to ask what has happened to the murderers, and then to utter brief exit lines so that they are off-stage before the end. These changes are very small in themselves, but their effect is enormous. Monsieur and Guise are now essentially the master-plotters to the end; the movement in Bussy's speeches towards reflection on Human Destiny is unsupported by the staging, and all the weight falls on the melodramatic plot. And yet no significant word of poetry is altered: so that I cannot think there was any *intention* to alter Chapman's final effect. I do not think it is too much to say that the last Act has been turned from tragedy into melodrama (rigged out with tragic trappings); and that this conversion was by sheer inadvertence.

Parrott suggested that the duologue on Nature's purpose was put earlier so that a heavy philosophical passage would not interrupt the final action. This may be true, however (as I think) misguided. But there is another possible reason: if the reviser's theatre did not possess a full balcony, he would need to set these long speeches below, and yet leave time for Monsieur and Guise to reappear above (perhaps at windows) before the murder.[1]

In all this, then, I trace a double 'theatrical' motive: a change of scene-order for stage convenience, and accompanying changes betraying a taste for melodramatic plots. And I have stressed the seemingly *accidental* nature of the radical change accomplished: the

[1] D'Urfey (see pp. lv–lvi) made them shoot Bussy themselves: he *may* have derived this from theatre tradition via Hart, but it seems to me very doubtful.

reviser does not delete the inconvenient philosophy; he respects all that Chapman has written; but he does not fully understand it. The one person who could *not* have done this is Chapman himself.[1]

If this argument is correct—and I would stress that it depends on no external evidence, but solely on my critical judgement—major revisions were carried out by someone other than Chapman, whose characteristics appear in this case to be both theatrical experience and theatrical taste. At the same time I must repeat that there are some passages of poetry peculiar to B which I cannot doubt are Chapman's. I must therefore assert that the play was twice revised, by Chapman himself and by someone else. This is not the most economical hypothesis (which is, as Ure insisted, that Chapman made all the changes that cannot be attributed to copyists and compositors); but it is the most economical that I find credible. It remains to consider the extent of each revision, and whether they can be separated.

The detailed discussion of every significant change must be left to the commentary. The general point to be made here is that the two kinds of revision, 'theatrical' and 'creative', seem to overlap. In Act v, where I find the 'theatrical' reviser's hand most obvious, there are also the lines

> And if Vespasian thought in majesty
> An Emperor might die standing, why not I?
> Nay without help, in which I will exceed him;
> For he died splinted with his chamber-grooms. (v. iii. 137–40)

whose genuineness seems to me so clear that I have included them in my text (I am only slightly less sure of v. iii. 84a–d, which I have excluded). Now just as I cannot believe that Chapman made the structural changes in Act v, so also I do not think he could have accepted them and touched only a few lines of verse after they were made. It follows that Chapman's work was done first.

It also follows that one kind of revision shades into another. In some places a bulky change whose character seems to me to suggest not-Chapman, contains some Chapman-like characteristic. So Ure quotes v. iii. 57a–b:

[1] Other major changes which I attribute to similar causes are at II. ii. 1–50, III. ii. 285.1–322, and v. iii. 193.

> And strike away this heartlesse trance of anguish,
> Be like the Sunne, and labour in eclipses,

as seeming 'to have the true accent of Chapman':[1] it occurs in a heavy revision covering some twenty lines which elsewhere seems to me characteristically not-Chapman. If Chapman revised first and did not work over his successor's version, stray lines of his authorship could not creep into the other reviser's work. It is not altogether convenient, but I am forced to postulate that the other reviser could write in Chapman's manner, and sometimes do it well. Further, he could add *Latin* stage-directions where A omits them.[2] If Chapman did not write the new scene for Maffé in III. ii (the theatrical motive for giving the comic actor something to do after I. i is so obvious that I am not altogether persuaded by Ure's eloquent defence of the dramatic propriety of the scene), then the other man could, besides writing several very Chapmanesque lines, introduce such a relatively rare direction as '*exiturus*' (III. ii. 294r).

Such a man was no hack. He was apparently a man of the theatre; he also had at least small Latin; and some literary talent, albeit imitative (he was not otherwise in the least like Shakespeare); he knew Chapman's work well, and very likely had Chapman's general permission for such extensive tampering. When I first reached this conclusion, it looked to me like a reduction to absurdity: the qualifications I needed for my not-Chapman were ones which only Chapman could possess; if anyone else, then I must produce him. Parrott suggested that Field was Chapman's adviser. Field certainly appeared in some if not all of Chapman's later tragedies; he was manager of the Children at the Whitefriars in 1609–10 when he probably staged his own comedy *A Woman is a Weathercock* and Chapman's *The Revenge of Bussy D'Ambois*. The *Weathercock* was printed in 1612 with commendatory verses by Chapman, who refers to Field as his 'Beloved son'. Jonson spoke of Field as a pupil. W. Peery in his edition of Field's plays[3] sees Chapman as the major influence in Field's original work (after *Amends for Ladies*, ?1609–12, all that is attributed to him is collaborations with Fletcher and

[1] Ure, p. 268.

[2] *Ascendit*, II. ii. 178.1; *Descendit*, III. i. 42q; *Moritur*, V. iii. 193.

[3] *The Plays of Nathan Field*, ed. W. Peery, Austin, 1950.

Massinger). So it was an obvious step to examine *A Woman is a Weathercock*: like Peery, I was struck by the obvious influence of Chapman in the verse—in oddities of syntax, as well as in grandiose rhetoric dependent on the kind of astronomical imagery so common in Chapman; the writing is never really distinguished, but it is often tolerably well done. I was equally struck (and more surprised) by frequent Latin stage-directions, including one instance of *exiturus* (I. i. 50). All this is found in a relatively trivial comedy; how much more like *Bussy* Field might have written if he had attempted an independent tragedy one can only guess.

This does *not* prove that Field revised *Bussy*; only that he *could* have done. The seemingly absurd position to which my opinions about the revision lead is not impossible. If Chapman was not responsible for the bulk of the revision, then I am inclined to believe that Field must have been. My guess is that Chapman did work over *Bussy* after the copy which became A left his hands (it may have been very soon after, perhaps on the prompt-copy, which would best explain corrected misprints and the repaired omission (III. ii. 199–201); or it may have been later, perhaps on a printed copy which he let Field see); that he made improvements to the verse which range from single word changes to the addition of several lines,[1] but that he did not alter the general layout and staging of his play; that Field knew Chapman's revisions and himself undertook to revise the play for revival when its sequel was produced;[2] that Field did this by copying out the entire play, often trusting his memory more than was justified by the event (hence the innumerable indifferent changes)[3] and altering freely wherever he thought fit because he had Chapman's warrant to do so; but most freely in

[1] As he did in his first revision of the *Iliads*, in which Miss Bartlett ('Chapman's Revisions in his Iliads', *ELH* II, 1925, 92) finds clear motives for all the changes—and my limited examination of the texts supports her conclusion. The motiveless tinkering which Ure finds so common in the revision of *Bussy* does not seem to be characteristic of the Homer revisions.

[2] Hence the rearranged end to Act V, to put the final stress on the living characters whose affairs are important to the new play.

[3] These tend to be more frequent and more obviously memorial around places where revision is heaviest, or in prose passages (where carelessness is likely): e.g. I. ii, III. ii. 166 ff., III. ii. 285.1–322.

prose scenes, and passages of relatively low pitch: he seldom tampers wilfully with significant poetry.

The one major exception to this is the omission of II. ii. 1–50, which is unquestionably deliberate because of the substitution of II. i. 209a–i. Parrott's suggestion that, despite the quality of Tamyra's long speech, 'this passage does not . . . contain anything of dramatic importance, and was advisedly cancelled' seems to me utterly mistaken. The dramatic significance was discussed on pp. xlii–xliii; omission here may go far to explain critical confusion over Chapman's attitude to Bussy (ll. 1–23), the Guise's legalist function (ll. 24–9), and the theory of passion governing the whole treatment of the affair, and specifically Comolet's rôle in it (ll. 30–49). I would tentatively suggest two reasons for B's omission: first, the unusual technique of making the time overlap with the end of II. i, so that Guise's revelation is already known to the audience whose attention is directed to the characters' reactions; second, the reviser's apparent distaste for Chapman's attitude to passion (see note on II. i. 210–11). The passage seems to me one of Chapman's most interesting achievements, omitted for quite inadequate reasons; the impossibility of retaining it in a reprint of B is a strong argument for reverting to A overall.

That is what I have done, acting on my imaginary picture of what happened. The difficulty is to decide how many 'improvements' to the verse to admit as Chapman's, how many may just be Field. There are so many cases where one could hesitate between the two that I have (after some experiment) decided not to attempt any full-scale 'reconstruction' of Chapman's own revised text. Instead, I have followed the principle that A is to be preferred except where *not* to print B would be painfully pedantic. This results in the use of only three passages[1] from the later text, two of them additions, the other a revision. Since their extent is so small, I have placed these passages in square brackets, so that Chapman's original version stands out clearly. This has the advantage of presenting a text

[1] I. ii. 14–15, III. ii. 152–6, V. iii. 137–40. I have been tempted to add I. i. 121a–d, V. i. 0a–d, V. iii. 84a–d. I have also accepted from B a few apparent corrections of misprints and the lines III. ii. 199–201 where I think an omission is repaired.

which can be confidently regarded as more or less wholly Chapman's, and as the play that he originally wrote. At the same time, since this decision is obviously controversial (and runs counter to what has been generally accepted for the last fifty years), I have tried to make the revised version as readably accessible as possible, without recourse to a parallel text edition, by printing all the most significant revisions in full lines in the collation.

7. MODERN EDITIONS

Dilke's modern-spelling edition (1814) was carefully based on B, with a few emendations, suggestions for more, and very inconsistent noting of A's variants. Pearson's reprint in old spelling (1873) (according to Parrott it was edited by Shepherd) claimed to reproduce B, but (as Boas noted) was in fact based on A inadequately corrected by B (there are twelve unacknowledged reversions to A in the first scene): wherever possible both texts were conflated, so that B's lines often lie alongside those they replaced in A (the most serious cases are retaining B's revised end to II. i as well as restoring A's II. ii. 1–50; and where B in re-siting V. iii. 265–74 very properly deleted ll. 265–7, which refer to Montsurry and Tamyra, Pearson includes them in the new place as though they referred to Bussy). Shepherd's modern-spelling edition (1874) was based on Pearson with some conjectural emendations of its misprints (e.g. V. iii. 152: A and B 'burning'; Pearson—and *O.E.D.*—'curning'; Shepherd 'cunning'). Phelps's Mermaid edition (1895) claimed to derive from Pearson, only using Shepherd for help; it very rarely differs from Shepherd. Boas (1905) went back to the originals, reprinting B very accurately, with a few emendations and additions from A when he thought their omission might be accidental (this includes II. ii. 1–50 after B's ending to II. i). Neilson (1911) claimed to follow Boas; but evidently his practice was to use a copy of Phelps, corrected where necessary by Boas (typographical details, unlike those in other Neilson plays, are imitated from Phelps); inevitably a fair number of Pearson's A readings survived, and the thoughtless duplications were included entire. Parrott (1910) once again returned to B, more strictly than Boas, using A only to correct misprints or replace expletives censored as blasphemous.

Parrott's has always been recognized as a first-class modern-spelling edition (Boas's, in old spelling, was scarcely inferior); yet only two of the subsequent editions have followed him. McIlwraith's (1953) is, as he states, a straight reprint; Baskervill, Heltzel, and Nethercot (1934) is the same, except where, with a conservatism that seems merely pedantic, they rejected emendations (e.g. II. ii. 146 and V. iii. 18–22). Brooke and Paradise (1933) claimed a fresh text from the originals, but they seem to have used Neilson, corrected very carefully by B; they do occasionally act independently, but the policy initiated by the egregious Shepherd is everywhere visible in punctuation and eclecticism. Spencer (1934) made a similar claim, but he also seems to have used Neilson with much less correction, and what there is appears to derive from Parrott; I can find no evidence that B was directly consulted. There is a moral to this sad tale: neither Brooke and Paradise nor Spencer, for such large collections as theirs, could undertake a full analysis of the relations of A and B, and without that all their labours are very little worth. The best recent editions are those whose editors did least work. The exception is probably Jacquot (1960), an old-spelling edition of B, except that he includes (within brackets) II. ii. 1–50 and V. iii. 69–74; the chief difference from Boas is in closer following of B's punctuation.

My policy in collating modern editions has therefore been: (1) to note all Dilke's deliberate departures from B; (2) to note the readings of Boas and Parrott whenever either departs from B; (3) to note the readings of other editors only where they offer emendations not found elsewhere.

In most respects this edition conforms to the general practice in this series, but a few points should be noted, besides those explained above (pp. lxxiii–lxxv).

Spelling has been modernized, except where real difference from the modern form seems to be implied (e.g. fivers, II. i. 100; implied, III. ii. 138).

Punctuation is as close as possible to that in A, except where a change is necessary to clarify the sense. As with all Chapman's works, heavy stops (colons and semi-colons) are very frequent, and this fits the weighty delivery his verse demands; but full stops are rarer than is usual nowadays. Colons frequently appear instead, indicating a significant pause, but yet a definite link between one sentence and the next. This usefully indicates the continuity of images and ideas usual in Chapman's writing. Jacobean punctuation is much more likely than modern to suggest how a passage should be *read*, as distinct from construed, and so (for instance) a semi-colon sometimes stands where a comma would be expected, to show a pause in speech where there is none in the grammar. It will be obvious that such usage cannot conform to the rigorous (and all too mechanical) consistency expected now: a flexible punctuation needs a flexible reader, and can often be helpfully expressive.

Capitals are also used very inconsistently in A, and I have kept closer to the text than is usual, though still not very close. Chapman's characteristic personifications justify an unusually free use of capitals, but it is difficult to know where to stop. He equally often gives some generic value to simple nouns (e.g. Haven, Port), and I have felt, rightly or wrongly, that capitals were often being used as an additional form of punctuation, to give prominence to particular words, so that to lower them was to lose a possible indication of expression. The result may sometimes look strange, but I hope it is not merely quaint. There can be no question at all of consistency in this matter, and I have only very rarely introduced a capital which is not in A, though commonly eliminating ones that are.

Stage-directions are normally from A; where B seems to reflect stage practice of the early seventeenth century, I have included its directions without the square brackets which mark off all modern additions, though such cases are always collated. Other directions are sparingly given: we do not know enough about the private theatres for which the play was written to guess at all accurately how it was staged; such guesses as I am tempted to make are recorded in the notes.

All definitions of words in the notes are supported by *O.E.D.*, except where specifically stated, or where a gloss is preceded by a question-mark.

BUSSY D'AMBOIS

Buſſy D'Ambois:

A TRAGEDIE:

As
it hath been often preſented
at Paules.

LONDON,
Printed for *William Aſpley.*
1607.

[*CHARACTERS*, in the order of their appearance:

BUSSY D'AMBOIS,[1] *an unemployed soldier.*
MONSIEUR, *the King's brother.*
MAFFÉ, *Monsieur's Steward.*
HENRY III, *King of France.*
THE DUKE OF GUISE.
THE COUNT OF MONTSURRY.
THE DUCHESS OF GUISE (named Elenor in some stage-directions).
TAMYRA, *Countess of Montsurry.*
BEAUPRÉ, *the Duchess' niece.*
PERO, *Tamyra's maid.*[2]
CHARLOTTE, *Beaupré's maid.*[2]
PYRHA, *a maid.*[2]
ANNABEL, *the Duchess' English maid.*[2]
BARRISOR, L'ANOU, PYRRHOT, } *Courtier-soldiers, Bussy's opponents.*
BRISAC, MELYNELL, } *Courtier-soldiers, Bussy's supporters.*
BEAUMOND, *Courtier.*
NUNCIUS.
Friar COMOLET, *Confessor to Montsurry and Tamyra. Later a ghost.*
BEHEMOTH, *a superior devil.*
CARTOPHYLAX, *a devil in charge of papers.*
Devils.
Murderers.

In addition, the text calls for fairly numerous male extras, variously described as Attendants, Servants, or Pages.

The action is set in and around the French Court in the 1570's.]

[1] Pronunciation of names in Jacobean plays was probably not consistent; the occurrence of the spellings 'Bucy' and 'Damboys' suggests that perhaps his name could rhyme with 'Lucy damn-boys'.

[2] Maids-in-waiting, not menials.

Bussy D'Ambois

Act I

[I. i]

Enter BUSSY D'AMBOIS, *poor.*

Buss. Fortune, not Reason, rules the state of things,
Reward goes backwards, Honour on his head;
Who is not poor, is monstrous; only Need
Gives form and worth to every human seed.
As cedars beaten with incessant storms,
So great men flourish; and do imitate
Unskilful statuaries, who suppose
(In forging a Colossus) if they make him
Straddle enough, strut, and look big, and gape,

Act I] Actus primi Scena prima. *A, B.* 0.1.] *B; Bussy solus. A.* 1. *Buss.*] *not in A, B.* 5. incessant] *A;* continuall *B.* 8. forging] *A;* forming *B.*

0.1.] A's '*Bussy solus*' emphasizes the semi-choric nature of this opening; B's '*poor*' supplies the appearance of poverty in contrast to Monsieur's magnificence.

1.] from Cicero or Plutarch: see Appendix B, p. 155.

3. *Need*] poverty, as well as necessity.

6–17.] loosely adapted from Plutarch: see Appendix B, p. 155.

6. *flourish*] (1) thrive; (2) swagger.

7 ff.] The same image occurs in *Byron's Conspiracy*, IV. i. 179 ff.

8. *forging*] could mean simply 'making' (which B 'modernized' as *forming*); but as the statues in l. 15 are clearly hollow metal, the foundry sense of *forge* is quite likely. 'Faking' may also be relevant (see II. i. 18).

9. *strut*] *O.E.D.* (s.v., 6a) cites this line to establish a distinct sense: 'To raise oneself to one's full height; to thrust up one's head and stand erect; to perk *up*.' I doubt the need for this: all the usual senses of the word apply here (except engineering ones), plus the obsolete 'bulge, swell' as in *Iliads* I. 464: 'The Misens strooted with the gale' (in 1598 'The misens then were fild with wind').

Their work is goodly: so our tympanous statists
(In their affected gravity of voice,
Sourness of countenance, manners' cruelty,
Authority, wealth, and all the spawn of Fortune)
Think they bear all the kingdom's worth before them;
Yet differ not from those colossic statues,
Which with heroic forms without o'erspread,
Within are nought but mortar, flint and lead.
Man is a torch borne in the wind; a dream
But of a shadow, summ'd with all his substance;
And as great seamen using all their powers
And skills in Neptune's deep invisible paths,
In tall ships richly built and ribb'd with brass,
To put a girdle round about the world—
When they have done it (coming near their Haven)
Are glad to give a warning-piece, and call
A poor staid fisherman, that never pass'd
His country's sight, to waft and guide them in:

10.] *A; B reads:*

Their work is goodly: so men meerely great

20. powers] *A;* wealth *B.* 25. glad] *A;* faine *B.*

---

10. *tympanous statists*] Ure (p. 260) believes that B's revision 'improves the sequaciousness' of the speech. It certainly has its own merits, and may well be Chapman's.

tympanous] apparently from tympany, a swelling on the body, sometimes pregnancy, *fig.* pride, arrogance, etc. Line 11 'gravity of voice' suggests tympanum=drum, not noted in *O.E.D.* before late 17th century, though Purchas used it for ear-drum in 1619.

statists] statesmen, politicians.

16. *without*] on the outside.

18–19. *a dream . . . shadow*] from Pindar, via Erasmus (see Appendix B, p. 154). Bussy recalls the phrase in V. iii. 131–4.

19. *substance*] (1) 'a solid or real thing as opposed to an appearance or shadow' (*O.E.D.*, s.v., 10a); (2) essential nature; (3) possessions, wealth.

23.] Cf. *M.N.D.*, II. i. 175–6. Parrott noted that the phrase was common, possibly deriving from an emblem of Providence's girdle encircling the globe and attached to a ship (Drake's), in G. Whitney's *A Choice of Emblemes*, Leyden 1586, p. 203 (c2) (facsimile, ed. H. Green, 1866).

25. *give a warning-piece*] discharge a signal-gun.

27. *waft*] Manwayring, *Sea-Mans Dictionary*, 1644: 'To Waft, is to guard any ship, or fleete at sea.'

So when we wander furthest through the waves
Of glassy Glory and the gulfs of State,
Topp'd with all titles, spreading all our reaches,
As if each private arm would sphere the world;
We must to Virtue for her guide resort,
Or we shall shipwrack in our safest Port. *He lies down.*

[*Enter*] MONSIEUR *with* two Pages.

Mons. There is no second place in numerous State
That holds more than a cipher: in a King
All places are contain'd. His words and looks
Are like the flashes and the bolts of Jove,
His deeds inimitable, like the sea
That shuts still as it opes, and leaves no tracts,
Nor prints of precedent for poor men's facts.
There's but a thread betwixt me and a Crown;
I would not wish it cut, unless by Nature;

31. world] *A;* earth *B.* 33. *He lies down*] *Procumbit A, B.* 34. *Mons.*] *not in A, B.* 40. precedent] *D;* President *A, B.* poor] *A;* meane *B.*

---

30. *Topp'd*] ? put a top-sail on: the strict nautical sense 'slanting a yard' is scarcely relevant.

reaches] presumably, maximum canvas (from 'a continuous stretch of some material thing', *O.E.D.*, s.v., 12a): the nautical 'run on one tack' is again irrelevant. The other sense here is 'range of mind', as commonly in the 17th century.

32. *Virtue*] used in the play in two senses, not always distinct: (1) good moral behaviour (as nowadays); (2) inherent quality, the spirit of greatness in a man (*O.E.D.* has this for divine beings only, but it was very commonly applied to great men). Here, rather unusually, only (1) seems required: but see Introduction, pp. xxix–xxxi.

33.] Cf. *Monsieur D'Olive*, I. i. 175; *Teares of Peace*, l. 942; *Justification of Andromeda Liberata, Dialogus*, l. 4. Perhaps from Quintilian via Erasmus: see Appendix B, p. 155.

34. *numerous*] (1) containing many individuals (*O.E.D.*, s.v., 3, cites *Iliads, To The Reader*, ll. 4–5); (2) musical, harmonious (*O.E.D.*, s.v., 5: see *Byron's Tragedy*, I. ii. 58, and *Chabot*, V. ii. 92–3, ''Tis dangerous to play too wild a descant / On numerous virtue').

38–40.] The sea closes behind a ship leaving no traces of its course for others to follow.

39. *tracts*] tracks.

40. *facts*] actions, deeds.

Yet to prepare me for that likely fortune,
'Tis fit I get resolved spirits about me.
I follow'd D'Ambois to this green retreat;
A man of spirit beyond the reach of fear,
Who (discontent with his neglected worth)
Neglects the light, and loves obscure abodes;
But he is young and haughty, apt to take
Fire at advancement, to bear state and flourish;
In his rise therefore shall my bounties shine:
None loathes the world so much, nor loves to scoff it,
But gold and grace will make him surfeit of it.
What, D'Ambois?
Buss. He sir.
Mons. Turn'd to earth, alive?
Up man, the sun shines on thee.
Buss. Let it shine.
I am no mote to play in 't, as great men are.
Mons. Think'st thou men great in state, motes in the sun?
They say so that would have thee freeze in shades,
That (like the gross Sicilian gourmandist)
Empty their noses in the cates they love,
That none may eat but they. Do thou but bring
Light to the banquet Fortune sets before thee,
And thou wilt loathe lean Darkness like thy Death.
Who would believe thy mettle could let sloth

43. likely] *A;* possible *B.* 44. fit I] *A;* good to *B.* 57. Think'st] *A;* Callest *B.* 64. mettle] *P;* Mettall *A, B.*

---

49. *haughty*] high-minded, aspiring: not necessarily pejorative.

50. *bear state*] *O.E.D.* (s.v. *state*, 16c) gives the phrase as 'to hold office'; of things only, 'to be of importance'; yet it is clearly the latter sense applied to Bussy. 'State' was used of 'greatness', 'power': cf. *Byron's Conspiracy*, IV. i. 113–14, 'you make all state before / Utterly obsolete'. (See l. 57.)

57. *state*] status, official rank; also, pomp (see l. 50).

59–81.] from Plutarch's *Moralia*, eked out in ll. 69–70 from the *Life of Camillus*: see Appendix B, pp. 155–7.

60. *cates*] delicacies.

64. *mettle*] originally only a variant spelling of 'metal', later confined to figurative senses. For Chapman, who spelt it 'mettall', the literal sense was still present in the figurative, hence 'Rust' (l. 65).

Rust and consume it? If Themistocles
Had liv'd obscur'd thus in th' Athenian state,
Xerxes had made both him and it his slaves.
If brave Camillus had lurk'd so in Rome,
He had not five times been dictator there,
Nor four times triumph'd. If Epaminondas
(Who liv'd twice twenty years obscur'd in Thebes)
Had liv'd so still, he had been still unnam'd,
And paid his country nor himself their right:
But putting forth his strength, he rescu'd both
From imminent ruin; and like burnish'd steel,
After long use he shin'd; for as the light
Not only serves to shew, but render us
Mutually profitable: so our lives
In acts exemplary, not only win
Ourselves good Names, but doth to others give
Matter for virtuous Deeds, by which we live.

Buss. What would you wish me do?

Mons. Leave the troubled streams,
And live as thrivers do at the well-head.

Buss. At the well-head? Alas what should I do
With that enchanted glass? See devils there?

80. doth] *A;* doe *B.* 82. do] *A; not in B.* 83. as] *A;* where *B.*

---

65. *Themistocles*] Athenian politician, *c.* 500 B.C., of dubious personal reputation, but responsible for enormous naval expansion, and success against Xerxes, at Salamis, etc.

67. *Xerxes*] King of Persia; personally conducted punitive expedition against Greeks in 480 B.C.

68. *Camillus*] re-founder of Rome after Gallic invasions of 387 B.C.: his career was embellished in official legends.

70. *Epaminondas*] Theban commander of high repute, notably successful in attacking Spartan power.

76–81.] The slight obscurity comes from conflating sources: see Appendix B, p. 157: I suggest, 'the example of our actions encourages similar virtue in others, by which our original virtue is perpetuated'.

85. *enchanted glass*] The Court is an enchanted glass because it looks splendid but is devilish, like a strumpet's face. Magic mirrors, like wells, are common properties in fairy tales and accounts of witchcraft; the phrase 'enchanted glass' occurs in Spenser, *Faerie Queene*, IV. vi. 26.6, in Bacon, *Advancement of Learning*, V. iv, and in Ford, *A Line of Life*, but never quite in the same sense.

Or (like a strumpet) learn to set my looks
In an eternal brake, or practise juggling,
To keep my face still fast, my heart still loose;
Or bear (like dames schoolmistresses their riddles)
Two tongues, and be good only for a shift;
Flatter great Lords, to put them still in mind
Why they were made Lords: or please portly Ladies
With a good carriage, tell them idle tales,
To make their physic work; spend a man's life
In sights and visitations, that will make
His eyes as hollow as his mistress' heart;
To do none good, but those that have no need;
To gain being forward, though you break for haste
All the Commandments ere you break your fast:
But believe backwards, make your period
And Creed's last article, *I believe in God*;
And (hearing villainies preach'd) t' unfold their art

89. dames] *A, B;* dame *P.* 92. portly] *A;* humorous *B.* 95. sights] *A, B;* sighs *D conj.* 101. article,] *B;* Article; *A.*

---

87. *brake*] a frame to hold wood- or metal-work steady; hence here, to keep the face set in one expression. Cf. *Byron's Tragedy*, IV. i. 84, 'See in how grave a brake he sets his vizard'.

juggling] used in general sense for trickery, deception; its strict sense included what is now called conjuring.

89. *dames . . . riddles*] This sounds like a proverb, but I can find no trace of it in Tilley.

90. *shift*] expedient, sophistry, etc. There may be a remote pun with underclothing. The phrase 'for a shift' was used for 'as a makeshift'.

92–4. *or . . . work*] I take this to refer to the habit of court ladies of taking laxatives (possibly for slimming ?); 'idle tales' being fictions, here frightening ones, always supposed to have the same effect.

92. *portly*] stately, handsome. The modern sense was also available, and no doubt affected the choice of word here; B's 'humorous' (=whimsical) is therefore less subtle.

100–1.] The inversion of parts of the liturgy was an accepted technique for conjuring devils.

102–4.] I take this to mean that a 'great man', on hearing a sermon against particular villainies, learns to commit them in order (supposedly) to investigate their technique—i.e., Machiavellian behaviour (see Bacon's essay on Cunning).

102. *unfold*] investigate, explain.

art] technique.

Learn to commit them—'Tis a great man's part.
Shall I learn this there?
Mons. No, thou need'st not learn,
Thou hast the theory, now go there and practise.
Buss. Ay, in a threadbare suit; when men come there,
They must have high naps, and go from thence bare:
A man may drown the parts of ten rich men
In one poor suit; brave barks, and outward gloss
Attract Court eyes, be in-parts ne'er so gross.
Mons. Thou shalt have gloss enough, and all things fit
T' enchase in all shew, thy long smother'd spirit:
Be rul'd by me then. The rude Scythians
Painted blind Fortune's powerful hands with wings,
To shew her gifts come swift and suddenly,
Which if her Favourite be not swift to take,
He loses them for ever. Then be rul'd:
Stay but a while here, and I'll send to thee.
Exit MONSIEUR [*and* Pages], *manet* BUSSY.
Buss. What will he send? some crowns? It is to sow them
Upon my spirit, and make them spring a Crown
Worth millions of the seed crowns he will send:

110. eyes] *A;* Loves *B.* 113. rude] *A;* old *B.* 117. rul'd] *A;* wise *B.*

---

107. *high naps*] the opposite of threadbare; nap is the pile on materials like velvet.

108. *parts*] shares; hence possessions.

109–10.] picking up the theme of Bussy's first speech.

109. *barks*] from tree bark, generalized to any covering, hence clothes.

112. *enchase*] serve as a setting for (jewels, etc.).

113–14.] This emblem is pictured and described in Cartari: *Le Imagini dei Dei degli Antichi* (1568) (see A. H. Gilbert: 'Chapman's Fortune with winged hands', *M.L.N.* LII, 1937, 190–2); see Appendix B, p. 149, for Chapman's use of Cartari for Plutarch. The Scythians were 'barbarians' in the region north of the Black Sea, thought of (e.g. in Seneca's *Hercules Oetaeus*, l. 40, etc.) as the extreme north (see v. iii. 51–2).

113. *rude*] ignorant, unrefined—not necessarily ill-mannered or brutal.

121–2.] B's lines, deliberately changing the poetry without theatrical motive, look very much like a revision by Chapman himself. They yield the admirable force of l. 121b; and the fuller comment on Policy; but the context suffers and the result is so clumsy as to need further 'tidying-up'. I have followed A with misgivings.

But he's no husband here; a smooth plain ground
Will never nourish any politic seed;
I am for honest actions, not for great:
If I may bring up a new fashion,
And rise in Court with virtue, speed his plough;
The King hath known me long as well as he,
Yet could my fortune never fit the length
Of both their understandings till this hour.
There is a deep nick in Time's restless wheel
For each man's good, when which nick comes it strikes;
As Rhetoric yet works not persuasion,
But only is a mean to make it work:
So no man riseth by his real merit,
But when it cries clink in his raiser's spirit.
Many will say, that cannot rise at all,
Man's first hour's rise, is first step to his fall:
I'll venture that; men that fall low must die,
As well as men cast headlong from the sky.

Enter MAFFÉ.

122.] *A; B reads:*

Like to disparking noble Husbandmen,
Hee'll put his Plow into me, Plow me up:
But his unsweating thrift is policie,
And learning-hating policie is ignorant
To fit his seed-land soyl; a smooth plain ground

126. with] *A;* for *B.*

---

123. *politic*] like policy, normally used with a strong pejorative sense, akin to the modern 'scheming'.

128. *fit the length*] *O.E.D.* does not give this phrase: I suppose 'length' to mean a tailor's length of cloth (remembering Bussy's clothes) applied satirically to the great length of 'their understandings'.

130. *nick*] The image seems to be of a striking mechanism: the clock strikes when the nick in the wheel releases the hammer. (Cf. 'In the nick of time'.)

132–3.] from Plutarch: see Appendix B, p. 157.

135. *cries clink*] *O.E.D.* (s.v. *clink*, 1b) gives this as 'to have a response', perhaps in the sense in which 'clink' was used of rhyming (s.v., 2); the 'spirit' in the same line suggests a pun with drink, where the glasses are clinked for a toast (cf. *Oth.*, II. iii. 72 ff.).

138. *fall low*] presumably, fall from a low level, only a short way.

Maff. [*aside*] Humour of Princes! Is this man indu'd
With any merit worth a thousand crowns?
Will my Lord have me be so ill a steward
Of his revenue, to dispose a sum
So great with so small cause as shews in him?
I must examine this.—Is your name D'Ambois?

Buss. Sir?

Maff. Is your name D'Ambois?

Buss. Who have we here?
Serve you the Monsieur?

Maff. How?

Buss. Serve you the Monsieur?

Maff. Sir, y' are very hot. I serve the Monsieur;
But in such place as gives me the command
Of all his other servants: and because
His Grace's pleasure is, to give your good
A pass through my Command; methinks you might
Use me with more good fashion.

Buss. Cry you mercy.
Now you have open'd my dull eyes, I see you;
And would be glad to see the good you speak of:
What might I call your name?

Maff. Monsieur Maffé.

140. *Maff.*] *not in A, B.* man] *A;* wretch *B.* 148. I serve] *A;* I doe serve *B.* 149–51.] *A; B adds in margin: Table Chesbord | & Tapers behind | the Arras.* 152. A] *A;* His *B.* 153. good fashion] *A;* respect *B.*

---

140. *Humour*] The humours were four fluids generated in the body, which conditioned temperament—blood, phlegm, choler, melancholy. Hence the word is used in various senses derived from this: (1) the fluids themselves; (2) qualities of temperament derived from them; (3) temperamental idiosyncrasies, whims (as here).

143. *revenue*] accented on the second syllable.

149–51.] B's marginal S.D. here is clearly a prompter's note to set properties for I. ii, probably on an inner stage.

151–2. *to give . . . Command*] 'to arrange for your money to reach you through forces I control'.

151. *good*] had a specific sense of 'money' (*O.E.D.*, s.v., C, 7d), as in l. 155.

152. *pass*] passage (esp. in military contexts).

Buss. Monsieur Maffé? Then good Monsieur Maffé,
Pray let me know you better.
Maff. Pray do so,
That you may use me better. For yourself,
By your no better outside, I would judge you
To be a poet; have you given my Lord
Some pamphlet?
Buss. Pamphlet?
Maff. Pamphlet sir, I say.
Buss. Did his wise Excellency leave the good
That is to pass your charge, to my poor use,
To your discretion?
Maff. Though he did not sir,
I hope 'tis no bad office to ask reason,
How that his Grace gives me in charge, goes from me?
Buss. That's very perfect sir.
Maff. Why very good sir;
I pray then give me leave: if for no pamphlet,
May I not know what other merit in you,
Makes his compunction willing to relieve you?
Buss. No merit in the world sir.
Maff. That is strange.
Y' are a poor soldier, are you?
Buss. That I am sir.
Maff. And have commanded?
Buss. Ay, and gone without sir.
Maff. [*aside*] I see the man: a hundred crowns will make him
Swagger, and drink healths to his Highness' bounty;

161. a] *A;* some *B.* 163. his wise Excellency] *A;* your great Masters goodnesse *B.* 166. bad] *A;* rude *B.* 176. Highness'] *A;* Graces *B.*

163. *his wise Excellency*] Changes in titles and styles are made in B, besides here, at I. i. 176, 188, 196, I. ii. 96, 97, and III. ii. 308; there does not seem to be any consistency to suggest deliberation, so this looks more like the working of an actor's memory. Changes at I. ii. 61, 62, 70 are of a similar kind.

168. *perfect*] correct, as in 'that's perfectly right' (not in *O.E.D.*).

174. *commanded*] Parrott notes that Bussy is punning: Maffé intends the military sense, Bussy takes it as for ordering a meal.

And swear he could not be more bountiful.
So there's nine hundred crowns, sav'd;—here tall soldier,
His Grace hath sent you a whole hundred crowns.

Buss. A hundred sir? Nay do his Highness right;
I know his hand is larger, and perhaps
I may deserve more than my outside shews:
I am a scholar, as I am a soldier,
And I can poetise; and (being well encourag'd)
May sing his fame for giving; yours for delivering
(Like a most faithful steward) what he gives.

Maff. What shall your subject be?

Buss. I care not much,
If to his Excellence I sing the praise
Of fair great noses, and to your deserts
The reverend virtues of a faithful steward;
What qualities have you sir (beside your chain
And velvet jacket)? Can your Worship dance?

Maff. [*aside*] A merry fellow faith: it seems my Lord
Will have him for his jester; and believe it,
Such men are now no fools, 'tis a Knight's place:
If I (to save my Lord some crowns) should urge him
T' abate his bounty, I should not be heard;

178. sav'd] *B;* saft *A.* 183. scholar] *A;* Poet *B.*
188–90.] *A; B reads:*
If to his bounteous Grace I sing the praise, 188
Of faire great Noses, And to you of long ones. 189–90
193. merry] *A;* pleasant *B.* 194. believe it] *A;* berlady *B.* 196. my Lord] *A;* his Grace *B.*

---

181. *larger*] more generous.

183. *scholar*] B's 'poet' is very clumsy with 'poetise' in the next line: it does not look like a compositor's error, but rather a trick of memory, copyist's or actor's.

188–9.] Alençon (Monsieur) was notoriously deformed, and his nose seems to have been both large and conspicuously pitted by smallpox.

191. *qualities*] accomplishments.

191–2. *chain / And velvet jacket*] 'the symbols of a steward's office' (Boas).

194. *believe it*] B's 'berlady' (=by our Lady) may be right if the A-text derives from compositor misreading manuscript.

195. *Knight's place*] alluding to James I's wholesale creation of knights after his accession (see I. ii. 111).

I would to heaven I were an arrant ass,
For then I should be sure to have the ears
Of these great men, where now their jesters have them:
'Tis good to please him, yet I'll take no notice
Of his preferment, but in policy
Will still be grave and serious, lest he think
I fear his wooden dagger; [*to him*] Here sir Ambo,
A thousand crowns I bring you from my Lord;
Serve God, play the good husband, you may make
This a good standing living, 'tis a bounty
His Highness might perhaps have bestow'd better.

Buss. Go, y' are a rascal; hence, away you rogue.
Maff. What mean you sir?
Buss. Hence; prate no more;
Or by thy villain's blood thou prat'st thy last:
A barbarous groom, grudge at his master's bounty:
But since I know he would as much abhor
His hind should argue what he gives his friend,
Take that sir, for your aptness to dispute. [*Hits him and*] *exit.*
Maff. These crowns are sown in blood, blood be their fruit. *Exit.*

204.] *A; B adds:*
D'Amb. How, Ambo sir?
Maff. I is not your name Ambo? 204a
D'Amb. You call'd me lately *D'Amboys*, has your Worship b
So short a head?
Maff. I cry thee mercy *D'Amboys.* c

206. Serve God,] *A, P;* If you be thriftie and *B.* 216. sown] *A;* set *B.* their] *A, B;* the *B* (*where type lost*).

---

199. *have the ears*] (1) have the attention; (2) have long ears like an ass or jester.

204. *wooden dagger*] part of the jester's traditional equipment.

204a–c.] B's lines look like comedian's gagging.

206. *Serve God*] Parrott and Ure attribute B's change to the 'Blasphemy' Act of 1606. It is odd that the verse line should be so completely destroyed: perhaps the correction is not fully recorded?

207. *standing*] *O.E.D.*, s.v., 14a: fixed, settled, not casual; i.e., a steady income.

211. *villain*] usually 'scoundrel' in the 16th century, but the earlier 'low-born' seems implied in this context.

214. *hind*] servant.

[I. ii]

[*Curtains drawn to reveal*] *Table, Chessboard, and tapers,* HENRY, GUISE [*playing chess*], MONTSURRY, DUCHESS, TAMYRA, BEAUPRÉ, PERO, CHARLOTTE, PYRHA, ANNABEL.

Hen. Duchess of Guise, your Grace is much enrich'd
In the attendance of this English virgin,
That will initiate her prime of youth
(Dispos'd to Court conditions) under hand
Of your preferr'd instructions and command,
Rather than any in the English Court,
Whose ladies are not match'd in Christendom
For graceful and confirm'd behaviours;
More than the Court where they are bred is equall'd.
Gui. I like not their Court-form, it is too crestfall'n
In all observance; making semi-gods

I. ii. 0.1. *Curtains . . . tapers*] *Table Chesbord & Tapers behind the Arras B at I. i. 149–51; not in A.* 0.2. *Duchess*] *Elenor A, B.* 0.3. *Annabel*] *Annable A, B.* 2. this] *A;* that *B.* 4. under hand] *A;* under the hand *B.* 10. Court-form] *A;* Court-fashion *B.* 11. semi-gods] *A;* Demi-gods *B.*

I. ii. 0.1.] Since the Table, etc., were provided for in B at I. i. 149–51, the Arras seems to have been curtains which could be drawn, and there must have been access to the inner playing space from back-stage. But in Act V (see V. i. 185.1–2 and V. iii. 56.1–2) 'arras' and 'canopy' seem to imply draperies independent of the curtains closing an inner stage. The terms seem to have been used for any hangings. I assume that here Henry and Guise are discovered playing, and the others move out on to the fore-stage; but the table itself may have been carried forward. They play chess throughout the scene.

0.3. *Annabel*] A always ends the name '-ble', which probably indicates pronunciation (B has 'Annabell' at III. ii. 0.2).

2. *this English virgin*] presumably Annabel, who serves the Duchess.

4–5. *under hand / Of*] under the charge of. *O.E.D.* (s.v. *hand*, 35a) has no knowledge of this form after 1340; with 'his', 'her', etc., before 'hand', later (35c); B's 'under the hand' is given (35d) only referring to signatures.

5. *preferr'd*] Annabel's preference flatters the Duchess.

8. *confirm'd*] emphatic for 'firm': firmly established, settled.

9. *More than*] any more than.

11. *observance*] ceremonial respect for rank, etc.

semi-gods] B's 'Demi-gods' may be right, but is probably normalizing.

Of their great nobles; and of their old Queen
An ever-young, and most immortal Goddess.
[*Mont.* No question she's the rarest Queen in Europe.
Gui. But what's that to her immortality?]
Hen. Assure you cousin Guise, so great a Courtier,
So full of majesty and royal parts,
No Queen in Christendom may boast herself,
Her Court approves it, that's a Court indeed;
Not mix'd with rudeness us'd in common houses;
But, as Courts should be th' abstracts of their Kingdoms,
In all the Beauty, State, and Worth they hold:
So is hers, amply, and by her inform'd.
The world is not contracted in a man
With more proportion and expression,
Than in her Court, her Kingdom: our French Court
Is a mere mirror of confusion to it:
The King and subject, Lord and every slave
Dance a continual Hay; our rooms of State,
Kept like our stables; no place more observ'd
Than a rude market-place: and though our custom

14–15.] *B; not in A.* 18. boast] *A;* vaunt *B.* 20. rudeness] *A;* Clowneries *B.*

12. *old Queen*] Elizabeth. Such a reference is unlikely in her lifetime (see Introduction, p. lvii).

14–15.] Ure listed these lines as good new dialogue. The sharpness of the wit seems to me more than good. (See Introduction, p. lxxiii, and cf. note on I. i. 121–2.)

16–27.] Cf. the account of Byron's visit to Elizabeth, *Byron's Conspiracy*, v. i.

19. *approves*] demonstrates, proves.

21. *abstracts*] representations in little, summing up the qualities of the greater (cf. 'epitome').

23. *inform'd*] given formative principle.

24.] The idea of man as a microcosm, an 'abstract' of the world, was a commonplace.

25. *proportion*] exactness in relation of parts to whole.

expression] exact representation (verb and adverb are still used in this sense).

29. *Hay*] or 'Hey', a country dance with a winding movement, sometimes like a reel; used figuratively of intertwining.

30. *observ'd*] respected.

Keep this assur'd deformity from our sight,
'Tis ne'ertheless essentially unsightly,
Which they would soon see, would they change their form
To this of ours, and then compare them both;
Which we must not affect, because in Kingdoms,
Where the King's change doth breed the subject's terror,
Pure innovation is more gross than error.

Mont. No question we shall see them imitate
(Though afar off) the fashions of our Courts,
As they have ever ap'd us in attire;
Never were men so weary of their skins,
And apt to leap out of themselves as they;
Who when they travel to bring forth rare men,
Come home deliver'd of a fine French suit:
Their brains lie with their tailors, and get babies
For their most complete issue; he's first-born
To all the moral virtues, that first greets
The light with a new fashion, which becomes them
Like apes, disfigur'd with the attires of men.

Hen. No question they much wrong their real worth,
In affectation of outlandish scum;

32. deformity] *A;* confusion *B.* sight] *A;* eyes *B.* 37. subject's] *D;* Subiects *A, B.* 47. first-born] *A;* sole heire *B.*

---

32. *assur'd*] certain, certified.

36. *affect*] aim at, aspire to.

38. *Pure*] mere or, more emphatically, sheer. I can find no support for Brooke and Paradise's 'intrinsically good'.

innovation] roughly equivalent to 'revolution' now: cf. *1H4*, v. i. 78, 'hurlyburly innovation'.

39–50.] Boas noted that this was a common satiric theme; see Nashe's *The Unfortunate Traveller* (ed. R. B. McKerrow in *The Works of Thomas Nashe*, Oxford, 1958, II, 297–302).

43. *leap out of themselves*] according to *O.E.D.* (s.v. *leap*, 2b), used as an expression of joy; Chapman seems to include this sense with a more literal one, 'change their skins'. (Cf. l. 75.)

44. *travel*] punning with 'travail': the spellings were interchangeable.

45–7.] The puns continue ('babies' was commonly used of dolls or puppets).

52. *scum*] The usual figurative sense is offscourings of humanity, which

But they have faults, and we; they foolish-proud,
To be the pictures of our vanity;
We proud, that they are proud of foolery.

Enter MONSIEUR, [BUSSY] D'AMBOIS [*in Court dress*].

Mons. Come mine own sweet heart I will enter thee.—
Sir, I have brought this Gentleman t' attend you;
And pray, you would vouchsafe to do him grace.
Hen. D'Ambois, I think.
Buss. That's still my name, my Lord,
Though I be something alter'd in attire.
Hen. I like your alteration, and must tell you,
I have expected th' offer of your service;
For we (in fear to make mild Virtue proud)
Use not to seek her out in any man.
Buss. Nor doth she use to seek out any man:
He that will win, must woo her; she's not shameless.

53. we] *A;* we more *B.*
54–5.] *A; B reads:*

To jet in others plumes so haughtely;
We proud, that they are proud of foolerie, 54
Holding our worthes more compleat for their vaunts. 55
55a

57. this Gentleman t' attend you] *A;* a Gentleman to court *B.* 59–60.] *D, Bo, P; as prose A, B.* 61. I] *A;* We *B.* 62. I] *A;* We *B.* 66. He] *A, Bo;* They *B.* her; she's not shameless] *A, Bo;* her *B.*

---

may apply; but the idea of 'scum' as the froth on a man, i.e. fantastic clothes, seems more appropriate.

54. *pictures*] visible imitations.

54–5.] Parrott and Ure see B's version as a successful clarification; it seems to me a rather clumsy simplification, for the double edge of Henry's 'our *vanity*; / We *proud* . . .' is lost, together with the near-rhyme 'vanity . . . foolery' which emphasized it. The revision seems to make 'our worthes' unequivocal.

59–73.] The whole passage is rhythmically a transition from verse to prose (Parrott noted at ll. 182–4 that this kind of overlapping is common in Chapman); but blank verse rhythm seems to dominate until Monsieur turns away from the King. Boas and Ure agree that B's truncating of l. 66 is regrettable, though Parrott thought it designedly terse: it may be only a careless omission. The trivial addition, l. 73a, is an obvious case of theatre influence on the revision.

Mons. I urg'd her modesty in him, my Lord,
And gave her those rites, that he says she merits.

Hen. If you have woo'd and won, then Brother wear him.

Mons. Th' art mine, my love; see here's the Guise's Duchess. The Countess of Montsurry; Beaupré, come I'll enseam thee; Ladies, y' are too many to be in Council: I have here a friend, that I would gladly enter in your Graces.

Duch. If you enter him in our Graces, methinks by his blunt behaviour, he should come out of himself.

Tam. Has he never been Courtier, my Lord?

Mons. Never, my Lady.

Beaup. And why did the toy take him in th' head now?

Buss. 'Tis leap-year, Lady, and therefore very good to enter a Courtier.

Tam. The man's a Courtier at first sight.

Buss. I can sing prick-song, Lady, at first sight; and why not be a Courtier as suddenly?

Beaup. Here's a Courtier rotten before he be ripe.

Buss. Think me not impudent, Lady, I am yet no Courtier, I

67–8.] *Bo, P; as prose A, B.* 70–3.] *A, B; as verse Bo, P.* 70. my love] *A;* sweet heart *B.* 71. Montsurry] Mountsurreaue *A, B.* Beaupré] *B;* Beaupres *A.* 73.] *A; B adds: D'Amb.* 'Save you Ladyes. [73a]
74. Graces] *A;* Graces, my Lord *B.*
80.] *A; B adds:*
Henr. Marke Duchesse of Guise, there is one is not bashfull. 80a
Duch. No my Lord, he is much guilty of the bold extremity. b

---

68. *rites*] often used for 'rights'; there seems to be a play between 'ceremonial attentions' and 'dues'.

71. *enseam*] bring together, introduce.

73.] *enter in*, gain admittance to; *your Graces*, (1) the society of you titled ladies, (2) your good graces. The Duchess's reply seems to depend (obscurely) on a courtly pun: 'enter in' sexually (cf. l. 79).

79. *leap-year*] Perhaps the primary sense is of the tradition that the lady may propose in leap-year (and so smooth a new courtier's way); but there is also a pun with 'leap' as used of rams mounting ewes in copulation, which connects with 'enter' (sexually as in l. 74). See also Introduction, p. lvii.

80a–b.] B's addition emphasizes the sexual implications of the dialogue.

82. *prick-song*] (1) singing from written notes, not memory or by ear; (2) punning with 'prick'=penis.

desire to be one, and [*to the Duchess*] would gladly take entrance, Madam, under your Princely Colours.

Gui. Sir, know you me?

Buss. My Lord?

Gui. I know not you: whom do you serve?

Buss. Serve, my Lord?

Gui. Go to companion; your courtship's too saucy.

Buss. [*aside*] Saucy? Companion? 'Tis the Guise, but yet those terms might have been spared of the Guiserd. Companion? He's jealous by this light: are you blind of

88–114.] *A; B reads:*

Enter Barrisor, L'Anou, Pyrlot.

Duch. Soft sir, you must rise by degrees, first being the servant of some common Lady or Knights wife, then a little higher to a Lords wife; next a little higher to a Countesse; yet a little higher to a Duchesse, and then turne the ladder.

D'Amb. Doe you alow a man then foure mistresses, when the greatest Mistresse is alowed but three servants?

Duch. Where find you that statute sir?

D'Amb. Why be judged by the Groome-porters.

Duchesse. The Groome-porters?

D'Amb. I Madam, must not they judge of all gamings i'th'Court?

Duchesse. You talke like a gamester.

Gui. Sir, know you me?

D'Amb. My Lord?

Gui. I know not you: Whom doe you serve?

D'Amb. Serve, my Lord?

Gui. Go to Companion; Your Courtship's too saucie.

D'Amb. Saucie? Companion? Tis the Guise, but yet those termes might have beene spar'd of the Guiserd. Compan-

---

86–7. *take entrance*] a form comparable with the phrase 'take leave'.

88–114.] B's added dialogue works up Bussy's courtship of the Duchess; it comes within a general rearrangement whose origin is most likely to be the theatre, and there is nothing distinctive of Chapman in it. See Introduction, p. lxii.

92, 93. *companion*] term of contempt, like 'fellow'.

92 ff. *courtship*] The word is being used in all possible senses: behaviour such as courtiers should use; such as satirically they were said to (flattery, etc.); paying court to a woman, either platonically or physically.

94. *Guiserd*] (1) partisan of the Guise; (2) masquerader (Brooke and Paradise say, with a false face: I have found no authority for this, but it makes sense).

95–6. *blind of that side*] evidently a variation on the phrase 'blind side', for which *O.E.D.*'s earliest date is 1655.

that side sir? I'll to her again for that. [*To the Duchess*] Forth Madam, for the honour of courtship.

Gui. Cease your courtship, or by heaven I'll cut your throat.

Buss. Cut my throat? cut a whetstone; good Accius Nævius, do as much with your tongue as he did with a razor; cut my throat?

Gui. I'll do 't by this hand.

Buss. That hand dares not do 't; y' have cut too many throats already Guise; and robbed the Realm of many thousand Souls, more precious than thine own. [*To the Duchess*]

ion? He's jealous by this light: are you blind of that side 95
Duke? Ile to her againe for that. Forth princely Mistresse, 96
for the honour of Courtship. Another Riddle. 97
Gui. Cease your Courtshippe, or by heaven Ile cut your throat. 98
D'Amb. Cut my throat? cut a whetstone; young *Accius Nævius,* 99
doe as much with your tongue as he did with a Rasor; cut 100
my throat? 101
Bar. What new-come Gallant have wee heere, that dares mate 108
the Guise thus? 109
L'An. Sfoot tis *D'Ambois*; The Duke mistakes him (on my life) 110
for some Knight of the new edition. 111
D'Amb. Cut my throat? I would the King fear'd thy cutting of 112
his throat no more than I feare thy cutting of mine. 113
Gui. Ile doe't by this hand. 102
D'Amb. That hand dares not doe't; y'ave cut too many / Throats 103
already Guise, and robb'd the Realme of / Many thousand 104
Soules, more precious than thine owne. / Come Madam, 105
talk on; Sfoot, can you not talk? / Talk on I say. Another 106
Riddle. 107

94. Guiserd.] *short line ends here A, B.* 103–7.] *Shepherd, Bo; as verse, lines ending:* many / of / owne. / talke? / it (Riddle). *A, B; as verse, lines ending:* do't. / Guise, / souls, / on. / say. *P.*

---

99. *Accius Nævius*] a Roman augur under Tarquinius Priscus: after a hostile prediction, Nævius was tested by being asked if what the king had in mind was possible; when he said it was, he was handed a whetstone which he promptly cut with a razor.

103–7.] B followed A's initial capitals, suggesting misaligned verse. Parrott believed his arrangement justified itself; blank verse rhythm does emerge briefly in ll. 103–5, but it seems to me better to set it out as prose, which overall it is.

103. *y' have cut too many throats*] Guise was notorious for the St Bartholomew's Day massacre of Protestants (1572): see Marlowe's *Massacre at Paris.*

Come Madam, talk on; 'sfoot, can you not talk? Talk on I say, more courtship, as you love it.

[*During the last speeches*] *enter* BARRISOR, L'ANOU, PYRRHOT.

Barr. What new-come gallant have we here, that dares mate the Guise thus?

L'An. 'Sfoot 'tis D'Ambois; the Duke mistakes him (on my life) for some Knight of the new edition.

Buss. Cut my throat? I would the King feared thy cutting of his throat no more than I fear thy cutting of mine.

Gui. So sir, so.

Pyrr. Here's some strange distemper.

Barr. Here's a sudden transmigration with D'Ambois, out of the Knights' ward, into the Duchess' bed.

L'An. See what a metamorphosis a brave suit can work.

Pyrr. 'Slight, step to the Guise and discover him.

Barr. By no means, let the new suit work, we'll see the issue.

Gui. Leave your courtship.

Buss. I will not. I say Mistress, and I will stand unto it, that if a woman may have three servants, a man may have threescore mistresses.

Gui. Sirrah, I'll have you whipped out of the Court for this insolence.

107.1. *Pyrrhot*] *Pyrlot A.* 119. 'Slight] *D;* Slight *A, B.* 121. courtship] *A;* Courting *B.*

107.1. During the last speeches] Barrisor, etc., must clearly overhear some of the quarrel. B's entry after l. 87 would do well enough, but as it is part of a considerable rearrangement, I have not specified it in the text.

108. *mate*] (1) match himself against, rival; (2) put out of countenance, put down (as in chess, to which there is also a direct reference here).

111. *Knight of the new edition*] In the first two months of his reign, James I created as many knights as Elizabeth in the previous ten years. Allusions are frequent: cf. I. i. 195; *Monsieur D'Olive*, IV. ii. 76 ff.; *Eastward Ho!*, IV. i. 179–80; Bacon's letter to Cecil, 3 July 1603, 'this almost prostituted title of knighthood'.

117. *Knights' ward*] one of the four parts of the Counter prison, discussed in *Eastward Ho!*, V. iii. 41 ff.

119. *discover him*] reveal his identity.

Buss. Whipped? Such another syllable out o' th' presence, if thou dar'st for thy Dukedom.

Gui. Remember, poltroon.

Mons. Pray thee forbear.

Buss. Passion of death! Were not the King here, he should strew the Chamber like a rush.

Mons. But leave courting his wife then.

Buss. I will not: I'll court her in despite of him. Not court her!—Come Madam, talk on; fear me nothing.—[*To Guise*] Well may'st thou drive thy master from the Court; but never D'Ambois.

Mons. [*aside*] His great heart will not down, 'tis like the sea
That partly by his own internal heat,
Partly the stars' daily and nightly motion,
Ardour and light, and partly of the place
The divers frames, and chiefly by the Moon,
Bristled with surges, never will be won
(No, not when th' hearts of all those powers are burst)
To make retreat into his settled home,
Till he be crown'd with his own quiet foam.

Hen. You have the mate. Another.

135–6. *To Guise*] *Bo; not in A, B.* 140. stars'] *P;* starr's *A, B.* 141. Ardour] *A;* Their heat *B.* place] *B;* place, *A.* 142. frames,] *B;* frames; *A.* and] *A;* but *B.*

---

127. *presence*] presence-chamber: king's reception room. Evidently there was a ban on brawling there (cf. III. ii. 66 ff.).

132. *rush*] The old practice of using rushes as floor-covering continued into the 17th century (cf. *The Gentleman Usher*, II. ii. 66).

138–46.] This is magnificent in general effect, but obscure in detail. I take ll. 139–42 to enumerate influences supposed to affect the incoming tide, which will not retreat until its waves have broken. In l. 143, 'Bristled' is a participle describing the sea: the only main verb is in 'never will be won'.

141. *Ardour*] burning heat.

142. *frames*] technically applied to heaven, earth, etc., regarded as a structure (*O.E.D.*, s.v., 8). Here in a more limited sense of the shape of the land which bounds the sea's movement, i.e. coasts, and perhaps (as Boas and Parrott thought) the sea-bed as well.

143. *surges*] waves, billows.

147.] referring to the game of chess (used as a dramatic comment on the quarrel).

Gui. No more.

Exit GUISE, *after him the* KING, MONSIEUR *whispering.*

Barr. Why here's the Lion, scared with the throat of a dunghill cock; a fellow that has newly shaked off his shackles; now does he crow for that victory.

L'An. 'Tis one of the best jigs that ever was acted.

Pyrr. Whom does the Guise suppose him to be, trow?

L'An. Out of doubt, some new-denizened Lord; and thinks that suit come new out o' th' Mercers' books.

Barr. I have heard of a fellow, that by a fixed imagination looking upon a bull-baiting, had a visible pair of horns grew out of his forehead: and I believe this Gallant overjoyed with the conceit of Monsieur's cast suit, imagines himself to be the Monsieur.

L'An. And why not? as well as the Ass, stalking in the Lion's case, bear himself like a Lion, roaring all the huger beasts out of the forest?

148.] *A; B adds: Flourish short.* 148.1. *King, Monsieur*] *A, B; King and Monsieur D, P.* 155. come new] *A;* newly drawne *B.* 162. roaring] *A;* braying *B.*

---

149. *throat*] i.e., voice.

149–50. *dunghill cock*] common as distinct from game-cock; as term of abuse, coward, etc. Cf. Gabriel Harvey, *Three Proper Wittie Letters* (1580), 'Asses in Lions skins; dunglecocks' (see ll. 161–3).

152. *jigs*] farcical entertainments (clowning, etc.) after a play.

153. *trow?*] think [you]?

154. *new-denizened*] newly naturalized. *O.E.D.* (s.v. *denizened*) cites this line and one from Ascham for a special sense: 'to furnish with denizens, people with settlers from another country'. I cannot see this sense in either instance. The allusion is to James I's Scottish entourage: the naturalization of the Scots was a repeated issue in James's efforts to unite his kingdom.

155. *Mercers*] fine clothiers.

156. *a fixed imagination*] Imagination was regarded as a faculty dependent entirely on the senses (and so possessed by animals), capable of constructing things not present, and often fantastic. So here, the fellow's sight was fixed (as in 'fixed attention') on the bull-baiting and governing his imagination.

159. *cast*] cast-off.

161–3.] referring to Aesop's fable (and see note on ll. 149–50).

162. *case*] covering; skin of an animal.

roaring] B's 'braying' has advantages, but could well derive from a trick of memory.

Pyrr. Peace, he looks this way.

Barr. Marry let him look sir, what will you say now if the Guise be gone to fetch a blanket for him?

L'An. Faith I believe it for his honour.

Pyrr. But, if D'Ambois carry it clean? *Exeunt* Ladies.

Barr. True, when he curvets in the blanket.

Pyrr. Ay marry sir.

L'An. 'Sfoot, see how he stares on 's.

Barr. Lord bless us, let's away.

Buss. Now sir, take your full view: how does the object please ye?

Barr. If you ask my opinion sir, I think your suit sits as well as if 't had been made for you.

Buss. So sir, and was that the subject of your ridiculous jollity?

L'An. What's that to you sir?

Buss. Sir, I have observed all your fleerings; and resolve yourselves ye shall give a strict account for 't.

Enter BRISAC, MELYNELL.

Pyrr. O strange credulity! Do you think yourself such a sin-

167. honour] *A;* honour sake *B.* 168. *Exeunt* Ladies.] *B; not in A.* 175. sits] *A, B;* fits *P.* 182. *Pyrr.* O strange credulity] *A; Bar.* O miraculous jealousie *B.* 182–4.] *D, Bo, P; as verse, lines ending:* selfe / into / you? *A, B.*

166. *blanket*] for traditional punishment, tossing in a blanket (cf. l. 169; *The Widow's Tears*, I. iii. 94–6; *2 H4*, II. iv. 239–40).

168. *carry it*] win, as in 'carry the day'.

clean] completely.

Exeunt *Ladies*] B's placing of this is quite arbitrary, but Chapman seems not to have provided an exit at all.

175. *sits*] (of clothes) fits.

180. *fleerings*] scornful laughter.

182–4.] A's initial capitals implying verse are obviously an error; that B retains them whilst making the words even more prosaic is clear evidence of its dependence. B's switching of speakers for this and the next two speeches seems quite pointless, and all the odder because Barrisor's 'jealousy' is carried back into his new speech, with clumsy results: once again, tricks of memory in the copyist-reviser seem the best explanation.

gular subject for laughter, that none can fall into our merriment but you?

Barr. This jealousy of yours sir, confesses some close defect in yourself, that we never dreamed of.

L'An. We held discourse of a perfumed Ass, that being disguised with a Lion's case, imagined himself a Lion: I hope that touched not you.

Buss. So sir: your descants do marvellous well fit this ground, we shall meet where your buffoonly laughters will cost ye the best blood in your bodies.

Barr. For life's sake let's be gone; he'll kill 's outright.

Buss. Go at your pleasures, I'll be your Ghost to haunt you, and ye sleep on 't, hang me.

L'An. Go, go sir, court your Mistress.

Pyrr. And be advised: we shall have odds against you.

Buss. Tush, valour stands not in number: I'll maintain it, that one man may beat three boys.

Bris. Nay you shall have no odds of him in number sir: he's a gentleman as good as the proudest of you, and ye shall not wrong him.

Barr. Not sir?

Mel. Not sir: though he be not so rich, he's a better man than the best of you; and I will not endure it.

L'An. Not you sir?

Bris. No sir, nor I.

Buss. I should thank you for this kindness, if I thought these

183. into our] *A;* into / The matter of our *B.* 185. *Barr.*] *A; L'An. B.* 187. *L'An.*] *A; Pyr. B.* 188. with] *A;* in *B.* 193. outright] *A;* outright else *B.*

---

185. *close*] hidden.

190. *descants . . . ground*] (1) *as musical terms:* 'ground'=plain-song (or tune) on which descant is raised; 'descant'=an air above (in pitch) and in harmony with the fixed (repeated) ground; (2) *in this context:* 'descant'= comments (criticisms); 'ground'=grounds for comment (Bussy's clothes and behaviour), and (more pertinently) the ground they stand on, the presence-chamber. (Brooke and Paradise gloss *descants* as flourishes, which would add a sense, if there is any authority for it.)

195. *and*] if.

perfumed musk-cats (being out of this privilege) durst but once mew at us.

Barr. Does your confident spirit doubt that sir? Come follow us and try.

L'An. Come sir, we'll lead you a dance. *Exeunt.*

211. Come] *A; not in B.* 213.] *A, B add: Finis Actus primi.*

---

209. *musk-cats*] any animals from which musk was extracted for perfume; hence fops.

privilege] Editors have assumed this refers to the ground on which the royal prerogative operated, i.e. the presence-chamber, etc., though *O.E.D.* does not give such a specific sense.

Act II

[II. i]

[*Enter*] HENRY, GUISE, BEAUMOND, *and* Attendants.

Hen. This desperate quarrel sprung out of their envies
To D'Ambois' sudden bravery, and great spirit.
Gui. Neither is worth their envy.
Hen. Less than either
Will make the gall of Envy overflow;
She feeds on outcast entrails like a kite:
In which foul heap, if any ill lies hid,
She sticks her beak into it, shakes it up,
And hurls it all abroad, that all may view it.
Corruption is her nutriment; but touch her

Act II] Actus secundi Scena prima. *A, B.* 0.1.] *Spencer; Henry, Guise, Beaumond, Nuncius. A; Henry, Guise, Montsurry, and Attendants. B;* Henry, Guise, Montsurry, [Beaumond] *and* Attendants *P.*

0.1.] A's *Nuncius* presumably derives from Chapman's list of characters for the scene (see Introduction, p. lxi). Boas thought that in B *Montsurry* was substituted for *Beaumond* to economize actors, and that the retention of *Beau.* at l. 105 and after l. 205 was due to careless correction. Parrott ingeniously suggested that Montsurry was brought on here to learn of Bussy's pardon when II. ii. 1–50 was cut, and that *Beaumond* was deleted in error. Either may be right; Chapman's original intention is not in doubt.

1. *sprung*] alternative form of sprang as a past tense: the participle is also possible, if Guise is assumed to interrupt Henry.

2. *bravery*] (1) fine clothes; (2) courage (a latent sense, linking with spirit).

4. *Envy*] The figure derives from traditional emblem pictures of the Seven Deadly Sins (see *The Faerie Queene*, I. iv. 30–2, for a similar method but different emblems). Chapman's Envy is half woman, half kite; but as his usage is not very close to visual picture, it is better described as simultaneously woman and kite. In *Chabot*, IV. i. 10–16, he uses the same idea as a simple image of the envious, without emblematic personification and so without the development which is possible here.

With any precious ointment, and you kill her:
When she finds any filth in men, she feasts,
And with her black throat bruits it through the world
(Being sound and healthful); but if she but taste
The slenderest pittance of commended virtue,
She surfeits of it, and is like a fly,
That passes all the body's soundest parts,
And dwells upon the sores; or if her squint eye
Have power to find none there, she forges some:
She makes that crooked ever which is straight;
Calls Valour Giddiness, Justice Tyranny:
A wise man may shun her, she not herself;
Whithersoever she flies from her harms,
She bears her foe still clasp'd in her own arms:
And therefore cousin Guise let us avoid her.

Enter NUNCIUS.

Nun. What Atlas, or Olympus lifts his head
So far past covert, that with air enough
My words may be inform'd? And from his height

11. When] *A;* Where *B.* 19. straight] *D, P;* strait *A, B.* 25. *Nun.*] *Nuncius B; not in A.* 27. his] *A;* their *B.*

---

12. *bruits*] noises, rumours.

13. (*Being . . . healthful*)] i.e., Envy, feeding on filth.

15–17.] Chapman uses the same image in *An Invective . . . against Mr. Ben: Johnson*, ll. 64–6.

17. *squint eye*] traditional attribute of Envy: see Spenser, *Shepheardes Calender*, August, l. 129, and E. K.'s gloss 'partiall iudgement'.

18. *forges*] (1) makes; (2) fakes (see I. i. 8).

19. *straight*] A and B 'strait' could involve the moral sense 'strict'.

24.1. *Nuncius*] The messenger-narrator derives from Greek tragedy via Seneca, whom Chapman imitates in deploying the grand manner of epic on the stage: see Introduction, pp. xl–xli.

25. *Atlas*] Titan who was punished by being made to support the heavens; hence mountains in North Africa.

Olympus] Greek mountain whose summit was supposed to be the residence of the gods.

26. *covert*] covering, shelter (especially of trees, etc.).

27. *inform'd*] (1) given form; (2) inspired.

his] its.

I may be seen, and heard through all the world?
A tale so worthy, and so fraught with wonder,
Sticks in my jaws, and labours with event.

Hen. Com'st thou from D'Ambois?

Nun. From him, and the rest
His friends and enemies; whose stern fight I saw,
And heard their words before, and in the fray.

Hen. Relate at large what thou hast seen and heard.

Nun. I saw fierce D'Ambois, and his two brave friends
Enter the field, and at their heels their foes;
Which were the famous soldiers, Barrisor,
L'Anou, and Pyrrhot, great in deeds of Arms:
All which arriv'd at the evenest piece of earth
The field afforded; the three challengers
Turn'd head, drew all their rapiers, and stood rank'd:
When face to face the three defendants met them,
Alike prepar'd, and resolute alike,
Like bonfires of contributory wood:
Every man's look shew'd, fed with either's spirit,
As one had been a mirror to another,
Like forms of life and death, each took from other;

43–5. alike, . . . wood: . . . spirit,] *A;* alike, . . . wood, . . . spirit, *B;* alike. . . . wood . . . spirit; *D, Bo, P.*

---

29. *fraught with*] filled with, attended with; with special reference to pregnancy (*O.E.D.*, s.v. *fraught*, 3b), 'big' with promise or menace of . . . (hence 'labours' in l. 30).

30. *event*] outcome, with special sense of birth (as in 'happy event'). The meaning 'outstanding happening' is apparently modern, though its germ is felt here.

35 ff.] Such a three-a-side duel took place in France in 1578 between partisans of the King and Guise; Bussy was not involved.

42–7.] The characteristic evolution of each clause from its predecessor here makes clear punctuation impossible; Boas's and Parrott's full stop after l. 43 destroys the sequence; and whilst B's comma after l. 44 is correct, A's colon offers a useful rhetorical pause, stressing that ll. 45–7 are all expanding the image of the 'bonfires of contributory wood', fed by each man's spirit, and reflected in their faces in the burning light which symbolizes equally the will to live, and to kill.

44. *contributory*] i.e., each piece of wood contributing to the one fire.

47. *Like*] adjective, not conjunction.

And so were life and death mix'd at their heights,
That you could see no fear of death, for life;
Nor love of life, for death: but in their brows
Pyrrho's Opinion in great letters shone,
That life and death in all respects are one.
Hen. Pass'd there no sort of words at their encounter?
Nun. As Hector, 'twixt the hosts of Greece and Troy
(When Paris and the Spartan King should end
The nine years' war) held up his brazen lance
For signal, that both hosts should cease from arms,
And hear him speak: so Barrisor (advis'd)
Advanc'd his naked rapier 'twixt both sides,
Ripp'd up the quarrel, and compar'd six lives
Then laid in balance with six idle words;
Offer'd remission and contrition too;
Or else that he and D'Ambois might conclude
The others' dangers. D'Ambois lik'd the last;
But Barrisor's friends (being equally engag'd
In the main quarrel) never would expose
His life alone, to that they all deserv'd.
And (for the other offer of remission)

60. lives] *Bo, P;* liues; *A;* lives, *B.* 61. words;] *Bo, P;* words, *A, B.*

---

48. *at their heights*] (1) the extremities of life and death; (2) the height of heroic spirit in the contestants.

51. *Pyrrho*] Greek founder of Sceptic philosophy, contemporary of Alexander the Great, preaching indifference. Ferguson (p. 6) quotes an Alexandrian epigram: 'Are you dead Pyrrho?' 'I do not know.'

54–8.] In *Iliad* III Paris proposed a duel with Menelaus to end the Trojan war. See *Iliads,* III. 73–85.

58. *advis'd*] having considered.

60. *Ripp'd up*] (1) literally, by putting his sword between the quarrellers; (2) (*O.E.D.*, s.v. *rip,* 4a) searched into, examined (the circumstances).

62. *remission*] 'Relaxation' (of anger) is possible, and more natural with contrition than 'forgiveness'; but that may be the sense if 'too' has the force of 'even'.

63. *conclude*] 'include' and 'finish'; i.e., settle the quarrel by single combat (see l. 55).

64. *dangers*] power to harm, as well as risk of harm (see l. 92).

D'Ambois (that like a laurel put in fire,
Sparkled and spit) did much much more than scorn,
That his wrong should incense him so like chaff,
To go so soon out; and like lighted paper,
Approve his spirit at once both fire and ashes:
So drew they lots, and in them Fates appointed,
That Barrisor should fight with fiery D'Ambois;
Pyrrhot with Melynell; with Brisac L'Anou:
And then like flame and powder they commix'd,
So spritely, that I wish'd they had been spirits,
That the ne'er-shutting wounds they needs must open,
Might as they open'd, shut, and never kill:
But D'Ambois' sword (that light'ned as it flew)
Shot like a pointed Comet at the face
Of manly Barrisor; and there it stuck:
Thrice pluck'd he at it, and thrice drew on thrusts,
From him, that of himself was free as fire;
Who thrust still as he pluck'd, yet (past belief!)
He with his subtle eye, hand, body, scap'd;
At last the deadly bitten point tugg'd off,
On fell his yet undaunted foe so fiercely,
That (only made more horrid with his wound)
Great D'Ambois shrunk, and gave a little ground;
But soon return'd, redoubled in his danger,
And at the heart of Barrisor seal'd his anger:

69–70.] Laurel burns explosively; and there may also be a reference to the hero's wreath (for Bussy).

71. *chaff*] husks (of corn, etc.) which burn out quickly; perhaps playing with fig. sense of 'ridicule' (not known in *O.E.D.* before 1648).

78. *spritely*] (1) vigorously; (2) ghostly (hence 'spirits').

79–80.] The wounds, which will never heal in men, would in angels ('spirits') heal instantly. Lamb compared Milton's angels, *Paradise Lost*, VI. 328–50.

84–7.] The pronouns are confusing: apparently 'he' is always Bussy, 'him' Barrisor.

88. *bitten*] having bitten, biting (*O.E.D.*, s.v., 4: only example is 1616).

90. *his*] Barrisor's.

93. *seal'd*] impressed (as with a seal).

Then, as in Arden I have seen an Oak
Long shook with tempests, and his lofty top
Bent to his root, which being at length made loose
(Even groaning with his weight) he gan to nod
This way and that, as loth his curled brows
(Which he had oft wrapp'd in the sky with storms)
Should stoop: and yet, his radical fivers burst,
Storm-like he fell, and hid the fear-cold Earth.
So fell stout Barrisor, that had stood the shocks
Of ten set battles in your Highness' war,
'Gainst the sole soldier of the world, Navarre.

Gui. O piteous and horrid murder!

Beaum. Such a life
Methinks had mettle in it to survive
An age of men.

Hen. Such, often soonest end.
Thy felt report calls on, we long to know
On what events the other have arriv'd.

Nun. Sorrow and Fury, like two opposite fumes
Met in the upper region of a cloud,

105. *Beaum.*] *A, B; Montsurry Bo.* 106. mettle] mettall *A, B;* metal *D, P.*

94–101.] apparently a re-creation from the *Aeneid*: see Appendix B, pp. 153–4.

94. *Arden*] derived (as in *As You Like It*) from Ardennes; perhaps confused with Arden in Warwickshire; it is always (as Parrott and Boas noted) a romantic site in Elizabethan literature.

99. *wrapp'd*] hidden.

100. *radical fivers*] apparently 'threads of life': 'fivers' was a common form of 'fibres'; *O.E.D.* (s.v. *fiver*, 2a) cites 1621 Sandys *Ovid's Metamorphoses* VI. 113, 'The threds / Of life, his fivers, wrathful Delius shreds'.

103–4.] Parrott noted that Henry of Navarre's military reputation depended on events well after Bussy's death.

106–7.] Classical mythology represented the four ages of Man as declining through golden, silver, brazen to iron.

106. *mettle*] (1) mettle; (2) metal (see I. i. 64).

108. *Thy felt report calls on*] primarily, calls for more; but 'calls on' was a hunting term, and 'report' has the sense of noise in l. 112, so that a hunting phrase seems likely here.

109. *other*] others, as in l. 128.

110–11. *like . . . cloud*] presumably a theory of thunderstorms.

At the report made by this worthy's fall
Brake from the earth, and with them rose Revenge,
Ent'ring with fresh powers his two noble friends;
And under that odds fell surcharg'd Brisac,
The friend of D'Ambois, before fierce L'Anou;
Which D'Ambois seeing, as I once did see
In my young travels through Armenia,
An angry Unicorn in his full career
Charge with too quick an eye a jeweller,
That watch'd him for the treasure of his brow;
And ere he could get shelter of a tree,
Nail him with his rich antler to the earth:
So D'Ambois ran upon reveng'd L'Anou,
Who eyeing th' eager point borne in his face,
And giving back, fell back, and in his fall
His foe's uncurbed sword stopp'd in his heart:
By which time all the life strings of the tw' other
Were cut, and both fell as their spirits flew
Upwards: and still hunt Honour at the view.
And now (of all the six) sole D'Ambois stood
Untouch'd, save only with the others' blood.

Hen. All slain outright?

Nun. All slain outright but he,
Who kneeling in the warm life of his friends
(All freckled with the blood his rapier rain'd),

120. quick an eye] *A;* swift a foot *B.* 129. spirits] *A, P;* spirit *B.* 133. outright?] *A, Bo;* outright but hee? *B.* 135. freckled] *B;* feebled *A.* blood] *B;* blood, *A.*

---

115. *surcharg'd*] overloaded.

118. *Armenia*] Seneca refers to Armenia as inhabited by wild animals (not unicorns) in *Hercules Oetaeus*, l. 241.

119–23.] The treasure of a unicorn's brow was of course its horn, especially prized as an antidote to all poisons. Unicorns were supposed to be caught by being tempted to charge a tree, and so impale their horns. See *Cæs.*, II. i. 203–4, and *The Faerie Queene*, II. v. 10.

130. *at the view*] at sight; i.e., their spirits still chase ardently after honour beyond death.

135. *freckled*] As Ure suggested, A's 'feebled' may have been a misread-

He kiss'd their pale cheeks, and bade both farewell;
And see the bravest man the French earth bears.

Enter MONSIEUR, [BUSSY] D'AMBOIS *bare.*

Buss. Now is the time, y' are Princely-vow'd my friend,
Perform it Princely, and obtain my pardon.
Mons. Else Heaven forgive not me: come on brave friend.
[*They kneel before* HENRY.]
If ever Nature held herself her own,
When the great trial of a King and subject
Met in one blood, both from one belly springing:
Now prove her virtue and her greatness One,
Or make the t' one the greater with the t' other
(As true Kings should), and for your brother's love
(Which is a special species of true virtue),
Do that you could not do, not being a King.
Hen. Brother I know your suit; these wilful murders
Are ever past our pardon.
Mons. Manly slaughter
Should never bear th' account of wilful murder;

136. cheeks] *A;* lips *B.* 138. Princely-vow'd] Princely vow'd *A, B.*
140.1.] *P, D subs.; not in A, B.*

---

ing (of, e.g., 'frekled'); if it was correct, 'feebled' = grown feeble. See *The Revenge of Bussy*, I. i. 117–18: 'the blood / She so much thirsts for, freckling hands and face', which is either a parallel phrase, or the source of B's revision.

137.1. bare] (1) unarmed (*O.E.D.*, s.v., 6b); (2) head uncovered.

140.1.] The action is indicated by l. 180.

141–8.] The contorted rhetoric makes Monsieur's preamble very obscure. But the effect of the lines depends on stressing the large abstractions (especially Nature, virtue, greatness) for their own sake, so that they are only secondarily linked by the particular meaning, which I suppose to be: 'If ever Nature could be true to herself in the conflict between our relationships as King and subject, and as brothers, either show that the family tie is as powerful as kingship or make your kingship greater by augmenting it with family loyalty, by granting your brother's suit by means available to you only as king (pardoning a murder).'

150. *Manly slaughter*] presumably a deliberate variant of manslaughter, playing on 'manly' = noble.

It being a spice of justice, where, with life
Offending past law, equal life is laid
In equal balance, to scourge that offence
By law of reputation (which to men
Exceeds all positive law); and what that leaves
To true men's valours (not prefixing rights
Of satisfaction, suited to their wrongs)
A free man's eminence may supply and take.
Hen. This would make every man that thinks him wrong'd,
Or is offended, or in wrong or right,
Lay on this violence, and all vaunt themselves
Law-menders and suppliers though mere butchers;
Should this fact (though of justice) be forgiven?
Mons. O no, my Lord; it would make cowards fear
To touch the reputations of full men;
When only they are left to imp the law,
Justice will soon distinguish murderous minds
From just revengers: had my friend been slain,

166. full] *A;* true *B.* men;] *D;* men, *A, B.*

---

152. *being a spice of*] having a touch of. (Brooke and Paradise gloss 'species of', but *O.E.D.* does not support this, although 'spice' can be 'species' in other senses; in any case it does not yield a likely reading here.)

153. *past law*] 'beyond the scope of regular law' (Brooke and Paradise).

156. *positive law*] formally laid down, as distinct from natural law.
that] i.e., positive law.

157. *prefixing*] settling in advance, determining (i.e., the legal code not providing for such circumstances).

163. *suppliers*] makers-up of deficiencies. Brooke and Paradise gloss 'deputies' but quote no authority; the word obviously derives from the use of 'supply' in II. ii. 147 and IV. i. 150, but *O.E.D.* has no other cases of this noun in this sense from the 17th century.

164. *fact*] deed (especially in legal usage).

165–7.] confusing pronouns: 'it' seems to go with 'This' in l. 160, i.e. private revenge by just men, and 'they' refers to 'full men'.

166. *full men*] complete, entire, perfect. See V. iii. 268 'complete man': this represents Chapman's positive as distinct from 'great men' (I. i. 6). Bacon's use of 'full man' (*O.E.D.*, s.v. *full*, 2d) as one whose mind is richly stored is similar, but narrower than Chapman's sense.

167. *imp*] engraft; hence eke out, mend (see *Monsieur D'Olive*, III. ii. 76–7: 'all my care is for followers to imp out my train').

His enemy surviving, he should die,
Since he had added to a murder'd fame
(Which was in his intent) a murder'd man;
And this had worthily been wilful murder:
But my friend only sav'd his fame's dear life
Which is above life, taking th' under-value
Which in the wrong it did was forfeit to him;
And in this fact only preserves a man
In his uprightness; worthy to survive
Millions of such as murder men, alive.

Hen. Well brother, rise, and raise your friend withal
From death to life: and D'Ambois, let your life
(Refin'd by passing through this merited death)
Be purg'd from more such foul pollution;
Nor on your 'scape, nor valour more presuming,
To be again so violent.

Buss. My Lord,
I loathe as much a deed of unjust death,
As law itself doth; and to tyrannise,
Because I have a little spirit to dare
And power to do, as to be tyrannis'd;
This is a grace that (on my knees redoubled) [*kneels again*]

185. violent] *A, Bo;* daring *B.*

---

170. *he*] i.e., the enemy.

173. *worthily*] justly (used with reference to demerit and its punishment, *O.E.D.*, s.v., 2d).

175–6.] The 'under-value' is life as distinct from fame; his enemy's life was forfeit because of the wrong he did.

179. *men, alive*] B's omission of the comma seems to make nonsense: I think it marks an ellision, 'such . . . [who are still] alive'.

190–204.] Boas notes that 'This' refers forward, and asserts that in ll. 194–202 Bussy explains the grace he asks for. Monsieur has argued Bussy's *right* to revenge his fame, but Henry only pardons him from 'merited death'; Bussy redoubles his knees for a grace not yet granted, i.e. to be above the reach of law in his innocence (l. 195) and native justice (l. 198). In short, Bussy refuses pardon because he does not acknowledge guilt (ll. 194–6). Compare Chabot's far clearer refusal of pardon for a crime of which he is innocent in *Chabot*, IV. i. 234 ff. Henry's equivocal reply here, 'we give but ours', keeps Bussy's freedom within the royal prerogative; but in III. ii

I crave to double this my short life's gift;
And shall your Royal bounty centuple,
That I may so make good what God and Nature
Have given me for my good: since I am free
(Offending no just law), let no law make
By any wrong it does, my life her slave:
When I am wrong'd and that law fails to right me,
Let me be King myself (as man was made)
And do a justice that exceeds the law:
If my wrong pass the power of single valour
To right and expiate; then be you my King,
And do a Right, exceeding Law and Nature:
Who to himself is law, no law doth need,
Offends no King, and is a King indeed.

Hen. Enjoy what thou entreat'st, we give but ours.

Exit KING *with* BEAUMOND [*and* Attendants].

Buss. What you have given, my Lord, is ever yours.

Gui. Mort Dieu, who would have pardon'd such a murder? *Exit.*

Mons. Now vanish horrors into Court attractions,
For which let this balm make thee fresh and fair.

193. God] *A, P;* law *B.* 204. no King] *A;* no Law *B.* 205.1.] *Exit Rex / cum Beau. A, B.* 207. Mort Dieu] *A, Bo, P; not in B.*

Henry upholds Bussy's assertion of man's 'native noblesse'. This conception of man's pre-lapsarian freedom to which he may return is central to all Chapman's later work: it is first clearly stated in *The Gentleman Usher*, v. iv. 56–62:

> And what's a prince? Had all been virtuous men,
> There never had been prince upon the earth,
> And so no subject; all men had been princes:
> A virtuous man is subject to no prince,
> But to his soul and honour; which are laws
> That carry fire and sword within themselves,
> Never corrupted, never out of rule.

192. *And shall*] 'i.e. And which grace shall' (Boas).

193. *God*] Parrott and Ure attribute B's change to the 'Blasphemy' Act.

197. *that*] when.

204. *no King*] Ure suggests B's change was a compositor's or copyist's error.

207. *Mort Dieu*] B's suppression may again be due to the 'Blasphemy' Act.

Buss. How shall I quite your love?
Mons. Be true to the end:
I have obtain'd a Kingdom with my friend. *Exeunt.*

[II. ii]

[*Enter*] MONTSURRY, TAMYRA, BEAUPRÉ, PERO *with a book,* CHARLOTTE, PYRHA.

Mont. He will have pardon sure.
Tam. 'Twere pity else:
For though his great spirit something overflow,
All faults are still-born, that from greatness grow:
But such a sudden Courtier saw I never.
Beaup. He was too sudden, which indeed was rudeness.
Tam. True, for it argu'd his no due conceit
Both of the place, and greatness of the persons;

210–11.] *A; B reads:*

And now forth with thy service to the Duchesse,
As my long love will to Montsurries Countesse. *Exit.*
D'Amb. To whom my love hath long been vow'd in heart,
Although in hand for shew I held the Duchesse.
And now through bloud and vengeance, deeds of height,
And hard to be atchiev'd, tis fit I make
Attempt of her perfection, I need feare
No check in his Rivality, since her vertues
Are so renown'd, and hee of all Dames hated. *Exit.*

211. *Exeunt.*] *Exit, A.*

II. ii. 0.1–50.] *A, Bo; not in B.* 0.1. *with a book*] *B at II. ii. 50; not in A.*
3. still-born] *this ed.;* still borne *A.*

---

210. *quite*] requite.

210–11.] B's substituted lines evidently prepare for the gap left by deleting II. ii. 1–50; but they are singularly inept both in their clumsy rhetoric, and in the suggestion that Bussy had 'long been vow'd' to Tamyra; there may have been a deliberate intention to gloss over the suddenness of Tamyra's passion, and Bussy's negative rôle in the wooing.

II. ii. 1–50.] See Introduction, pp. xlii–xliii and lxxiii.

3. *still-born*] the spelling in A is ambiguous: Brooke and Paradise read 'still borne', which is possible (still=ever); my text seems more probable, and is supported in *O.E.D.* from 1607.

6. *conceit*] conception; hence esteem.

7. *the place*] the presence-chamber.

Nor of our sex: all which (we all being strangers
To his encounter) should have made more manners
Deserve more welcome.
Mont. All this fault is found
Because he lov'd the Duchess and left you.
Tam. Alas, love give her joy; I am so far
From envy of her honour, that I swear,
Had he encounter'd me with such proud sleight,
I would have put that project face of his
To a more test than did her Duchess-ship.
Beaup. Why, by your leave my Lord, I'll speak it here
(Although she be my Aunt), she scarce was modest,
When she perceiv'd the Duke her husband take
Those late exceptions to her servant's courtship,
To entertain him.
Tam. Ay, and stand him still,
Letting her husband give her servant place:
Though he did manly, she should be a woman.

Enter GUISE.

Gui. D'Ambois is pardon'd: where's a King? Where law?
See how it runs, much like a turbulent sea;
Here high, and glorious, as it did contend

24. *Gui.*] *not in A.*

---

9. *encounter*] with stronger sense of 'accosting', especially sexually.
14. *sleight*] adroitness (of wit); coloured by sense of 'trickery'.
15. *project*] a use peculiar to Chapman; *O.E.D.* glosses 'abandoned, ab-
ect, base', but it seems to be nearer to the Latin, implying forward-thrust-
ng, self-asserting. See *Iliads*, III, Comm. ll. 15–16, 'For which yet his
Criticus hath the project impudence to taxe Homer', and *Hymn to Apollo*,
. 707.
20. *late*] recent.
21. *entertain*] admit his conversation; but there was a special sense of
aking someone as a servant (*O.E.D.*, s.v., 5 and 6, not noted in the amorous
ense of servant).
stand] an odd use, not represented in *O.E.D.*: perhaps the result of play-
ng between the senses 'put up with' (as in 'I can't stand so-and-so') and
encounter' (opponent, not lover, *O.E.D.*, s.v., 52a, citing *Iliads*, XXI. 508).
22. *servant*] playing between 'menial' and 'lover'.

To wash the heavens, and make the stars more pure:
And here so low, it leaves the mud of hell
To every common view; come Count Montsurry
We must consult of this.

Tam. Stay not, sweet Lord.

Mont. Be pleas'd, I'll straight return. *Exit with* GUISE.

Tam. Would that would please me.

Beaup. I'll leave you Madam to your passions.
I see, there's change of weather in your looks.
Exit with [CHARLOTTE *and* PYRHA].

Tam. I cannot cloak it: but, as when a fume,
Hot, dry and gross (within the womb of Earth
Or in her superficies begot),
When extreme cold hath struck it to her heart,
The more it is compress'd, the more it rageth;
Exceeds his prison's strength that should contain it,
And then it tosseth Temples in the air;
All bars made engines to his insolent fury:
So, of a sudden, my licentious fancy
Riots within me: not my name and house
Nor my religion to this hour observ'd
Can stand above it: I must utter that
That will in parting break more strings in me,
Than death when life parts; and that holy man
That from my cradle counsell'd for my soul,
I now must make an agent for my blood.

31. *with*] *cum A.* 33.1.] *Exit cum suis. A.*

34–41.] a classical theory of earthquakes as caused by the compression of hot air in the earth. See Seneca, *Nat. Quaest.*, VI, especially his own theory, sections 17, 18.

35. *gross*] dense, thick.

36. *superficies*] i.e., outer crust.

37. *her*] i.e., Earth's.

39. *his*] i.e., the fume's.

41. *engines*] tools.

49.] illustrating the phrase 'All bars made engines' in l. 41, which is the key to all Tamyra's subsequent hypocrisy.

blood] regarded as one of the four humours from which the physical and

Enter MONSIEUR.

Mons. Yet, is my Mistress gracious?
Tam. Yet unanswer'd?
Mons. Pray thee regard thine own good, if not mine,
And cheer my love for that; you do not know
What you may be by me, nor what without me;
I may have power t' advance and pull down any.
Tam. That's not my study: one way I am sure
You shall not pull down me: my husband's height
Is crown to all my hopes: and his retiring
To any mean state, shall be my aspiring:
Mine honour's in mine own hands, spite of Kings.
Mons. Honour, what's that? your second maidenhead:
And what is that? a word: the word is gone,
The thing remains: the rose is pluck'd, the stalk
Abides: an easy loss where no lack's found:
Believe it there's as small lack in the loss,
As there is pain i' th' losing; archers ever
Have two strings to a bow: and shall great Cupid
(Archer of archers both in men and women)
Be worse provided than a common archer?
A husband and a friend all wise wives have.
Tam. Wise wives they are that on such strings depend,
With a firm husband, weighing a dissolute friend.
Mons. Still you stand on your husband, so do all

49.1.] *A, Bo; Enter Monsieur, Tamyra, and Pero with a Booke. B, before 51.*
71. weighing a dissolute] *A;* joyning a lose *B.*

---

psychological nature of man was composed (see note on ll. 234–5): blood conveyed passion in general, sexual passion in particular.

60 ff.] Monsieur's language is persistently suggestive, not often specifically enough for comment.

60–2.] a common form of argument, depending on the distinction (from the sceptical philosophy Monsieur represents) of nominal and real, word and thing. Falstaff follows the same formula in *1 H4*, v. i. 131–43. The 'thing' of l. 62 is of course the female genitals, unaffected by loss of *second* maidenhead; 'thing' commonly refers to penis, hence 'the stalk / Abides'.

71.] Boas asserted a play between the senses of 'firm' and 'loose' in archery and morals, which is clarified in B.

The common sex of you, when y' are encounter'd
With one ye cannot fancy: all men know
You live in Court here by your own election,
Frequenting all our solemn sports and triumphs,
All the most youthful company of men:
And wherefore do you this? To please your husband?
'Tis gross and fulsome: if your husband's pleasure
Be all your object, and you aim at Honour
In living close to him, get you from Court,
You may have him at home; these common put-offs
For common women serve: my honour? husband?
Dames maritorious, ne'er were meritorious:
Speak plain and say I do not like you sir,
Y' are an ill-favour'd fellow in my eye,
And I am answer'd.

Tam. Then I pray be answer'd:
For in good faith my Lord I do not like you
In that sort you like.

Mons. Then have at you here:
Take (with a politic hand) this rope of pearl;
And though you be not amorous, yet be wise:
Take me for wisdom; he that you can love
Is ne'er the further from you.

Tam. Now it comes
So ill prepar'd, that I may take a poison
Under a medicine as good cheap as it:

76. solemn] *A;* common *B.*

---

76. *solemn*] (1) formal; (2) sumptuous (*O.E.D.*, s.v., 4a). Parrott thought B's change deliberate to avoid suggesting Tamyra confined herself to solemn occasions; I suspect a trick of memory depending on the aural likeness of 'common' and 'solemn'.

sports and triumphs] entertainments and spectacles.

84. *maritorious*] nonce-word: *O.E.D.* glosses 'fond of their husbands'; presumably excessively so, equivalent to 'uxorious'.

meritorious] probably playing with sense 'that earns money (by prostitution)' (*O.E.D.*, s.v., 5).

95. *Under*] disguised beneath.

good cheap] intensive form of cheap, commonly in moral as well as economic sense.

I will not have it were it worth the world.
Mons. Horror of death: could I but please your eye,
You would give me the like, ere you would loose me:
Honour and husband!
Tam. By this light my Lord
Y' are a vile fellow: and I'll tell the King
Your occupation of dishonouring Ladies
And of his Court: a Lady cannot live
As she was born, and with that sort of pleasure
That fits her state, but she must be defam'd
With an infamous Lord's detraction:
Who would endure the Court if these attempts
Of open and profess'd lust must be borne?
Who's there? come on Dame, you are at your book
When men are at your mistress; have I taught you
Any such waiting woman's quality?
Mons. Farewell good husband. *Exit* MONSIEUR.
Tam. Farewell wicked Lord.

Enter MONTSURRY.

Mont. Was not the Monsieur here?
Tam. Yes, to good purpose.
And your cause is as good to seek him too
And haunt his company.
Mont. Why what's the matter?
Tam. Matter of death, were I some husbands' wife:
I cannot live at quiet in my chamber
For opportunities almost to rapes
Offer'd me by him.

111. *Tam.*] *Tamira. B; Mont. A.* 117. opportunities] *A, B;* importunities *D conj.*

---

106. *attempts*] in special sense of sexual assault (*O.E.D.*, s.v., 3b).
108–10.] a conventional comic formula: see *All Fools*, II. i. 282–5, and *Monsieur D'Olive*, V. i. 190–200.
110. *quality*] accomplishment.
115.] i.e., most husbands would challenge Monsieur.
117. *opportunities*] importunities.

Mont. Pray thee bear with him:
Thou know'st he is a bachelor, and a Courtier,
Ay, and a Prince: and their prerogatives
Are, to their laws, as to their pardons are
Their reservations: after Parliaments
One quits another; form gives all their essence:
That Prince doth high in virtue's reckoning stand
That will entreat a vice, and not command:
So far bear with him: should another man
Trust to his privilege, he should trust to death;
Take comfort then, my comfort, nay triumph,
And crown thyself, thou part'st with victory:
My presence is so only dear to thee,
That other men's appear worse than they be.
For this night yet, bear with my forced absence:
Thou know'st my business; and with how much weight
My vow hath charg'd it.
Tam. True my Lord, and never
My fruitless love shall let your serious profit,
Yet, sweet Lord, do not stay, you know my soul
Is so long time without me, and I dead,
As you are absent.
Mont. By this kiss, receive
My soul for hostage, till I see my love.
Tam. The morn shall let me see you.

122. reservations:] reseruations, *A, B.* Parliaments] *A;* Parliaments, *B;* Parliaments— *Bo, P.* 135. profit] *A;* honour *B.* 136. not] *D, P;* no *A, B.* 140. you.] *B;* you: *A.*

120–3.] The general sense is that as Princes qualify (and effectively negate) their pardons with reservations, so their devotion to law manifested while Parliament sits is negated by use of the prerogative during a recession. Hence their mercy and their constitutionalism are mere matters of form, not reality.

122. *reservations*] in technical sense of reserving right, power, or privilege.

123. *quits*] balances; hence cancels out.

129. *part'st*] comest away.

134. *charg'd*] loaded.

135. *let*] hinder, obstruct.

Mont. With the sun
I'll visit thy more comfortable beauties.
Tam. This is my comfort, that the sun hath left
The whole world's beauty ere my sun leaves me.
Mont. 'Tis late night now indeed: farewell my light. *Exit.*
Tam. Farewell my light and life—But not in him.
Alas, that in the wane of our affections
We should supply it with a full dissembling,
In which each youngest maid is grown a mother:
Frailty is fruitful, one sin gets another:
Our loves like sparkles are that brightest shine,
When they go out; most vice shews most divine.—
Go maid, to bed, lend me your book I pray:
Not like yourself, for form; I'll this night trouble
None of your services: make sure the doors,
And call your other fellows to their rest.
Per. [*aside*] I will, yet I will watch to know why you watch. *Exit.*
Tam. Now all ye peaceful regents of the night,
Silently-gliding exhalations,
Languishing winds, and murmuring falls of waters,

145.] *A; B reads:*
Tam. Farewell my light and life: But not in him,
In mine owne dark love and light bent to another.
146. wane] *D, Bo, P;* waue *A;* wave *B, Baskervill etc.* 157. ye] *B;* the *A.*

---

143. *my sun*] a common comparison of the power of love to that of the sun controlling its satellite planets.

145a.] Ure speaks of this as a clarification of the figure, strikingly like Chapman; Brooke and Paradise found it an unmetrical and difficult line. It is its obscurity which makes it look genuine, but it does attempt a coherent extension of the image.

146. *wane*] Dilke's emendation is certainly right: A invariably prints 'v' as 'u', so that a turned 'n' gave 'waue', which B normalized to 'wave'.

147. *supply*] make up for, compensate.

148. *maid . . . mother*] i.e., girls instinctively become mature in the art of dissembling; also, to dissemble is to give birth to another personality different from yourself, which suggests the images of the next line.

151. *most vice . . . divine*] Dissembled love looks more convincing than sincere feeling.

157. *ye*] A probably confused 'ye' with the abbreviation 'y^{e}'='the'.

158. *exhalations*] mists, vapours.

Sadness of heart, and ominous secureness,
Enchantments, dead sleeps, all the friends of rest,
That ever wrought upon the life of man,
Extend your utmost strengths; and this charm'd hour
Fix like the Centre; make the violent wheels
Of Time and Fortune stand; and great Existence
(The Maker's treasury) now not seem to be,
To all but my approaching friends and me:
They come, alas they come, fear, fear and hope
Of one thing, at one instant fight in me:
I love what most I loathe, and cannot live
Unless I compass that that holds my death:
For love is hateful without love again,

171. that that] *A;* that which *B.*
172–8.] *A; B reads:*

For lifes meere death loving one that loathes me, 172
And he I love, will loath me, when he sees 173
The Vault opens.
I flie my sex, my vertue, my Renowne, 174
To runne so madly on a man unknowne. 175
See, see a Vault is opening that was never 176
Knowne to my Lord and husband, nor to any 176a
But him that brings the man I love, and me; b
How shall I looke on him? how shall I live c
And not consume in blushes, I will in; 177
And cast my selfe off, as I ne're had beene. *Exit.* 178

---

160. *Sadness*] firmness, security.

ominous secureness] 'Ominous' could have the sense of good as well as evil, so this presumably implies the omens were of security (=freedom from anxiety).

164. *Centre*] i.e., of the revolving spheres of the Ptolemaic universe.

164–5. *make . . . stand*] Time and Fortune were both emblematically represented as a wheel which turned on inexorably, so that a fall is sure to follow a rise. This image springs from the last, but with variation, since there the reference was to the still centre of a turning system, here to the stopping of a whole wheel.

165. *Existence*] all that exists; hence the created universe (*O.E.D.* does not give this before 1751).

171. *death*] possibly playing with use of 'death' for 'orgasm' (*O.E.D.* 'swoon').

172.] Parrott suggested B's change was made to connect with the antithesis in l. 173; the elaborate verbal patterning (which echoes l. 170 as well) might be Chapman's, but is hardly an improvement.

And he I love, will loathe me, when he sees *The Vault opens.*
I fly my sex, my virtue, my renown,
To run so madly on a man unknown.
See, see the gulf is opening, that will swallow
Me and my fame for ever; I will in,
And cast myself off, as I ne'er had been. *Exit.*

Friar [COMOLET] *and* [BUSSY] D'AMBOIS *ascend.*

Com. Come worthiest son, I am past measure glad,
That you (whose worth I have approv'd so long)
Should be the object of her fearful love;
Since both your wit and spirit can adapt
Their full force to supply her utmost weakness:
You know her worths and virtues, for report
Of all that know, is to a man a knowledge:
You know besides, that our affections' storm,
Rais'd in our blood, no Reason can reform.
Though she seek then their satisfaction
(Which she must needs, or rest unsatisfied),
Your judgement will esteem her peace thus wrought,
Nothing less dear, than if yourself had sought:
And (with another colour, which my Art
Shall teach you to lay on) yourself must seem

173. *The Vault opens.*] *B; not in A.* 178.1.] *Ascendit Frier and D'Ambois. B; not in A.*

---

175. *run . . . on*] not in *O.E.D.*: the context suggests a close likeness to the modern 'run after'.

176–7.] Parrott called B's new lines 'explanatory', Ure listed them as 'good reflection of the action'. They seem to me to give unnecessary explanation in bad verse at the expense of a strikingly effective image.

178.] The meaning is not clear: 'cast . . . off' can refer to clothes, or more generally 'disown', 'abandon'; Boas assumed the former, Parrott thought a higher key indicated here, and supposed Tamyra meant to renounce her meeting with Bussy. I suspect Chapman was hovering between different meanings: (1) a wish, born of panic, to evaporate; (2) a withdrawal to prepare herself for a rôle which she has defined as quite alien to her former self.

180. *approv'd*] put to the proof.

192. *colour*] manner of presentation: used of rhetoric, etc.

The only agent, and the first Orb move,
In this our set and cunning world of Love.
Buss. Give me the colour, my most honour'd Father,
And trust my cunning then to lay it on.
Com. 'Tis this, good son; Lord Barrisor (whom you slew)
Did love her dearly, and with all fit means
Hath urg'd his acceptation, of all which
She keeps one letter written in his blood:
You must say thus then, That you heard from me
How much herself was touch'd in conscience
With a report (which is in truth dispers'd)
That your main quarrel grew about her love,
Lord Barrisor imagining your courtship
Of the great Guise's Duchess in the Presence,
Was by you made to his elected mistress:
And so made me your mean now to resolve her,
Choosing (by my direction) this night's depth,
For the more clear avoiding of all note
Of your presumed presence; and with this
(To clear her hands of such a lover's blood)
She will so kindly thank and entertain you
(Methinks I see how), ay, and ten to one,
Shew you the confirmation in his blood,
Lest you should think report and she did feign,
That you shall so have circumstantial means
To come to the direct, which must be used:

194. move] Moue *A*, *B*. 195. set] *Bo*, *P;* set, *A*, *B*.

---

194. *first Orb move*] set the Primum Mobile (the outer sphere which impelled the rest) in motion. A's cap. M for Move is strange, as caps. are not elsewhere used for verbs, and I wonder if Chapman actually wrote 'Mover' which would make slightly easier sense.

195. *set*] may imply 'static', i.e. until Bussy makes a move. I have wondered whether Orb in l. 194 can also refer to a tennis ball, and 'set' to the game which Bussy must start. Such a double meaning would explain the strained syntax in these lines.

212. *presumed*] 'presumptuous' (Brooke and Paradise). *O.E.D.* has this sense only for the noun 'presume'=presumption (see l. 275).

For the direct is crooked; Love comes flying;
The height of love is still won with denying.
Buss. Thanks honour'd Father.
Com. She must never know
That you know anything of any love
Sustain'd on her part: for learn this of me:
In any thing a woman does alone,
If she dissemble, she thinks 'tis not done;
If not dissemble, nor a little chide,
Give her her wish, she is not satisfy'd;
To have a man think that she never seeks,
Does her more good than to have all she likes:
This frailty sticks in them beyond their sex;
Which to reform, reason is too perplex:
Urge reason to them, it will do no good;
Humour (that is the chariot of our food
In every body) must in them be fed,
To carry their affections by it bred.
Stand close.

Enter TAMYRA *with a book.*

Tam. [*aside*] Alas, I fear my strangeness will retire him:
If he go back, I die; I must prevent it,

234. food] *A, B;* blood *T.* 237.1. *with a book*] *B; not in A.*

220. *Love comes flying*] playing between a reference to Cupid's wings and the paradox 'comes, fleeing' developed in l. 221.

232. *perplex*] *O.E.D.* has only 'puzzled, bewildered', which could be right if 'reason' is personified.

234–5. *Humour* (*that . . . body*)] The four humours were thought to be distilled from the elements received as food in the stomach-liver organs, and conveyed vital properties via the blood to the body, at the same time by their proportionate mixture conditioning temperament (see I. i. 140). (Emendation is quite unnecessary: blood could be said to carry the humours, not vice versa.)

234. *chariot*] used figuratively for a physiological vehicle (*O.E.D.*, s.v., 2).

235–6. *must . . . bred*] One must 'humour them', if the feelings their humours have bred are to find a healthy passage.

238. *strangeness*] aloofness.

And cheer his onset with my sight at least,
And that's the most; though every step he takes
Goes to my heart, I'll rather die than seem
Not to be strange to that I most esteem.

Com. Madam.

Tam. Ah.

Com. You will pardon me, I hope,
That, so beyond your expectation
(And at a time for visitants so unfit),
I (with my noble friend here) visit you:
You know that my access at any time
Hath ever been admitted; and that friend
That my care will presume to bring with me,
Shall have all circumstance of worth in him,
To merit as free welcome as myself.

Tam. O Father, but at this suspicious hour
You know how apt best men are to suspect us,
In any cause, that makes suspicious shadow
No greater than the shadow of a hair:
And y' are to blame: what though my Lord and husband
Lie forth to-night? and since I cannot sleep
When he is absent, I sit up to-night,
Though all the doors are sure, and all our servants
As sure bound with their sleeps; yet there is One
That sits above, whose eye no sleep can bind:
He sees through doors, and darkness, and our thoughts;
And therefore as we should avoid with fear
To think amiss ourselves before his search,
So should we be as curious to shun
All cause that other think not ill of us.

Buss. Madam, 'tis far from that: I only heard
By this my honour'd Father, that your conscience

255. suspicious] *A, B;* suspicions *Jacquot.* 262. sits] *A;* wakes *B.*

---

262. *sits*] B's 'wakes', as Parrott noted, makes an effective antithesis with 'sleeps'; see note on l. 172 for a similar alteration on a larger scale.

266. *curious*] careful, fastidious.

Was something troubled with a false report
That Barrisor's blood should something touch your hand,
Since he imagin'd I was courting you,
When I was bold to change words with the Duchess,
And therefore made his quarrel; which my presence
Presum'd on with my Father at this season
(For the more care of your so curious honour),
Can well resolve your Conscience, is most false.

Tam. And is it therefore that you come good sir?
Then crave I now your pardon and my Father's,
And swear your presence does me so much comfort,
That all I have, it binds to your requital:
Indeed sir, 'tis most true that a report
Is spread, alleging that his love to me
Was reason of your quarrel; and because
You shall not think I feign it for my glory
That he importun'd me for his Court service,
I'll shew you his own hand, set down in blood
To that vain purpose: good sir, then come in.
Father I thank you now a thousandfold.

Exeunt TAMYRA *and* [BUSSY] D'AMBOIS.

Com. May it be worth it to you honour'd daughter.

Friar [COMOLET] *descends.*

270. Was something troubled] *A;* Made some deepe scruple *B.* 271. hand] *A;* honour *B.*
274.] *A; B reads:*

> And therefore made his quarrell, his long love 274
> And service, as I heare, being deepely vowed 274a
> To your perfections, which my ready presence b

274–6. And . . . (For . . . honour),] (And . . . For . . . honour) *A;* And . . . For . . . honour, *B.* 280. comfort] *A;* good *B.* 289.1.] *B (Exit); not in A.* 290.1.] *Descendit Fryar. / Finis Actus secundi. B; Finis Actus secundi. A.*

---

271. *hand*] B's 'honour' is an unnecessary change: it is common to speak of a murderer's hands being stained by the blood of his victim (as with Lady Macbeth).

274.] Like Ure, I see no special need for B's explanatory addition.

Act III

[III. i]

Enter BUSSY, TAMYRA.

Tam. O my dear servant, in thy close embraces,
I have set open all the doors of danger
To my encompass'd honour, and my life:
Before, I was secure against death and hell;
But now am subject to the heartless fear
Of every shadow, and of every breath,
And would change firmness with an aspen leaf:
So confident a spotless conscience is;
So weak a guilty: O the dangerous siege
Sin lays about us! and the tyranny
He exercises when he hath expugn'd:
Like to the horror of a winter's thunder,
Mix'd with a gushing storm, that suffer nothing

Act III] Actus Tertij Scena Prima. *A, B.* 0.1.] *Bucy, Tamyra. A; Enter D'Ambois, Tamyra, with a Chaine of Pearle. B.*
1.] *A; B adds:*
D'Amb. Sweet Mistresse cease, your conscience is too nice, oa
And bites too hotly of the Puritane spice. b

0.1.] For B's Chain of Pearl, here and in l. 42q, see II. ii. 90.

0a–b.] Parrott suggested that this reference to puritans, taken with the pruning of the attack on Latin prayers (V. iii. 5–12), implied a new sympathy with the Roman church in the revision. The evidence seems to me quite inadequate for such a conclusion: there is obvious theatrical convenience in these words for Bussy before Tamyra embarks on a long speech; the puritan reference is quite conventional; and the pruning in Act V is not a cancellation.

3. *encompass'd*] totally surrounded, either by defence or attack; the latter is more obvious here, but both can apply, since danger is similarly ambiguous (see II. i. 64).

5. *heartless*] lacking courage.

11. *expugn'd*] vanquished, overpowered.

To stir abroad on earth, but their own rages;
Is sin, when it hath gather'd head above us:
No roof, no shelter can secure us so,
But he will drown our cheeks in fear or woe.

Buss. Sin is a coward Madam, and insults
But on our weakness, in his truest valour:
And so our ignorance tames us, that we let
His shadows fright us: and like empty clouds
In which our faulty apprehensions forge
The forms of dragons, lions, elephants,
When they hold no proportion, the sly charms
Of the witch Policy makes him like a monster
Kept only to shew men for Goddess Money:
That false hag often paints him in her cloth
Ten times more monstrous than he is in troth.
In three of us, the secret of our meeting
Is only guarded, and three friends as one

26. Goddess] *A;* Servile *B.* 27. him] *B;* him: *A.* 28. troth.] *Bo;* troth: *A*, *B.*

---

15. *gather'd head*] used of collecting an army (here, of storms); but also of boils, sores, etc. Compare *2 H4*, III. i. 76–7: 'foul sin, gathering head, / Shall break into corruption'.

17. *drown our cheeks*] The literal sense of sin's storms is conscience: hence they break in tears.

18–19. *insults / But on*] triumphs only over.

19. *in his truest valour*] 'at his best' (Parrott).

21–4.] a common emblem of illusion: see *Monsieur D'Olive*, II. ii. 92–4; *Ham.*, III. ii. 400–6; *Ant.*, IV. xii. 2–3.

22. *apprehensions*] understandings, fears. The apprehension was the faculty of understanding; but often, as here, by imagination rather than by intellect. See *M.N.D.*, V. i. 18–20, 'Such tricks hath strong imagination, / That, if it would but apprehend some joy, / It comprehends some bringer of that joy'.

24. *proportion*] likeness of shape.

24–8.] Policy (=political cunning, associated with Machiavelli) has 'sly charms', 'magical' powers used to exhibit sin like a 'monster' on a painted cloth: the reality is far less monstrous.

25. *monster*] fairground freak. See *Mac.*, V. vii. 54–5.

27. *cloth*] painted cloth: a cheap substitute for tapestry; emblematic pictures, e.g. of the Seven Deadly Sins, were common. For their use outside freak shows, see *Tp.*, II. ii. 29–31.

Have ever been esteem'd: as our three powers
That in our one soul are, as one united:
Why should we fear then? for my truth I swear
Sooner shall Torture be the sire to Pleasure,
And health be grievous to men long time sick,
Than the dear jewel of your fame in me
Be made an outcast to your infamy;
Nor shall my value (sacred to your virtues)
Only give free course to it, from myself:
But make it fly out of the mouths of Kings
In golden vapours, and with awful wings.

Tam. It rests as all Kings' seals were set in thee.

Exit [BUSSY] D'AMBOIS, *manet* TAMYRA.

32. our] *A, Bo; not in B.* 33. truth] *A;* selfe *B.* 35. men] *A;* one *B.*
38. value] *A, B;* valour *Shepherd.*
42.1.] *A; B reads:*

Now let us call my Father, whom I sweare
I could extreamly chide, but that I feare
To make him so suspicious of my love
Of which (sweet servant) doe not let him know
For all the world.
D'Amb. Alas! he will not think it?
Tam. Come then—ho? Father, ope, and take your friend.
Ascendit Frier.
Frier. Now honour'd daughter, is your doubt resolv'd.
Tam. I Father, but you went away too soone.
Fryer. Too soone?

---

31. *our three powers*] Man was thought to have three faculties associated with the three regions of his body: the vegetative (Liver, etc.); sensitive (Heart); reasoning (Brain).

32. *our*] Ure supposes B's omission to be an error.

38. *value*] valour (*O.E.D.*, s.v., 2b, has also a doubtful example meaning 'valuation' which could be involved here).

38–41.] Far from bringing infamy on Tamyra, Bussy will not only proclaim her virtue, but will cause kings to do so. The image in l. 41 may refer to a known emblem; it suggests the qualities of angels.

42. *as*] as if.

42a–q.] Parrott and Ure see this as bringing out the action more fully; it does, but not in a necessary way. Tamyra's calculated hypocrisy is displayed effectively (especially in ll. 42d–e) but gratuitously (it is more subtly done in ll. 69 ff.); and the intrusion of this passage weakens the context of Tamyra's great speech which follows.

It is not I, but urgent destiny,
That (as great statesmen for their general end
In politic justice, make poor men offend)
Enforceth my offence to make it just:
What shall weak Dames do, when th' whole work of Nature
Hath a strong finger in each one of us?
Needs must that sweep away the silly cobweb
Of our still-undone labours: that lays still
Our powers to it, as to the line the stone,
Not to the stone the line should be oppos'd;
We cannot keep our constant course in virtue;
What is alike at all parts? every day
Differs from other: every hour and minute:

Tam. Indeed you did, you should have stayed; 42i
Had not your worthy friend beene of your bringing, j
And that containes all lawes to temper me, k
Not all the fearefull danger that besieged us, l
Had aw'd my throat from exclamation. m
Fryer. I know your serious disposition well. n
Come sonne the morne comes on.
D'Amb. Now honour'd Mistresse o
Till farther service call, all blisse supply you. p
Tamy. And you this chaine of pearle, and my love onely. q
Descendit Frier and D'Amb.

43. It] *B; Ta.* It *A.*

43–67.] I have slightly lightened the punctuation to make the sequence clearer; in A, the heavy stops are even more frequent than usual, which may suggest a slow or broken delivery (see especially l. 55).

43–8.] The idea of individual evil submitting to universal good may be behind these lines: see Pope's *Essay on Man* (ed. Mack, 1950), ll. 291–2, 'All Discord, Harmony, not understood; / All partial Evil, universal Good'. But Tamyra's 'destiny' is ironically compared to *politic* justice.

45. *politic*] Cf. the use of 'Policy' in l. 25 for the idea of justifying means by end.

46.] The offence must be carried through to become a part of the just end.

50. *still-undone*] ever-undone. Whether this implies that the labour of making the cobweb is never completed, or that it is unravelled and so rendered worthless, I am not sure—possibly both. The ambiguity does not weaken the force of the words.

50–2.] In wall-building, the stones are laid to a plumb-line suspended from above. The proverb is from Plutarch, possibly via Erasmus: see Appendix B, p. 157.

52. *oppos'd*] set over against.

Ay, every thought in our false clock of life
Ofttimes inverts the whole circumference:
We must be sometimes one, sometimes another;
Our bodies are but thick clouds to our souls,
Through which they cannot shine when they desire;
When all the stars, and even the sun himself,
Must stay the vapours' times that he exhales
Before he can make good his beams to us—
O how can we, that are but motes to him,
Wand'ring at random in his order'd rays,
Disperse our passions' fumes, with our weak labours,
That are more thick and black than all earth's vapours?

Enter MONTSURRY.

Mont. Good day, my love: what up and ready too!
Tam. Both, my dear Lord: not all this night made I
Myself unready, or could sleep a wink.
Mont. Alas, what troubled my true love, my peace,
From being at peace within her better self?
Or how could Sleep forbear to seize thy beauties
When he might challenge them as his just prize?

62. times] *A, B;* fumes *Shepherd.* 73. thy beauties] *A;* thine eyes *B.*

56–7.] The effective compression of ideas makes commentary difficult and clumsy: 'thought' is the final diminutive in the series 'day—hour—minute', but it opens out its own general sense as well: it is the capriciousness of thought which is expanded in l. 58, and its power to effect instantaneously radical moral change which 'inverts the circumference' (turned upside down, virtue becomes vice). Behind the whole image is the use of circles as emblems of infinity and perfection, contrasted with Time as inevitable mutability, the enemy of immortality.

61–3.] Even the sun cannot shine on us until the mists he has himself raised have dispersed.

62. *exhales*] draws up (from the sea, etc.).

66. *fumes*] distilled in lower organs of the body by the heat of passion, and rising to the brain to cloud reason.

68. *ready*] fully dressed.

73. *thy beauties*] Parrott suspected B's 'thine eyes' (which entirely destroys the image of sleep as a lover) of being introduced for the sake of a rhyme.

Tam. I am in no power earthly, but in yours;
To what end should I go to bed my Lord,
That wholly miss'd the comfort of my bed?
Or how should sleep possess my faculties,
Wanting the proper closer of mine eyes?
Mont. Then will I never more sleep night from thee:
All mine own business, all the King's affairs
Shall take the day to serve them: every night
I'll ever dedicate to thy delight.
Tam. Nay, good my Lord esteem not my desires
Such doters on their humours, that my judgement
Cannot subdue them to your worthier pleasure:
A wife's pleas'd husband must her object be
In all her acts, not her sooth'd fantasy.
Mont. Then come my love, now pay those rites to Sleep
Thy fair eyes owe him: shall we now to bed?
Tam. O no my Lord, your holy Friar says,
All couplings in the day that touch the bed
Adulterous are, even in the married;
Whose grave and worthy doctrine, well I know,
Your faith in him will liberally allow.
Mont. He's a most learned and Religious man;
Come to the Presence then, and see great D'Ambois
(Fortune's proud mushroom shot up in a night)
Stand like an Atlas underneath the King;

99. underneath the King] *A;* under our Kings arme *B.*

---

85. *humours*] The technical sense is still present, but the looser sense 'whims' is needed here.

88. *fantasy*] *O.E.D.* (s.v., 7) gives 'desire': I suggest sensuality in its widest sense, as the fantasy or imagination unites all experience of the senses.

92–3.] apparently derived from Plutarch: see Appendix B, p. 158.

95. *liberally*] freely.

allow] approve.

99. *Atlas . . . King*] The image primarily refers to Bussy supporting the divine majesty as Atlas held up the heavens; but its grotesque impact is part of its value; B's effort to eliminate this results in absurdity, and suggests to me a mind unlike Chapman's.

Which greatness with him Monsieur now envies
As bitterly and deadly as the Guise.

Tam. What, he that was but yesterday his maker?
His raiser and preserver?

Mont. Even the same.
Each natural agent works but to this end,
To render that it works on, like itself;
Which since the Monsieur in his act on D'Ambois
Cannot to his ambitious end effect,
But that (quite opposite) the King hath power
(In his love borne to D'Ambois) to convert
The point of Monsieur's aim on his own breast,
He turns his outward love to inward hate:
A Prince's love is like the lightning's fume,
Which no man can embrace, but must consume. *Exeunt.*

[III. ii]

[*Enter*] HENRY, [BUSSY] D'AMBOIS, MONSIEUR, GUISE, DUCHESS, ANNABEL, Attendants.

Hen. Speak home my Bussy, thy impartial words

III. ii. 0.1–2.] *this ed.; Henry, D'Ambois, Monsieur, Guise, Monts. / Elenor, Tam. Pero. A; Henry, D'Ambois, Monsieur, Guise, Dutches / Annabell, Charlot, Attendants. B.* 1. my] *A, Bo; not in B.*

---

100. *greatness*] intimacy; with a play on the common meaning.

100–1. *envies . . . Guise*] probably meant to rhyme.

104–5.] The idea derives from Platonic theory: the 'soul' endeavours to produce an image of itself from the material body it inhabits; always unsuccessfully because of the inherent imperfection of matter.

113. *but must consume*] 'which' (=the lightning) is understood as subject.

III. ii. 0.1–0.2.] I take A's list to be for the whole scene: although no entry is given for Montsurry and Tamyra, they can hardly have entered at once. The absence of attendants suggests that it was Chapman rather than a prompter who made the list (see II. i. 0.1). B's direction swells the court with Annabel, and presumably Charlotte is there for the same reason, although her mistress, Beaupré, is not (unless it is an error of the corrector's).

1. *my*] Ure (and presumably Boas) took B's omission for a slip; Parrott thought it like Chapman to introduce a 'syncopated foot' for emphasis.

Are like brave Falcons that dare truss a fowl
Much greater than themselves; flatterers are Kites
That check at nothing; thou shalt be my Eagle,
And bear my thunder underneath thy wings:
Truth's words like jewels hang in th' ears of Kings.
Buss. Would I might live to see no Jews hang there
Instead of jewels; sycophants I mean,
Who use Truth like the Devil, his true foe,
Cast by the Angel to the pit of fears,
And bound in chains; Truth seldom decks Kings' ears:
Slave Flattery (like a Rippier's legs roll'd up
In boots of hay-ropes) with Kings' soothed guts
Swaddled and strappled, now lives only free:
O 'tis a subtle knave; how like the plague
Unfelt, he strikes into the brain of Truth,
And rageth in his entrails when he can,
Worse than the poison of a red-hair'd man.

4. nothing] *A;* Sparrowes *B.* 16. Truth] *A;* man *B.*

---

2. *truss*] of birds of prey, seize prey in talons (especially in the air as opposed to on the ground).

4. *check at nothing*] in hawking, go after baser game instead of proper prey.

nothing] Ure suggested an unhappy ambiguity; I agree that B's sparrows is clearer.

4–5. *thou . . . wings*] Jove's eagle carried thunder beneath his wings. Chapman 'mythologized' it more elaborately in *Eugenia*, ll. 742–5: 'Her selfe being th'Eagle . . . beares beneath her wings / The dreadfull Thunder, the Almightie word; / All which (called fiction) with sure Truth accord.' (See also his marginal gloss on this passage.)

12. *Rippier*] itinerant fishmonger.

12–14.] Imaginative agility is required here because the Rippier's legs are strongly visualized, whilst the swaddled Flattery is not; yet in successively different modes the idea becomes concrete, and the connections are powerfully made in 'Swaddled and strappled'. The difficulty may be more acute for the analysing, than for the imaginatively listening, mind.

13. *boots of hay-ropes*] bands of hay used instead of gaiters.

14. *Swaddled*] bandaged.

strappled] protected on the shin.

16. *Truth*] B's 'man' is slightly simpler, but obviously weaker: Ure suggested a printer's error; perhaps 'man' was picked up from l. 18?

18. *red-hair'd*] Boas notes that Judas was represented as red-haired, and Parrott cites Middleton's *The Witch* (ed. Bullen, 1885), ll. 55–6, when

Hen. Fly at him and his brood, I cast thee off,
And once more give thee surname of mine Eagle.
Buss. I'll make you sport enough then, let me have
My lucerns too (or dogs inur'd to hunt
Beasts of most rapine) but to put them up,
And if I truss not, let me not be trusted:
Shew me a Great Man (by the people's voice,
Which is the voice of God) that by his greatness
Bombasts his private roofs, with public riches;
That affects royalty, rising from a clapdish;
That rules so much more than his suffering King,
That he makes kings of his subordinate slaves:
Himself and them graduate like woodmongers
(Piling a stack of billets) from the earth,
Raising each other into steeples' heights;
Let him convey this on the turning props

29. than] *A, Bo;* by *B.*

Hecate adds to the brew 'three ounces of the red-hair'd girl / I kill'd last midnight'.

22. *lucerns*] lynxes. *O.E.D.* assumes that the word is here being used of hunting dogs, but there is no support or need for this. Lynxes were known for courageous attacks on beasts of prey, though it was not usual for them to be trained for this. See *Iliads,* XI. 417–23, where lucerns attack a wounded hart, and are put to flight by a lion: there, 'lucerns' translates 'θῶες' = beasts of prey, and that is probably all Chapman intends by the word.

25–6. (*by the people's . . . God*)] i.e., whose greatness is acclaimed by popular vote, vulgarly accepted as the voice of God.

27. *Bombasts*] stuffs; inflates (not necessarily of words).

28. *clapdish*] beggar's alms-dish.

29. *than*] B's 'by' makes (as Ure noted) alternative sense; Parrott (unlike Boas) assumed it was deliberate; I don't see why.

suffering] permitting; but the usual sense is also involved.

31–3.] Ferguson (p. 10) suggested a parody of the myth of the Giants piling mountains to reach heaven.

31. *graduate*] rise by degrees (Brooke and Paradise); *O.E.D.* (s.v., 4d) has a similar usage for 1694 only.

32. *billets*] firewood.

34–6.] another difficult passage of super-imposed images: the 'turning props' seem first to suggest wheels of a cart, but then as props that keep all upright are presumably supports, 'turning' in the sense of changing with the various legal devices used to maintain the position. These possibilities stem from the various senses of the word 'convey'.

Of Protean Law, and (his own counsel keeping)
Keep all upright; let me but hawk at him,
I'll play the Vulture, and so thump his liver,
That (like a huge unlading Argosy)
He shall confess all, and you then may hang him.
Shew me a Clergyman, that is in voice
A Lark of Heaven, in heart a Mole of Earth;
That hath good living, and a wicked life;
A temperate look, and a luxurious gut;
Turning the rents of his superfluous Cures
Into your pheasants and your partridges;
Venting their Quintessence as men read Hebrew:
Let me but hawk at him, and, like the other,
He shall confess all, and you then may hang him.
Shew me a Lawyer that turns sacred Law
(The equal rend'rer of each man his own,
The scourge of Rapine and Extortion,
The Sanctuary and impregnable defence
Of retir'd Learning, and oppressed Virtue)

53. oppressed] *A;* besieged *B.*

---

34. *convey*] The usual sense is coloured by the legal term.

35. *Protean*] Proteus, the old man of the sea, changed shape at will to avoid questioning.

(*his . . . keeping*)] (1) retaining his own advisers; (2) being secretive.

37.] apparently an allusion to Prometheus, chained to Caucasus where an eagle fed on his liver by day.

38. *unlading*] unloading.

Argosy] largest size of merchant ship (usually Italian).

41. *Lark . . . Mole*] Larks are proverbial for divine song, moles for blindness, which is only remotely relevant: the sense would seem to be earth-bound, worldly, and perhaps unable to look towards heaven.

42. *good living*] playing between 'bon vivant' and 'living'=clergyman's appointment.

43. *gut*] stomach; hence, appetite.

44. *rents*] revenues.

superfluous Cures] 'Bussy is thinking of a pluralist clergyman' (Parrott).

46. *Venting*] evacuating (from bowels)—i.e., both cures and pheasants, etc.

Quintessence] substance of which heavenly bodies were composed; hence loosely for 'best part' (of pheasants, etc.).

read Hebrew] i.e., backwards.

Into a Harpy, that eats all but 's own;
Into the damned sins it punisheth;
Into the Synagogue of thieves and atheists;
Blood into gold, and Justice into lust:
Let me but hawk at him, as at the t' other,
He shall confess all, and you then may hang him.

Enter MONTSURRY, TAMYRA, *and* PERO.

Gui. Where will you find such game as you would hawk at?
Buss. I'll hawk about your house for one of them.
Gui. Come, y' are a glorious ruffi'n, and run proud
Of the King's headlong graces; hold your breath,
Or by that poison'd vapour not the King
Shall back your murderous valour against me.
Buss. I would the King would make his Presence free
But for one charge betwixt us: by the reverence
Due to the sacred space 'twixt kings and subjects,
Here would I make thee cast that popular purple,
In which thy proud soul sits and braves thy Sovereign.
Mons. Peace, peace, I pray thee peace.
Buss. Let him peace first

58. t' other] *A;* rest *B.* 59.1.] *B; not in A.* 67. charge] *A;* bout *B.*
71–2. Let . . . war.] *Bo, P; as one line A, B.*

54. *Harpy*] Greek fabulous monster, rapacious and filthy, with a woman's face and body, and a bird's wings and claws; supposed to act as minister of divine vengeance.

56. *Synagogue*] meeting place, not necessarily Jewish.

57.] depending on 'turns' in l. 49.

59.1.] See note on ll. 0.1–2. An entry here is quite arbitrary, but as good as any other place.

61. *one of them*] presumably the Great Man; though Guise did not rise from a clapdish, Bussy does refer in l. 75 to the 'people's voice' of l. 25.

62. *glorious*] vainglorious, boastful.

62–3. *run proud / Of*] not in *O.E.D.* Presumably 'swell', 'get puffed out with'. A proud sail is one full of wind; 'proud' is also used of animals on heat.

63. *headlong*] rash.

67. *charge*] bout (as B reads).

69. *popular purple*] Purple was normally an imperial colour; Guise in wearing it (says Boas) made his popularity an affront to the king.

That made the first war.
Mons. He's the better man.
Buss. And therefore may do worst?
Mons. He has more titles.
Buss. So Hydra had more heads.
Mons. He's greater known.
Buss. His greatness is the people's, mine's mine own.
Mons. He's nobler born.
Buss. He is not, I am noble.
And noblesse in his blood hath no gradation,
But in his merit.
Gui. Th' art not nobly born,
But bastard to the Cardinal of Ambois.
Buss. Thou liest proud Guiserd; let me fly, my Lord.
Hen. Not in my face; my Eagle, violence flies
The Sanctuaries of a Prince's eyes.
Buss. Still shall we chide? and foam upon this bit?
Is the Guise only great in faction?
Stands he not by himself? proves he th' opinion
That men's souls are without them? Be a Duke,
And lead me to the field.
Gui. Come, follow me.
Hen. Stay them, stay D'Ambois; Cousin Guise, I wonder
Your equal disposition brooks so ill
A man so good, that only would uphold

76. nobler] *Neilson;* noblie *A;* nobly *B;* noblier *Bo, P.* 89. equal] *A;* honour'd *B.*

75.] See ll. 25 and 61.

76. *nobler*] 'er' could easily be misread as 'ie', and so this reading seems better than Boas's improbable 'noblier'.

77, 78. *his*] its, here with some personal force.

79. *Cardinal of Ambois*] George, Archbishop of Rouen, d. 1509: he was in fact Bussy's great-uncle.

81. *in my face*] in my presence (cf. 'in the face of').

83. *foam upon this bit*] i.e., like eager horses under restraint.

84. *great in faction*] i.e., dependent on his supporters.

86. *without*] outside.

86–7. *Be . . . field*] playing with derivation of Duke from 'dux' = leader.

89. *equal*] equitable, just.

Man in his native noblesse, from whose fall
All our dissensions rise; that in himself
(Without the outward patches of our frailty,
Riches and honour) knows he comprehends
Worth with the greatest: Kings had never borne
Such boundless eminence over other men,
Had all maintain'd the spirit and state of D'Ambois;
Nor had the full impartial hand of Nature
That all things gave in her original,
Without these definite terms of Mine and Thine,
Been turn'd unjustly to the hand of Fortune—
Had all preserv'd her in her prime, like D'Ambois;
No envy, no disjunction, had dissolv'd
Or pluck'd out one stick of the golden faggot
In which the world of Saturn was compris'd,
Had all been held together with the nerves,
The genius and th' ingenuous soul of D'Ambois.
Let my hand therefore be the Hermean rod
To part and reconcile, and so conserve you,
As my combin'd embracers and supporters.

96. eminence] *A;* Empire *B.* 104. out one stick] *A;* one stick out *B.* 105. was compris'd] *A;* bound our lifes *B.* 107. ingenuous] *A;* ingenious *B.*

---

93. *patches*] things which patch up (*O.E.D.* does not note the fig. sense).

94–5. *comprehends . . . with*] includes . . . [to compare] with (*O.E.D.*, s.v. *comprehends*, 8b, + with).

96. *eminence*] B's 'Empire' may be a trick of memory.

97. *state*] natural status. Like 'spirit', it implies nobility.

99. *original*] beginning.

103–5.] i.e., the Golden Age would have remained intact, if Man had not fallen from his 'native noblesse'. This is the Greek version of the Eden myth, stressing human greatness rather than simple happiness.

103. *dissolv'd*] loosened; put asunder (see IV. ii. 142).

105. *world of Saturn*] the Golden Age.

106. *nerves*] were thought of as literally tying the body together, as well as uniting its parts in intelligence. 'nerve' (=sinew) implied 'strength'.

107. *ingenuous*] B's 'ingenious' does not imply any difference, the forms being interchangeable.

108. *Hermean rod*] the Caduceus: representing two serpents twined, as an emblem of peace.

110. *supporters*] (1) politically; (2) heraldic term: the figures supporting a shield.

Buss. 'Tis our King's motion, and we shall not seem
(To worst eyes) womanish, though we change thus soon
Never so great grudge for his greater pleasure.
Gui. I seal to that, and so the manly freedom
That you so much profess, hereafter prove not
A bold and glorious licence to deprave:
To me his hand shall prove the Hermean rod
His grace affects, in which submissive sign
On this his sacred right hand, I lay mine.
Buss. 'Tis well my Lord, and so your worthy greatness
Engender not the greater insolence,
Nor make you think it a Prerogative,
To rack men's freedoms with the ruder wrongs:
My hand (stuck full of laurel, in true sign
'Tis wholly dedicate to righteous peace)
In all submission kisseth th' other side.
Hen. Thanks to ye both: and kindly I invite ye
Both to a banquet where we'll sacrifice
Full cups to confirmation of your loves;
At which, fair Ladies, I entreat your presence.
Exeunt HENRY, [BUSSY] D'AMBOIS, Ladies.

117. prove] *A;* hold *B.* rod] *A;* vertue *B.* 121. Engender not] *A;* Decline not to *B.* 129. your] *B;* yours *A.*
130.] *A; B adds:*

And hope you Madam will take one carowse
For reconcilement of your Lord and servant.
Duches. If I should faile my Lord, some other Lady
Would be found there to doe that for my servant.
Mons. Any of these here?
Duches. Nay, I know not that.
D'Amb. Think your thoughts, like my Mistresse, honour'd Lady.
Tamy. I think not on you Sir, y'are one I know not.
D'Amb. Cry you mercy Madam.
Monts. Oh Sir, has she met you?

130.1.] *B; Exeunt / Henry, / D'Amb. / Ely. Ta. A.*

114. *and so*] so long as, provided that.

117. *prove . . . rod*] B's 'hold . . . vertue' may be, as Ure suggests, an improvement.

121. *Engender not*] B's tinkering here may be a simplification in the memory.

[For notes on ll. 123–30 see over.]

Mons. What had my bounty drunk when it rais'd him?
Gui. Y' have stuck us up a very proper flag
That takes more wind than we with all our sails.
Mons. O so he spreads and flourishes.
Gui. He must down,
Upstarts should never perch too near a crown.
Mons. 'Tis true my Lord; and as this doting hand,
Even out of earth (like Juno) struck this giant,
So Jove's great ordnance shall be here implied
To strike him under th' Ætna of his pride:
To which work lend your hands and let us cast
Where we may set snares for his gadding greatness:
I think it best, amongst our greatest women:
For there is no such trap to catch an upstart
As a loose downfall; and indeed their falls
Are th' ends of all men's rising: if great men
And wise make 'scapes to please advantage

132. proper] *A;* worthy *B.* 138. ordnance] *B;* ordinance *A.* implied] *A, B;* employ'd *D.* 141. gadding] *A;* ranging *B.* 144. and indeed] *A;* for you know *B.* 146. advantage] *A, B;* advantage[s] *P.*

---

123. *rack*] oppress (as by torture).
ruder] more brutal.
124. *laurel*] evidently as emblem of peace rather than victory.
130.] B's addition here gives the silent ladies words at last, and by its effective ironic comedy completes the first part of this scene more fully; it is not necessary, but would be likely to help on the stage.
134. *spreads*] used of flags or sails.
flourishes] shows off generally.
137–9.] The giant is Typhon, a hundred-headed monster, child of Tartarus and Ge (Earth), or of Juno. Jove destroyed him with a thunderbolt.
137. *struck*] like a coin: a common metaphor for the creation of man out of clay. The verb is used in the usual sense as well in l. 139.
138. *Jove's great ordnance*] thunderbolt.
implied] employed.
140. *cast*] plan, decide (*O.E.D.*, s.v., VII); in this context it seems also to echo both senses of 'strike'.
141. *gadding*] roving; perhaps also implying 'flaunting' (not in *O.E.D.*)?
144–5.] The bland platitude doubles an obscene development of the previous line: the rise and fall of a penis.
146. *'scapes*] escapades.
please advantage] apparently, give an opening to their enemies (*O.E.D.* is no help).

'Tis with a woman: women that worst may
Still hold men's candles: they direct and know
All things amiss in all men; and their women
All things amiss in them: through whose charm'd mouths
We may see all the close 'scapes of the Court:
[When the most royal beast of chase, the Hart
(Being old, and cunning in his lairs and haunts)
Can never be discover'd to the bow,
The piece or hound: yet where (behind some queich)
He breaks his gall, and rutteth with his hind,]
The place is mark'd, and by his venery
He still is taken. Shall we then attempt
The chiefest mean to that discovery here,
And court our greatest Ladies' greatest women

152–6.] *B; A reads:*
When the most royall beast of chace (being old,
And cunning in his choice of layres and haunts)
Can neuer be discouered to the bow
The peece or hound: yet where his custome is
To beat his vault, and he ruts with his hinde,

160. greatest women] *A;* chiefest women *B.*

147–8. *women . . . candles*] Tilley (p. 78, C40) has the proverb 'He that worst may must hold the Candle'. So here: 'the most unsuitable women ever guide men'. The obscene undercurrent of Monsieur's speech is sustained in the phallic suggestion of 'candles'.

152–6.] not an addition but a radical revision; the passage is so strikingly improved that it would be pedantic to stick to A. The result is certainly clearer, but such additions as 'behind some queich' are not solely for clarity, nor can they derive from a trick of memory. All in all, Chapman's responsibility seems more than probable.

155. *piece*] gun.

queich] thicket. See *Homer's Hymn to Apollo*, ll. 375–6, 'and in some queach / (Or strength of shade)'.

156. *breaks his gall*] *O.E.D.* (s.v. *gall*, 3c) glosses 'breaks his spirit', in the sense of 'lets go his rancour'. The gall-bladder was regarded as the seat of bitterness; to break it=empty it.

rutteth] copulates (*O.E.D.*'s earliest date is 1625).

157. *mark'd*] noticed (by the hounds).

venery] sexual activity; also, hunting game, which gives it additional point here.

159. *mean*] means.

160. *greatest . . . greatest*] (a) highest in rank; (b) most intimate [rare].

With shews of love, and liberal promises?
'Tis but our breath: if something given in hand
Sharpen their hopes of more, 'twill be well ventur'd.
Gui. No doubt of that: and 'tis an excellent point
Of our devis'd investigation.
Mons. I have already broke the ice, my Lord,
With the most trusted woman of your Countess,
And hope I shall wade through to our discovery.
Mont. Take 'ssay of her my Lord, she comes most fitly,
And we will to the other.

Enter CHARLOTTE, ANNABEL, PERO.

Gui. Y' are engag'd.
Ann. Nay pray my Lord forbear.

164. an excellent] *A;* the cunningst *B.*
166–70.] *A; B reads:*

Mons. I have broken 166
The yce to it already with the woman 166a
Of your chast Lady, and conceive good hope, 167
I shall wade thorow to some wished shore 168
At our next meeting.
Monts. Nay, there's small hope there. 168a
Guise. Take say of her my Lord, she comes most fitly. 169
Mons. Starting back?
Enter Charlot, Anable, Pero.
Gui. Y'are ingag'd indeed. 170

170–5.] *as prose Bo, P.* 171. *Ann.*] *A, Bo, P; Char. B, T.*

---

165. *devis'd*] planned.

166 ff.] The revision is unusually heavy in the next fifty lines or so. For ll. 166–9 this is clearly deliberate, thereafter it seems quite casual: perhaps the reviser, once started on independent action, ignored his copy more than usual (the density of revision thins out progressively); in any case memorial variants are more frequent in prose passages. A shows a gradual transition from verse to prose; B's verse is far more 'correct' but very feeble. It rather looks as though the reviser, using printed copy, thought improvement necessary; his only independent achievement is to stress Montsurry's false confidence.

169. *Take 'ssay of*] make trial of (assay).

170. *engag'd*] either (1) caught (cf. *Ham.*, III. iii. 68–9); or (2) fig. use of military sense, joined battle (cf. use of 'encounter' in military and sexual contexts).

171. *Ann.*] B's change to *Char.* assumes that the line is spoken to Guise, but this coy remark is a prelude to Montsurry's words. Parrott apparently

Mont. What skittish, servant?

Ann. No my Lord, I am not so fit for your service.

Char. Pray pardon me now my Lord! my Lady expects me.

Gui. I'll satisfy her expectation, as far as an uncle may.

Mons. Well said: a spirit of courtship of all hands.— Now mine own Pero: hast thou remembered me for the discovery I entreated thee to make concerning thy Mistress? speak boldly, and be sure of all things I have promised.

Pero. Building on that you have sworn, my Lord, I may speak: and much the rather, because my Lady hath not trusted me with that I can tell you; for now I cannot be said to betray her.

Mons. That's all one: so it be not to one that will betray thee: forth I beseech thee.

Pero. To tell you truth, my Lord, I have made a strange discovery.

Mons. Excellent Pero thou reviv'st me: may I sink quick into earth here, if my tongue discover it.

Pero. 'Tis thus then: this last night my Lord lay forth: and I wondering my Lady's sitting up, stole at midnight from my pallet: and (having before made a hole both through the wall and arras to her inmost chamber) I saw D'Ambois and she set close at a banquet.

176. me for] *Bo, P;* mee / For *A, B.* 177. concerning thy] concerning / Thy *A;* of thy *B.* 178–9. promised] *A;* sworne to thee *B.* 180. you have sworn] *A;* assurance *B.* 184. it be not to one that will betray thee] *A;* wee reach our objects *B.* 188. Excellent Pero] *A, Bo;* Excellent! Pero *B.* 188–9. into earth here] *A;* to perdition *B.* 191. wondering] *A;* watching *B.* stole] *A;* stole up *B.* 194. she set close at a banquet] *A;* her selfe reading a letter *B.*

---

followed Boas in printing A without collation; that Boas was following Pearson was presumably coincidence.

skittish] coy (*O.E.D.*, s.v., 5, earliest date 1648): Montsurry obviously means this sense; Annabel affects to understand it in the more usual sense of 'frivolous'.

172. *service*] punning on the sense in which a dog serves a bitch.

174. *uncle*] Guise was Beaupré's uncle (II. ii. 18).

194. *banquet*] possibly not implying food at all, but simply sexual satis-

Mons. D'Ambois?

Pero. Even he my Lord.

Mons. Dost thou not dream wench?

Pero. No my Lord, he is the man.

Mons. The devil he is, and thy Lady his dam: why this was the happiest shot that ever flew! the just plague of hypocrisy levelled it! O the infinite regions betwixt a woman's tongue and her heart: is this our Goddess of chastity? I thought I could not be so slighted, if she had not her freight besides: and therefore plotted this with her woman—dear Pero I will advance thee for ever: but tell me now—God's precious it transforms me with admiration—sweet Pero, whom should she trust with his con-

198. No my Lord] *A;* I sweare *B.* 199–201. why this . . . O the] *B; not in A.* 200. shot that ever flew!] shot? that ever flewe *B uncorr.;* shot that ever flew, *B corr.* 201. it!] it. *Bo;* it, *B.* 203. slighted,] *P;* sleighted, *B;* sleighted: *A.* 204. freight] *A;* fraught *B.* 205. woman—] woman: *A;* woman: never dreaming of *D'Amboys. B.* 207. his] *A;* this *B.*

---

faction. *O.E.D.* does not have such a distinct sense, but (s.v., 1b) cites Dunbar, 'To furnyse a bancat / In Venus chalmer'; the same sense occurs in the title of Chapman's poem *Ovid's Banquet of Sense.* Chapman may have supposed (rightly or wrongly) that this was a general rather than a fig. use of the word. Perhaps some earlier use of this kind lies behind the strange bedroom feast in Keats's *St Agnes' Eve*? B's change is obviously to avoid the obscurity, and refers (as Parrott suggested) to Barrisor's letter. I do not accept Parrott's further suggestion that the reviser wished to leave Tamyra's adultery in doubt.

199. *dam*] female animal, commonly in connection with the devil in numerous proverbs, e.g. *Oth.*, IV. i. 151, 'Let the devil and his dam haunt you!'

199–201. *why . . . O the*] A could just make sense, and Parrott thought B added deliberately; but it looks to me (as presumably to Boas) much more likely that A omitted words that had stood in Chapman's MS.

201. *regions*] spaces.

204. *freight*] implying lover on board.

205.] B's addition may indicate another omission in A: it is effective, but not necessary.

206–7. *admiration*] wonder, surprise.

207–8, 209. *his conveyance*] (1) transporting; (2) trickery: the second sense is emphasized by B's 'this' in l. 207, which may be preferred.

veyance? Or, all the doors being made sure, how could his conveyance be performed?

Pero. Nay my Lord, that amazes me: I cannot by any study so much as guess at it.

Mons. Well, let's favour our apprehensions with forbearing that a little: for if my heart were not hooped with adamant, the conceit of this would have burst it: but hark thee— *Whispers.*

Char. I swear to your Grace, all that I can conjecture touching my Lady your niece, is a strong affection she bears to the English Milor.

Gui. All quod you? 'tis enough I assure you; but tell me— [*Whispers.*]

Mont. I pray thee resolve me—the Duke will never imagine that I am busy about 's wife—hath D'Ambois any privy access to her?

Ann. No my Lord, D'Ambois neglects her (as she takes it) and is therefore suspicious that either your Countess, or the Lady Beaupré hath closely entertained him.

Mont. Berlady a likely suspicion, and very near the life, if she marks it; especially of my wife.

Mons. Come we'll put off all, with seeming only to have

208. could] *A;* should *B.* 209. performed] *A;* made *B.* 215. *Whispers.*] *B; not in A.* 216–19.] *A; not in B.* 224–5. your Countess, or the Lady] *this ed.;* your Lady, or the Countesse *A;* your Lady, or the Lady *B.* 226–7. if she marks it] *A; not in B.* 228. put off] *A;* disguise *B.*

---

212. *apprehensions*] understandings (imaginations): see note on III. i. 22.

213–14. *adamant*] legendary mineral of supreme hardness.

214. *conceit*] imagining.

216–19.] As Parrott suggested, this looks like an omission in B: possibly because the direction *Whispers* was added after ll. 215 and 219, so that the compositor skipped from one to the other.

218. *Milor*] French designation for English lord (*O.E.D.* has Scots use in 1596, no English one before Byron).

224. *and is*] i.e., and she is.

224–5. *your Countess, or the Lady*] B's emendation recognizes that Beaupré is not a countess; mine assumes that A transposed the titles.

225. *closely*] secretly.

228. *put off*] pass off as other than what it is, i.e. disguise.

courted—Away dry palm: sh' has a liver as hard as a biscuit: a man may go a whole voyage with her, and get nothing but tempests at her windpipe.

Gui. Here's one, I think, has swallowed a porcupine, she casts pricks from her tongue so.

Mont. And here's a peacock seems to have devoured one of the Alps, she has so swelling a spirit, and is so cold of her kindness.

Char. We be no windfalls my Lord; ye must gather us with the ladder of matrimony, or we'll hang till we be rotten.

Mons. Indeed that's the way to make ye right open-arses. But alas ye have no portions fit for such husbands as we wish you.

Pero. Portions my Lord, yes and such portions as your principality cannot purchase.

Mons. What, woman? what are those portions?

Pero. Riddle my riddle my Lord.

Mons. Ay marry wench, I think thy portion is a right riddle, a man shall never find it out: but let's hear it.

Pero. You shall my Lord.

229. hard] *A;* dry *B.* 231. at] *A;* from *B.* 237. be] *A;* are *B.* 244. What,] *Bo, P;* What *A, B.*

---

229. *dry palm*] Cf. Tilley, 'A moist hand argues an amorous nature' (H86). See also *Oth.*, III. iv. 37–48, esp. 'Give me your hand. This hand is moist, my lady. / *Des.* It yet has felt no age nor known no sorrow. / *Oth.* This argues fruitfulness and liberal heart.' (And cf. *Chabot*, II. iii. 172.)

229. *sh' has a liver as hard*] she is as unresponsive to passion (seated in the liver).

230–1.] rather obscurely bawdy: sea voyages are supposed to be sexually exciting. The windpipe is both ends (i.e., speech and fart: see l. 239).

233. *pricks*] punning obliquely on 'prick'=penis.

235. *swelling*] playing on 'proud' as opposed to pregnancy.

237. *windfalls*] Fruit is commonly an image of sexual ripeness: 'windfall' indicates over-eagerness to 'fall'.

239. *open-arses*] Schmidt, *Shakespeare-Lexicon* (Berlin, 1923), gives it as vulgar name for the medlar: see l. 268; hence it implies vagina as well as anus. Monsieur plays between promiscuous life and the open skeleton of death.

240–4. *portions*] (1) dowries; (2) parts, here hymen, virginity.

What's that, that being most rare 's most cheap?
That if you sow, you never reap?
That when it grows most, most you in it?
And still you lose it when you win it:
That when 'tis commonest, 'tis dearest,
And when 'tis farthest off 'tis nearest?

Mons. Is this your portion?

Pero. Even this my Lord.

Mons. Believe me I cannot riddle it.

Pero. No my Lord, 'tis my chastity, which you shall neither riddle nor fiddle.

Mons. Your chastity? let me begin with the end of you; how is a woman's chastity nearest a man, when 'tis furthest off?

Pero. Why my Lord, when you cannot get it, it goes to th' heart on you; and that I think comes most near you: and I am sure it shall be far enough off; and so I leave you to my mercy. *Exeunt* Women.

Mons. Farewell Riddle.

Gui. Farewell Medlar.

250. if] *A;* when *B.* 251. in] *A, B;* thin *Bo.* 255. your] *A;* your great *B.* 260. you] *A;* it *B.* 265–6. I . . . my mercy] *A;* wee . . . our mercies *B.* 266. *Exeunt* Women] *B; Exit A.*

249–54.] Pero's riddle is her hymen, representing chastity. Compare Cupid's riddle, *Byron's Tragedy*, II. i. 87–94, representing the penis.

251. *in*] Parrott glosses as a verb meaning 'harvest', which is possible as a pun following 'grows'. The preposition, however, yields the obvious sense of the hymen stretched by an erect penis. Boas's emendation seems to me pointless.

253. *commonest*] the commoner chastity is, the rarer is intercourse, hence: *dearest*] most passionately sought, and expensive.

259. *riddle*] punning with sense 'make holes in'.

fiddle] play about with, esp. sexually. *O.E.D.* (s.v., 5) 'take liberties with a woman', cites Chapman (?) and Shirley, *The Ball*, II. ii. 15; but it is still current slang.

264. *comes most near you*] affects you most.

268. *Medlar*] fruit eaten when rotten; hence licentiousness. See *Rom.*, II. i. 35–8, 'And wish his mistress were that kind of fruit / As maids call medlars, when they laugh alone. / O Romeo! that she were, O! that she were / An open *et cætera* [i.e. open-arse, as in l. 239].

Mont. Farewell Winter Plum.

Mons. Now my Lords, what fruit of our inquisition? feel you nothing budding yet? Speak good my Lord Montsurry.

Mont. Nothing but this: D'Ambois is negligent in observing the Duchess, and therefore she is suspicious that your niece or my wife closely entertains him.

Mons. Your wife, my Lord? think you that possible?

Mont. Alas, I know she flies him like her last hour.

Mons. Her last hour? why that comes upon her the more she flies it: does D'Ambois so, think you?

Mont. That's not worth the answering: 'tis horrible to think with what monsters women's imaginations engross them when they are once enamoured, and what wonders they will work for their satisfaction. They will make a Sheep valiant, a Lion fearful.

Mons. And an Ass confident, my Lord, 'tis true, and more will come forth shortly, get you to the banquet.

Exit GUISE *with* MONTSURRY.

O the unsounded Sea of women's bloods,
That when 'tis calmest, is most dangerous;
Not any wrinkle creaming in their faces,
When in their hearts are Scylla and Charybdis,
Which still are hid in monster-formed clouds,
Where never day shines, nothing ever grows,
But weeds and poisons, that no statesman knows;
Not Cerberus ever saw the damned nooks
Hid with the veils of women's virtuous looks:
I will conceal all yet, and give more time
To D'Ambois' trial, now upon my hook;
He awes my throat; else like Sibylla's Cave
It should breathe oracles; I fear him strangely,
And may resemble his advanced valour
Unto a spirit rais'd without a circle,
Endangering him that ignorantly rais'd him,
And for whose fury he hath learn'd no limit.

[text continued on p. 80]

272. negligent] *A;* thought negligent *B.* 279. horrible] *A;* miraculous *B.*
284. my Lord, 'tis true, and] *A;* well my Lord, *B.* 285.1. *with*] *cum A.*
285.1–322.] *A; B reads:*

Guise. Come my Lord, I have the blind side of one of them. 285a
Exit Guise cum Mont.
Mouns. O the unsounded Sea of womens bloods, 286
That when tis calmest, is most dangerous; 287
Not any wrinkle creaming in their faces, 288
When in their hearts are *Scylla* and *Caribdis,* 289

---

269. *Winter Plum*] fruit which ripens very late, or possibly never, thus contrasting with 'Medlar'. Cf. Webster, *The White Devil* (ed. J. R. Brown, 1960), v. vi. 65, and Wilson, *The Arte of Rhetorique,* 1560 (ed. G. H. Mair, Oxford, 1909, p. 83): 'Among fruite we see some apples are sone ripe, and fal from the Tree in the middest of Sommer, other be still greene and tary til Winter, and hereupon are commonly called Winter fruite'.

272. *observing*] paying court to.

280. *engross*] become absorbed with: coloured by senses of 'gross', (1) huge, (2) obscene.

284. *'tis true*] Parrott thought B's 'well' was substituted to conceal Monsieur's knowledge, which is barely plausible.

285.1–322.] The revision here, including over sixty added lines, is so considerable that it must be set out in full in the collation. It may, of course, be Chapman's own work, but for lack of positive evidence I have preferred to stick to the original version. Line 285a was presumably added to give Guise an exit line, and the motive for most of the added material is also theatrical, to bring back the comedian playing Maffé after his brief appearance in I. i. The reviser is noticeably careful to retain the original lines, working in 298–303 well on in his new scene; only ll. 295–8 are lost, because it is their material that is worked up in the addition. It is more difficult to attribute ll. 294a–o to another hand, especially ll. 294a–c and 294j–l which are striking in Chapman's manner. The main point of these lines, however, is to emphasize a point of plot—that Monsieur must shift the revenge on to Montsurry's shoulders—which does not need labouring. It is noticeable that (as in ll. 166 ff.) the reviser carries on beyond his main need, and once more (ll. 314a–315) achieves an effective line. If it is not Chapman, it is good pastiche (including the S.D. *Exiturus,* l. 294r): I have argued in the Introduction (pp. lxxi–lxxiii) that Field *could* have written it; decision is impossible, preference a matter of critical judgement. Ure felt that the farcical interlude stressing Monsieur's panic was well-judged between his discovery and his next seeing Bussy; I see the force of this, but nonetheless find the labouring of Monsieur's fears clumsy and unconvincing compared with the original, whilst Maffé's contribution is tedious stuff leading to the irrelevance of Monsieur's commentary in ll. 294ww–ba. For lines which look like *mere* pastiche I would point to ll. 294bc–bi, attenuated rhetoric which both anticipates and makes absurd the retention of 'I feare him strangely', etc., ll. 298–303.

[For notes on ll. 286–302 see pp. 79–80.]

Which still are hid in dark and standing foggs,
Where never day shines, nothing ever growes,
But weeds and poysons, that no States-man knowes;
Not *Cerberus* ever saw the damned nookes
Hid with the veiles of womens vertuous lookes.
But what a cloud of sulphur have I drawne
Up to my bosome in this dangerous secret?
Which if my hast (with any spark) should light
Ere *D'Ambois* were engag'd in some sure plot
I were blowne up; He would be sure, my death.
Would I had never knowne it, for before
I shall perswade th'importance to *Montsurry*,
And make him with some studied stratagem,
Train *D'Ambois* to his wreak, his maid may tell it,
Or I (out of my fiery thirst to play
With the fell Tyger, up in darknesse tyed,
And give it some light) make it quite break loose.
I feare it afore heaven, and will not see
D'Ambois againe,[till I have told *Montsurry*,
And set a snare with him to free my feares: whose there?
Enter Maffe.

Maffe. My Lord?
Mons. Goe call the Count *Montsurry*,
And make the dores fast, I will speak with none
Till he come to me.
Maffe. Well my Lord. *Exiturus.*
Mons. Or else
Send you some other, and see all the dores
Made safe your selfe I pray, hast, flie about it.
Maffe. You'l speak with none but with the Count *Montsurry*.
Mont. [*sic*] With none but hee except it be the Guise.
Maffe. See even by this, there's one exception more,
Your Grace must be more firme in the command,
Or else shall I as weakly execute.
The Guise shall speak with you?
Mons. He shall I say.
Maffe. And Count *Montsurry*?
Mons. I, and Count *Montsurry*.
Maffe. Your Grace must pardon me, that I am bold
To urge the cleare and full sence of your pleasure;
Which when so ever I have knowne, I hope
Your Grace will say, I hit it to a haire.
Mons. You have.
Maffe. I hope so, or I would be glad.—
Mons. I pray thee get thee gone, thou are so tedious
In the strickt forme of all thy services,
That I had better have one negligent.
You hit my pleasure well, when *D'Ambois* hit you,
Did you not, think you?

Maffe. *D'Ambois*? why my Lord?
Mons. I pray thee talk no more, but shut the dores.
Doe what I charge thee.
Maffe. I will my Lord, and yet
I would be glad the wrong I had of *D'Ambois*—
Mons. Precious! then it is a Fate that plagues me
In this mans foolery, I may be murthered
While he stands on protection of his folly.
Avant about thy charge.
Maffe. I goe my Lord.
I had my head broke in his faithfull service,
I had no suit the more, nor any thanks,
And yet my teeth must still be hit with *D'Ambois*.
D'Ambois my Lord shall know.—
Mons. The devill and *D'Ambois*. *Exit Maffe.*
How am I tortur'd with this trusty foole?
Never was any curious in his place
To doe things justly, but he was an Asse:
We cannot finde one trusty that is witty,
And therefore beare their disproportion.
Grant thou great starre, and angell of my life,
A sure lease of it but for some few dayes,
That I may cleare my bosome of the Snake
I cherisht there, and I will then defie
All check to it but Natures, and her Altars
Shall crack with vessels crown'd with ev'ry liquor
Drawn from her highest, and most bloudy humors.
I feare him strangely, his advanced valour
Is like a spirit rais'd without a circle,
Endangering him that ignorantly rais'd him,
And for whose fury he hath learnt no limit.

Enter Maffe hastily.

Maffe. I cannot help it, what should I do more?
As I was gathering a fit Guard to make
My passage to the dores, and the dores sure,
The man of bloud is enter'd.
Mons. Rage of death.
If I had told the secret, and he knew it,
Thus had I bin endanger'd:—My sweet heart!

286–9.] possibly derived from Seneca: see Appendix B, pp. 149–50.

286. *unsounded*] in nautical sense; cf. 'unfathomed'.

288. *creaming*] forming scum or froth (used of either stagnant or rushing water); see *Mer. V.*, I. i. 88–9.

289. *Scylla and Charybdis*] a monster in a cave and a whirlpool on either side of the straits of Messina (see *Odyssey*, XII).

290. *monster-formed*] very compressed image: the clouds are formed by the monsters (Scylla and Charybdis) to conceal their presence; at the same

Enter [BUSSY] D'AMBOIS.

How now, what leap'st thou at?
Buss. O royal object.
Mons. Thou dream'st awake: object in th' empty air?
Buss. Worthy the head of Titan, worth his chair.
Mons. Pray thee what mean'st thou?
Buss. See you not a Crown
Empale the forehead of the great King Monsieur?

How now? what leap'st thou at?
Enter D'Ambois.
D'Amb. O royall object.
Mons. Thou dream'st awake: Object in th'empty aire?
D'Amb. Worthy the browes of *Titan*, worth his chaire.
Mons. Pray thee what mean'st thou?
D'Amb. See you not a Crowne
Empale the forehead of the great King Monsieur?

---

time the clouds themselves are monstrous and threatening: thus echoing the imagery of III. i. 21–8.

292. *that . . . knows*] i.e., unknown *even* to statesmen.

293. *Cerberus*] the monstrous watchdog of Hades.

297. *awes my throat*] frightens me into silence.

Sibylla's Cave] Sibylla was the name of several female prophets, of whom the most celebrated was the Cumaean Sibyl, whose cave Aeneas visited before his descent to hell.

299. *advanced*] developed, in opprobrious sense implying *over*-advanced (cf. use of 'advanced' nowadays re morals or politics).

300. *rais'd without a circle*] The circle drawn round the magician conjuring devils to serve him protected him from their malice. Cf. *Teares of Peace*, ll. 674–5, 'and (like to Spirits raisde / Without a Circle) neuer is appaisde.'

302.] Monsieur (the magician) cannot control Bussy's (the spirit's) fury.

303. *How . . . at?*] B's misplacing above Bussy's entry may indicate that the main MS. addition ended here in the printer's copy: if so, the compositor read MS. here more accurately than in Act V (see Introduction, p. lxii).

leap'st] *O.E.D.* does not specify 'leap' used like 'jump' = start; 'leap at' may mean 'reach after'.

305. *Titan*] seems to be the early sun-god, Hyperion; 'Titan' might be any one of the gods who preceded Zeus.

chair] evidently chariot (of the sun), though not in *O.E.D.* in this sense. Ferguson (p. 12) points out that Monsieur is compared to Phaeton in his disastrous attempt to drive the sun's chariot.

307. *Empale*] encircle (esp. for adornment).

Mons. O fie upon thee.
Buss. Sir, that is the subject
Of all these your retir'd and sole discourses.
Mons. Wilt thou not leave that wrongful supposition?
This still hath made me doubt thou dost not love me.
Wilt thou do one thing for me then sincerely?
Buss. Ay, anything, but killing of the King.
Mons. Still in that discord, and ill-taken note?
Buss. Come, do not doubt me, and command me all things.
Mons. I will not then, and now by all my love
Shewn to thy virtues, and by all fruits else
Already sprung from that affection,
I charge thee utter (even with all the freedom

Mons. O fie upon thee.
D'Amb. Prince, that is the Subject
Of all these your retir'd and sole discourses.
Mons. Wilt thou not leave that wrongfull supposition?
D'Amb. Why wrongfull? to suppose the doubtlesse right
To the succession worth the thinking on.
Mons. Well, leave these jests, how I am over-joyed
With thy wish'd presence, and how fit thou com'st,
For of mine honour I was sending for thee.
D'Amb. To what end?
Mons. Onely for thy company,
Which I have still in thought, but that's no payment
On thy part made with personall appearance.
Thy absence so long suffered oftentimes
Put me in some little doubt thou do'st not love me.
Wilt thou doe one thing therefore now sincerely?
D'Amb. I, any thing, but killing of the King.
Mons. Still in that discord, and ill taken note?
How most unseasonable thou playest the Cucko,
In this thy fall of friendship?
D'Amb. Then doe not doubt,
That there is any act within my nerves,
But killing of the King that is not yours.
Mons. I will not then; to prove which by my love
Shewne to thy vertues, and by all fruits else
Already sprung from that still flourishing tree,
With whatsoever may hereafter spring,
I charge thee utter (even with all the freedome

---

309. *sole*] solitary.

Both of thy noble nature and thy friendship)
The full and plain state of me in thy thoughts.
Buss. What, utter plainly what I think of you?
Why this swims quite against the stream of greatness:
Great men would rather hear their flatteries,
And if they be not made fools, are not wise.
Mons. I am no such great fool, and therefore charge thee
Even from the root of thy free heart, display me.
Buss. Since you affect it in such serious terms,
If yourself first will tell me what you think
As freely and as heartily of me,
I'll be as open in my thoughts of you.
Mons. A bargain of mine honour; and make this,
That prove we in our full dissection
Never so foul, live still the sounder friends.
Buss. What else sir? come begin, and speak me simply.
Mons. I will I swear. I think thee then a man,
That dares as much as a wild horse or tiger;
As headstrong and as bloody; and to feed
The ravenous wolf of thy most Cannibal valour
(Rather than not employ it), thou would'st turn
Hackster to any whore, slave to a Jew

Both of thy noble nature and thy friendship) 320
The full and plaine state of me in thy thoughts. 321
D'Amb. What, utter plainly what I think of you? 322
Mons. Plaine as truth. 322a

335. begin, and speak me simply] *A;* pay me home, ile bide it bravely *B.*
338. to] *A, Bo, P;* so *B.*

322a.] a good case of an addition which seems to derive from stage practice, probably via memory.

325. *are not wise*] i.e., in their own estimation.

328. *affect*] aspire to, crave (from 'affectare'; usual senses are from 'afficere').

330. *heartily*] sincerely.

332. *this*] i.e., another bargain.

334. *live*] i.e., we shall live.

335. *come . . . simply*] Parrott is surely right that B retains 'come' by an error in conflating the printed text with the MS.

simply] sincerely.

341. *Hackster*] cut-throat, etc.; *O.E.D.* gives this as a nonce-use for

Or English usurer, to force possessions
(And cut men's throats) of mortgaged estates;
Or thou wouldst tire thee like a tinker's wife,
And murder market folks; quarrel with sheep,
And run as mad as Ajax; serve a butcher,
Do anything but killing of the King:
That in thy valour th' art like other naturals,
That have strange gifts in nature, but no soul
Diffus'd quite through to make them of a piece,
But stop at humours that are more absurd,
Childish and villainous than that hackster, whore,
Slave, cut-throat, tinker's bitch, compar'd before:
And in those humours wouldst envy, betray,
Slander, blaspheme, change each hour a religion;
Do anything, but killing of the King;
That in that valour (which is still my dunghill,
To which I carry all filth in thy house)
Th' art more ridiculous and vainglorious
Than any mountebank; and impudent
Than any painted bawd; which, not to soothe

342. possessions] *Bo, P;* possessions, *A, B.* 343. (And . . . throats)] *Bo, P;* And . . . throates *A, B.* 344. wife] *A;* strumpet *B.*
357–8.] *A; B reads:*

That in thy valour (which is still the dunghill,
To which hath reference all filth in thy house)

361. which, not to soothe] *A, B;* which not to sooth, *Bo, P.*

'prostitute's bully', presumably one who protects her and lives on her earnings.

344. *tire*] attire.

tinker's wife] roughly equivalent to 'gangster's moll' (see l. 353).

345–6. *quarrel . . . Ajax*] Ajax went mad when not awarded the arms of Achilles, and slaughtered a flock of sheep believing them to be Greeks.

348. *naturals*] half-wits.

349. *strange gifts in nature*] presumably a reference to the supernatural gifts sometimes ascribed to half-wits.

357–8.] Parrott supposed B's revision was to avoid the ridiculous image of a Prince carrying a servant's filth to his own dunghill. Jacobean ideas of decorum in imagery make this possible. Ure thought the change an improvement: it is clearly deliberate, though I do not prefer it.

361. *soothe*] flatter.

And glorify thee like a Jupiter Hammon,
Thou eat'st thy heart in vinegar; and thy gall
Turns all thy blood to poison, which is cause
Of that toad-pool that stands in thy complexion;
And makes thee (with a cold and earthy moisture,
Which is the dam of putrefaction,
As plague to thy damn'd pride) rot as thou liv'st;
To study calumnies and treacheries;
To thy friend's slaughters like a Screech-owl sing,
And to all mischiefs, but to kill the King.

Buss. So: have you said?

Mons. How thinkest thou? Do I flatter?
Speak I not like a trusty friend to thee?

Buss. That ever any man was bless'd withal;
So here's for me. I think you are (at worst)
No devil, since y' are like to be no King;
Of which, with any friend of yours I'll lay
This poor stillado here, 'gainst all the stars,

367. dam] damme *A*, *B*. 371. to all] *A*, *B;* do all *T*.

---

362. *Jupiter Hammon*] the title derived from association of Zeus, and thus Jupiter, with the Egyptian ram-god, Ammon. Chapman's allusion is obscure: Boas referred to Alexander the Great worshipping Ammon, but I do not see the relevance of this.

363. *eat'st thy heart*] common phrase for brooding melancholy.

vinegar] used figuratively of 'sour' or 'bitter' humours.

365. *toad-pool*] *O.E.D.* cites this as a nonce-use, glossing 'mass of corrupted matter'. Toads were supposed to be poisonous; the phrase seems to imply an unhealthy complexion; cf. Webster, *The Duchess of Malfi* (ed. Lucas, 1927), I. i. 158–60: 'he is a mellancholy Churchman: The Spring in his face, is nothing but the Ingendring of Toades', and *Mer. V.*, I. i. 88–9: 'There are a sort of men whose visages / Do cream and mantle like a standing pond'.

complexion] presumably in modern sense of skin, as well as temperament.

366–8. *with . . . pride*] Pride derived from the hot and dry humours, and so would be plagued by cold and moist elements from earth. 'dam' = mother (i.e., moisture gives birth to putrefaction) and also plays with 'damn', as 'damn'd' in l. 368 plays with 'dammed', changing the metaphor from plaguing to obstruction.

370. *like . . . sing*] Screech-owls were supposed to be ominous of misfortune, esp. death.

378. *stillado*] *O.E.D.* knows no other use of this form; it may be an error for 'stiletto'.

Ay, and 'gainst all your treacheries, which are more:
That you did never good, but to do ill;
But ill of all sorts, free and for itself:
That (like a murdering piece, making lanes in armies,
The first man of a rank, the whole rank falling)
If you have once wrong'd one man, y' are so far
From making him amends, that all his race,
Friends and associates fall into your chase:
That y' are for perjuries the very Prince
Of all intelligencers; and your voice
Is like an eastern wind, that where it flies,
Knits nets of caterpillars, with which you catch
The prime of all the fruits the Kingdom yields.
That your political head is the curs'd fount
Of all the violence, rapine, cruelty,
Tyranny and atheism flowing through the realm.
That y' have a tongue so scandalous, 'twill cut
A perfect Crystal; and a breath that will
Kill to that wall a spider; you will jest
With God, and your soul to the devil tender
For lust; kiss horror, and with death engender.

384. once] *A; not in B.* y' are] *A, B uncorr.;* you are *B corr.* 396. A perfect] *A;* The purest *B.* 398. tender] *A, B;* tender; *P.* 399. lust;] *A, B;* lust *P.*

---

382. *piece*] gun.

making lanes] Chapman uses similar phrases in *Sir Giles Goosecap*, I. ii. 15–17, and *Fragment of The Teares of Peace* (Bartlett, p. 235), l. 44.

386. *chase*] hunt.

388. *intelligencers*] spies, informers.

388–90. *and ... caterpillars*] Cf. *Fragment of The Teares of Peace*, ll. 16–18, 'And for free bounties (like an Easterne wind) / Knits nets of Caterpillars, that all fruites / Of planting peace, catch with contentious suites'. The image is obscure: 'caterpillars' are (1) larvae, eating fruit; (2) (from old sense of 'piller') plunderers, parasites (*O.E.D.*, s.v., 2); Monsieur's voice is the 'eastern wind' nipping off the fruit, and commands the 'nets of caterpillars' waiting to catch and devour it.

395. *scandalous*] uttering scandal.

399. *kiss ... engender*] Cf. *Revenge of Bussy*, I. ii. 32, 'Learn to kiss horror, and with death engender'. I do not see any need for Parrott's repunctuation.

That your foul body is a Lernean fen
Of all the maladies breeding in all men.
That you are utterly without a soul:
And, for your life, the thread of that was spun
When Clotho slept, and let her breathing rock
Fall in the dirt; and Lachesis still draws it,
Dipping her twisting fingers in a bowl
Defil'd, and crown'd with Virtue's forced soul.
And lastly (which I must for gratitude
Ever remember) that of all my height
And dearest life, you are the only spring,
Only in royal hope to kill the King.

Mons. Why now I see thou lov'st me, come to the banquet. *Exeunt.*

412. *Exeunt.*] *Exeunt.* / *Finis Actus tertij. B; Finis Actus tertij. A.*

---

400. *Lernean fen*] near Argos, where lived the Hydra that Hercules killed.

403–7.] The detail of the imagery is slightly obscure, though its rhetorical development is effective. Presumably Monsieur's life-thread is doubly defiled, by the dirt in which Clotho drops it, and the bowl in which Lachesis dips her fingers; 'crown'd' only faintly depends on the bowl image, serving chiefly to suggest the climax of defilement.

404–5. *Clotho . . . Lachesis*] The Fates, spinning the thread of life: Clotho held the distaff, Lachesis drew the thread, and Atropos cut it off.

404. *breathing*] giving life.

rock] distaff.

407. *crown'd*] topped (with foam, on a brimful glass).

forced] violated.

409. *height*] high position, rank.

Act IV

[IV. i]

[*Enter*] HENRY, MONSIEUR *with a letter*, GUISE, MONTSURRY, BUSSY, DUCHESS, TAMYRA, BEAUPRÉ, PERO, CHARLOTTE, ANNABEL, PYRHA, *with* four Pages.

Hen. Ladies, ye have not done our banquet right,
Nor look'd upon it with those cheerful rays
That lately turn'd your breaths to floods of gold;
Your looks, methinks, are not drawn out with thoughts
So clear and free as heretofore, but fare
As if the thick complexions of men
Govern'd within them.

Buss. 'Tis not like, my Lord,

Act IV] Actus Quarti Scena Prima. *A, B.* 0.1. *with a letter*] *B; not in A.* 0.2. *Duchess*] *Elynor A, B.* 5. fare] *A, T;* foule *B.*

2–3.] an elaborately courtly image of the ladies' presence in terms of sunbeams, contrasting with Bussy's moon images below.

5. *free*] unimpeded; frank.

fare] evidently a submerged pun with 'fair'; B's change to 'foul' looks like a trick of memory.

6. *thick complexions*] a 'thick' (muddy, etc.) as opposed to a 'clear', 'free', and 'fair' mixture of humours.

7–20.] The structure of this speech depends on the double sense of 'image': (1) as reflection or metaphor; (2) as created object, real as distinct from imaginary. The moon is a metaphoric reflection of the character of women (changeable, lovely, etc.), but also in fact exercises direct influence on them, so that *they* are creations (images) of *it*. Hence women are 'images' of men's instability, and as they also influence men, can be said to make men images of them. Latent in all this is the whole range of traditional associations with Moon and Sun: the sublunary world is mortal, changeable; Moon=Cynthia, goddess of chastity; moonlight is imaginative (female) experience, contrasted with reasonable, logical, permanent (male) sunlight. Humanity ('made of nothing') is fundamentally committed to change and so finds its values (images to be adored) in moon-like beauty, absurdity, immaturity, as well as knowing a different range of values by its

That men in women rule; but contrary,
For as the Moon (of all things God created)
Not only is the most appropriate image
Or glass to shew them how they wax and wane,
But in her light and motion, likewise bears
Imperial influences that command
In all their powers, and make them wax and wane;
So women, that (of all things made of nothing)
Are the most perfect images of the Moon
(Or still-unwean'd sweet Moon-calves with white faces),
Not only are patterns of change to men:
But as the tender Moonshine of their beauties
Clears or is cloudy, make men glad or sad.

Mons. But here the Moons are chang'd (as the King notes)
And either men rule in them, or some power
Beyond their voluntary motions:

12. light] *A;* height *B.* 16. images] *A;* Idols *B.* 20. sad.] *A;* sad, *B.*
20.] *A; B adds:*
So then they rule in men, not men in them.
23. motions] *A;* faculty *B.*

---

intellectual (sun) power. The result is a difficult but impressive balance of response to the limitations and glories of sublunar life, fundamental to the play's tragic sense in general, and to Tamyra's function in particular (cf. her acceptance of the 'imperial' commands of passion in II. ii). See also Introduction, p. xlvi.

11. *them*] i.e., women.

12. *light*] B's 'height' may be correct, if A misread MS.; but light is important in the passage (esp. in ll. 2 and 19). The moon's influences referred to as real, not imaginary, seem to involve lunacy (moon-calves), which may suggest 'light' as the source of influence, and the physical cycle of menstruation.

13. *Imperial*] doubling the idea of a wide sphere of influence, with the suggestion of 'imperious', irresistible commands.

16. *images*] B's 'idols' emphasizes the relevant sense of an object of worship, but it avoids the repetition from l. 10 which is vital to grasping the passage.

17. *Moon-calves*] congenital idiots, or deformed embryos; *O.E.D.* (s.v., 2b) cites this as earliest use of special sense 'children' of the moon (lunatic or not); but the other senses are clearly involved.

19. *Moonshine*] Cf. 'Moon-calves' for the double sense of beauty and nonsense.

23. *motions*] Parrott thought B's 'faculty' was intended to avoid trisyl-

For nothing can recover their lost faces.
Buss. None can be always one: our Griefs and Joys
Hold several sceptres in us, and have times
For their predominance: which Grief now, in them
Doth claim, as proper to his diadem:
And Grief's a natural sickness of the blood,
That time to part asks, as his coming had;
Only slight fools griev'd, suddenly are glad;
A man may say t' a dead man, be reviv'd,
As well as to one sorrowful, be not griev'd.
And therefore, Princely mistress, in all wars
Against these base foes that insult on weakness,
And still fight hous'd behind the shield of Nature,
Of tyrannous law, treachery, or beastly need,
Your servant cannot help; authority here
Goes with corruption; something like some States,
That back worst men: valour to them must creep
That (to themselves left) would fear him asleep.

25. *Buss.*] *A; Montsur. B.* 27. predominance] *A;* divided Empires *B.* 28. claim] *A;* prove *B.* 29.] *A; B prefixes: D'Amb.* 37. tyrannous] *A;* priviledge *B;* privilege, *D, P;* privilegd *P conj.*

---

labic sounding of motions, which does not seem to me necessary anyhow; 'motions' is effective in sustaining the moon image, which 'faculty' forgets.

25–8.] Parrott suggested that B transferred these lines to give Montsurry some part in the dialogue: they were obviously conceived as part of Bussy's argument.

27. *predominance*] in astrology, period of ascendance of star, moon, etc., when it has major influence; hence applied to correspondent humours. B's alternative again forgets the moon image.

which] Editors refer this to 'times': the whole phrase 'times . . . predominance' seems more appropriate.

29. *natural . . . blood*] The psychological humours were thought to be dependent on the physical—a connection more intelligible now than in the three centuries between.

34. *Princely mistress*] the Duchess; Bussy's speech is still keyed to courtliness, though its reference is of course to his relations with Tamyra.

35–7.] i.e., the weakness inherent in the nature of humanity is manifest as tyranny or treachery to our 'better nature', or simply as animal necessity; the stress has shifted from grief in particular to passion in general.

38–9. *authority . . . corruption*] Authority is in the hands of corrupt forces.

Duch. Ye all take that for granted, that doth rest
Yet to be prov'd; we all are as we were,
As merry, and as free in thought as ever.
Gui. And why then can ye not disclose your thoughts?
Tam. Methinks the man hath answer'd for us well.
Mons. The man? why madam d'ee not know his name?
Tam. Man is a name of honour for a King:
Additions take away from each chief thing;
The School of Modesty, not to learn, learns Dames:
They sit in high forms there, that know men's names.
Mons. Hark sweetheart, here's a bound set to your valour:
It cannot enter here; no, not to notice
Of what your name is; your great Eagle's beak
(Should you fly at her) had as good encounter
An Albion cliff, as her more craggy liver.
Buss. I'll not attempt her sir; her sight and name
(By which I only know her) doth deter me.
Hen. So do they all men else.
Mons. You would say so
If you knew all.
Tam. Knew all my Lord? what mean you?
Mons. All that I know Madam.
Tam. That you know? speak it.
Mons. No 'tis enough I feel it.
Hen. But methinks

52. bound] *A;* bar *B.*

46.] The submerged reference to the Bussy-Tamyra affair is brought nearer to the surface in Tamyra's endorsement, which leads to the verbal battle with Monsieur in ll. 47–62.

49. *Additions*] styles of address, titles, etc.

50. *learns*] teaches.

51. *high forms*] presumably akin to dunce's stools.

54–6.] Monsieur is picking up the eagle and Prometheus references in III. ii. 4–5 and 37. The 'liver' as seat of passion is in Tamyra craggy because of her declared imperviousness.

57. *name*] with a play on 'reputation'.

59.] As Parrott noted, Monsieur deliberately misunderstands Henry.

62–5.] Henry's observation of Tamyra's new maturity makes an impressive final comment on this oblique discussion of her passion.

Her courtship is more pure than heretofore:
True Courtiers should be modest, but not nice:
Bold, but not impudent: pleasure love, not vice.
Mons. [*aside to Bussy*] Sweetheart: come hither, what if one should make
Horns at Montsurry? would it strike him jealous
Through all the proofs of his chaste Lady's virtues?
Buss. No I think not.
Mons. Not if I nam'd the man
With whom I would make him suspicious
His wife hath arm'd his forehead?
Buss. So, you might
Have your great nose made less indeed: and slit:
Your eyes thrust out.
Mons. Peace, peace, I pray thee peace.
Who dares do that? the brother of his King?
Buss. Were your King brother in you: all your powers
(Stretch'd in the arms of great men and their bawds)

64. but] *A;* and *B.* 67. it] *A;* it not *B.*
69–73.] *A; B reads:*
D'Amb. If he be wise, not. 69
Mons. What? not if I should name the Gardener, 70
That I would have him think hath grafted him? 71
D'Amb. So the large licence that your greatnesse uses 71a
To jest at all men, may be taught indeed b
To make a difference of the grounds you play on, c
Both in the men you scandall, and the matter. d
Mons. As how? as how? e
D'Amb. Perhaps led with a traine, where you may have f
Your nose made lesse, and slit, your eyes thrust out. 72
Mons. Peace, peace, I pray thee peace. 73
71e–73.] *as three lines, ending:* traine, / slit, / peace. *Bo, P.*

69–73.] Ure regards B's addition as good: it may well be Chapman's, though it does not strike me as an unquestionable gain over the terseness of the text.

71. *arm'd*] furnished with horns (emblem of cuckoldry).

72. *great nose*] See I. i. 188–9.

slit] punishment branding the criminal, esp. for traitors.

75. *powers*] personal powers; but also servants, armies, etc.

76. *arms*] (1) military sense (from 'powers'); (2) lasciviously, implying corruption.

Set close down by you; all your stormy laws
(Spouted with lawyers' mouths; and gushing blood,
Like to so many torrents); all your glories
(Making you terrible, like enchanted flames
Fed with bare coxcombs and with crooked hams);
All your prerogatives, your shames and tortures:
All daring heaven, and opening hell about you—
Were I the man ye wrong'd so and provok'd:
(Though ne'er so much beneath you) like a box-tree
I would (out of the toughness of my root)
Ram hardness in my lowness, and like death
Mounted on earthquakes, I would trot through all
Honours and horrors: through foul and fair,
And from your whole strength toss you into air.

Mons. Go, th' art a devil; such another spirit
Could not be still'd, from all th' Armenian dragons.

79–81. glories (Making . . . flames . . . coxcombs . . . hams);] glories: (Making . . . flames . . . cockescombes: . . . hammes) *A;* glories, (Making . . . flames, . . . cockscombs, . . . hammes) *B;* glories (Making . . . flames) . . . cockscombs . . . hams, *P.* 86. toughness] *A, Spencer;* roughnesse *B.* 89. through] *A;* thorow *B.* 90. into air] *A;* into the aire *B.*

---

77. *stormy*] i.e., as they affect people, violent and tyrannical: the image develops into the torrents of the next two lines.

81. *bare . . . hams*] gestures of servility: caps off, and kneeling.

82. *shames*] inflictions of shame on others.

85. *box-tree*] known both for the hardness of its root (Parrott cites Gerard's *Herball*, 1597, recommending it for dagger hafts) and its lowness. In *Byron's Tragedy*, V. iii. 13–14, Byron contrasts himself and his judges as a cedar of Lebanon and box-trees.

87. *Ram*] stuff; see Jonson, *Poetaster* (ed. Herford and Simpson, Oxford, 1932), V. i. 136, 'And for his poesie, 'tis so ramm'd with life'. (For common sense of pressing down in gun-loading, see IV. ii. 17.)

87–8. *death . . . earthquakes*] The context suggests a familiar emblem, though I have not found any analogues.

88. *trot*] emphasizing briskness.

89. *horrors:*] A's punctuation makes an effective rhetorical break: it has no logical significance.

90. *strength*] Cf. 'powers' (l. 75): personal, and supporters, armies, etc.

92. *still'd*] distilled: used in alchemy for any process aimed at extracting the essence (or quintessence) of a substance.

Armenian dragons] See II. i. 118. Parrott refers to the gold-guarding griffins of Scythia in Herodotus, IV. 27.

O my Love's glory: heir to all I have—
That's all I can say, and that all I swear—
If thou outlive me, as I know thou must,
Or else hath Nature no proportion'd end
To her great labours: she hath breath'd a spirit
Into thy entrails, of effect to swell
Into another great Augustus Caesar:
Organs, and faculties fitted to her greatness:
And should that perish like a common spirit,
Nature's a Courtier and regards no merit.

Hen. Here's nought but whispering with us: like a calm
Before a tempest, when the silent air
Lays her soft ear close to the earth to hearken
For that she fears is coming to afflict her;
Some fate doth join our ears to hear it coming.
Come, my brave Eagle, let's to covert fly:
I see Almighty Æther in the smoke
Of all his clouds descending: and the sky
Hid in the dim ostents of Tragedy.

Exit HENRY *with* [BUSSY] D'AMBOIS *and* Ladies.

Gui. Now stir the humour, and begin the brawl.

93–4. have—That's . . . swear—] *Bo, P subs.;* haue: That's . . . sweare. *A, B.* 97. spirit] *A;* minde *B.* 98. effect] *A;* desert *B.*
106.] *A; B reads:*
For that she feares steales on to ravish her;
111.1. *and* Ladies] *B; not in A.*

---

96. *proportion'd*] proportionate: the purposive or fortuitous working of Nature, questioned in I. i, is directly confronted here and in the rest of Monsieur's speech, in terms that anticipate V. iii. 1–56.

98. *effect*] B's 'desert' could easily be confused with 'effect' in MS., and either may derive from a misreading.

103–11.] Henry (as in ll. 62–5) identifies finally the relation of surface and undercurrent in this scene as directly bearing on the tragedy.

106. *is . . . her*] Ure and Parrott both praise B's revision.

109. *Almighty Æther*] Æther was commonly identified with Jove. The line can be traced to Virgil or Lucretius: see Appendix B, p. 154.

111. *ostents*] portents (cf. Marlowe, *Hero and Leander*, IV, Argument, l. 4).

112. *stir*] excite (feeling, passion, etc.).

brawl] the name of a dance; usual senses also relevant.

Mont. The King and D'Ambois now are grown all one.
Mons. Nay, they are two my Lord.
Mont. How's that?
Mons. No more.
Mont. I must have more my Lord.
Mons. What more than two?
[*Making horns.*]
Mont. How monstrous is this!
Mons. Why?
Mont. You make me horns.
Mons. Not I, it is a work without my power,
Married men's ensigns are not made with fingers:
Of divine fabric they are, not men's hands;
Your wife, you know, is a mere Cynthia,
And she must fashion horns out of her nature.
Mont. But doth she? dare you charge her? speak, false Prince.
Mons. I must not speak my Lord: but if you'll use
The learning of a nobleman, and read,
Here's something to those points: soft you must pawn
Your honour having read it to return it.
Mont. Not I, I pawn mine Honour, for a paper?
Mons. You must not buy it under. *Exeunt* GUISE *and* MONSIEUR.

Enter TAMYRA, PERO.

128. *Exeunt Guise and Monsieur.*] *B; not in A.* 128.1.] *A; Enter Tamira & Pero. B, line 126.*

---

118. *ensigns*] characteristic marks.

120. *mere*] (1) pure, perfect; (2) nothing else than (as nowadays).

Cynthia] Goddess of Chastity, and of the moon.

121. *fashion . . . nature*] referring to the 'horned' appearance of the new moon.

123. *not speak*] See his oath to Pero, III. ii. 188–9. Parrott supposes the paper to be a proof of Tamyra's guilt and refers to a letter the historical Bussy wrote to Alençon, boasting of his conquest. This is surely wrong: Chapman is vague about papers in the play, but the implication seems to be that Monsieur has *written* what he has sworn not to *speak* (see l. 196 and IV. ii. 87). I wonder whether Parrott's suggestion may depend on IV. ii. 9a–b, which is a later addition adding to the confusion.

128. *under*] at a lower price (*O.E.D.*, s.v., 5, earliest date 1632).

128.1. Enter *Tamyra, Pero*] B, shifting this up two lines, very likely reflects theatre practice: Tamyra must see Monsieur go.

Mont. Keep it then!
And keep fire in your bosom.
Tam. What says he?
Mont. You must make good the rest.
Tam. How fares my Lord?
Takes my Love anything to heart he says?
Mont. Come y' are a—
Tam. What my Lord?
Mont. The plague of Herod
Feast in his rotten entrails.
Tam. Will you wreak
Your anger's just cause given by him, on me?
Mont. By him?
Tam. By him my Lord, I have admir'd
You could all this time be at concord with him,
That still hath play'd such discords on your honour.
Mont. Perhaps 'tis with some proud string of my wife's.
Tam. How's that, my Lord?
Mont. Your tongue will still admire,
Till my head be the miracle of the world.
Tam. O woe is me. *She seems to swoon.*
Pero. What does your Lordship mean?
Madam, be comforted; my Lord but tries you.
Madam? Help good my Lord, are you not mov'd?
Do your set looks print in your words, your thoughts?
Sweet Lord, clear up those eyes, for shame of Noblesse:

141. *She seems to swoon.*] *B; not in A.*
145–6.] *A; B reads:*
Sweet Lord, cleare up those eyes, unbend that masking forehead, 145
Whence is it you rush upon her with these Irish warres, 145a
More full of sound then hurt? but it is enough, 146

---

129. *keep fire*] Cf. 'to keep one's fire' = to stay at home (*O.E.D.*, s.v. *fire*, 3), i.e., keep quiet. But here the stress is equally on the suppressed heat.

132. *plague of Herod*] worms; see *Acts*, xii. 23.

138. *proud string*] 'proud' is playing with the sense 'on heat' of animals; 'string' continues the musical metaphor, and plays on 'string' for nerve.

144. *print*] fig.: impress, give form to. The line is elliptical: Montsurry's words are as set as his looks—does this represent his thoughts?

145–6.] B's addition is clumsily made, but Parrott's reading is plausible;

Merciless creature; but it is enough,
You have shot home, your words are in her heart;
She has not liv'd to bear a trial now.
Mont. Look up my Love, and by this kiss receive
My soul amongst thy spirits for supply
To thine, chas'd with my fury.
Tam. O my Lord,
I have too long liv'd to hear this from you.
Mont. 'Twas from my troubled blood, and not from me—
[*aside*] I know not how I fare; a sudden night
Flows through my entrails, and a headlong Chaos
Murmurs within me, which I must digest;
And not drown her in my confusions,
That was my life's joy, being best inform'd.
[*To her*] Sweet, you must needs forgive me, that my love
(Like to a fire disdaining his suppression)
Rag'd being discourag'd; my whole heart is wounded
When any least thought in you is but touch'd,
And shall be till I know your former merits,
Your name and memory altogether crave

145–6.] *as B, in four lines, ending:* eyes, / it, / warres, / enough, *Bo; 145 as A, remainder as Bo P.* 154. *aside*] *P; not in A, B.* 163. merits,] *Bo, P;* merits: *A, B.*

---

the only point seems to be an allusion to Irish wars, which Parrott dates 1607–8, and takes as dating the revision. Irish troubles were persistent in the late 16th and early 17th centuries, and their proverbial indecisiveness does not help to establish date.

151. *chas'd with*] chased away by.

153. *troubled blood*] blood stirred by passion: both literally 'blood', and the humour.

154. aside] evident in l. 157 'her'.

156. *digest*] disperse; get over the effects of.

157. *drown*] The image is sustained from 'blood' in l. 153, through 'Flows' in l. 155.

158. *inform'd*] ambiguous, perhaps accidentally. It may mean she was his joy when he had no evil information; or, because she was formed perfect ('informed' was commonly used in this sense: see I. ii. 23); or, when he was best formed, before his confusions, as Parrott suggests. Or perhaps an amalgam of these senses explains the awkward construction.

In loath'd oblivion their eternal grave;
And then you must hear from me, there's no mean
In any passion I shall feel for you:
Love is a razor cleansing being well us'd,
But fetcheth blood still being the least abus'd:
To tell you briefly all; the man that left me
When you appear'd, did turn me worse than woman,
And stabb'd me to the heart thus, with his hand.
[*Making horns.*]

Tam. O happy woman! Comes my stain from him?
It is my beauty, and that innocence proves,
That slew Chimæra, rescu'd Peleus
From all the savage beasts in Pelion,
And rais'd the chaste Athenian Prince from Hell:
All suffering with me; they for women's lusts,
I for a man's, that the Augean stable
Of his foul sin would empty in my lap:

165. loath'd] *A;* just *B.* 172. hand] *A;* fingers *B.* 173. him?] *A, B;* him, *Bo.* 179. Augean] *P;* Egean *A, B.*

---

166. *mean*] moderation.

172. Making horns] B's reading makes this clear.

173–4. *Comes . . . beauty*] Boas, printing 'him,', glosses 'if he is the source of the blot on my honour, it becomes a beauty, not a blemish'. I think that is the general sense, but it does not require the emendation.

174–7.] Schoell points to Comes, *Mythologiae,* IX. iv, *De Bellerophonte*: these stories are told there successively as instances of Innocence; there is no verbal echo.

174. *and . . . proves*] The beauty is proved innocent because it is abused by the evil it has resisted, as in the classical stories cited.

175. *Chimæra*] a monster with a lion's head, goat's body, and dragon's tail; Bellerophon was sent to be killed by it as punishment for an adultery he had not committed; in the event, he killed it.

Peleus] also falsely accused of adultery; he was exposed on Mount Pelion, but survived when his magic knife was restored.

176. *Pelion*] celebrated for savage beasts: see V. i. 86.

177. *Athenian Prince*] Hippolytus, son of Theseus and Hippolyta, devotee of Artemis and purity. He was torn to pieces in revenge for his supposed adultery with his step-mother Phaedra, but was restored to life by Artemis.

179. *Augean*] Cleaning the Augean stables was one of Hercules' labours.

180. *lap*] genitals, as well as more general senses.

How his guilt shunn'd me! Sacred Innocence
That where thou fear'st, art dreadful; and his face
Turn'd in flight from thee, that had thee in chase:
Come, bring me to him: I will tell the serpent
Even to his teeth (whence, in mine honour's soil,
A pitch'd field starts up 'twixt my Lord and me)
That his throat lies, and he shall curse his fingers,
For being so govern'd by his filthy soul.

Mont. I know not, if himself will vaunt t' have been
The princely author of the slavish sin,
Or any other; he would have resolv'd me,
Had you not come; not by his word, but writing,
Would I have sworn to give it him again,
And pawn'd mine honour to him for a paper.

Tam. See how he flies me still: 'tis a foul heart
That fears his own hand: good my Lord make haste
To see the dangerous paper: be not nice
For any trifle, jewell'd with your honour,

182. art] *A;* are *B.*
185.] *A; B reads:*
Even to his venom'd teeth (from whose curst seed
197–9.] *A; B reads:*
To see the dangerous paper: Papers hold
Oft-times the formes, and copies of our soules,
And (though the world despise them) are the prizes
Of all our honors, make your honour then
A hostage for it, and with it conferre

---

181. *shunn'd*] avoided, turned away from (the point is clarified in l. 183).

182–3.] Innocence frightens what it is frightened by, and makes the hunter turn away from what he chases.

185–6.] referring to Cadmus or Jason, who both had to sow dragon's teeth from which a hostile army sprang up.

185. *soil*] (1) earth; (2) ruin.

187. *his fingers*] i.e., making horns.

196. *fears . . . hand*] Tamyra evidently supposes the paper is in Monsieur's writing: Parrott supports his conjecture about l. 123 by suggesting Tamyra takes the letter to be a forgery: this is not implied by IV. ii. 87.

197–9.] Parrott is no doubt right in thinking the philosophical tone of B's version typical of Chapman; but the new lines fit awkwardly.

198–9.] 'trifle' refers to the paper; but its frequent use for trivial orna-

To pawn your honour; and with it confer
My nearest woman here, in all she knows;
Who (if the Sun or Cerberus could have seen
Any stain in me) might as much as they:
And Pero, here I charge thee by my love,
And all proofs of it (which I might call bounties),
By all that thou hast seen seem good in me,
And all the ill which thou shouldst spit from thee,
By pity of the wound my Lord hath given me,
Not as thy Mistress now, but a poor woman
(To death given over): rid me of my pains,
Pour on thy powder: clear thy breast of me:
My Lord is only here: here speak thy worst,
Thy best will do me mischief; if thou spar'st me,
Never shine good thought on thy memory:
Resolve my Lord, and leave me desperate.

Pero. My Lord? My Lord hath play'd a prodigal's part,
To break his stock for nothing; and an insolent,
To cut a Gordian when he could not loose it:
What violence is this, to put true fire
To a false train? To blow up long crown'd peace
With sudden outrage? and believe a man

202. much] *A;* well *B.*   207. my Lord] *A;* this touch *B.*

---

ments (brooches, etc.) suggests 'jewell'd' as governing its value, and hence 'pawn' in common sense.

199. *confer*] apparently combining 'compare' and 'consult'. Chapman used a rather similar combination of 'collect' and 'inform' in *Odysses*, XXII. 619, 'That all the Handmaids she should first confer'.

201. *Cerberus*] Parrott notes that the monstrous guardian of Hades is contrasted with the sun as darkness opposed to light.

210. *powder*] (1) medicinal powder; (2) violent force (*O.E.D.*, s.v., *sb.* 2).

214. *Resolve*] free from doubt.

216. *break his stock*] Brooke and Paradise gloss 'bankrupt himself', presumably understanding 'stock' as property; following 'prodigal', this seems likely, though I know no analogues.

insolent] presumptuous.

217. *Gordian*] the legendary knot which Alexander the Great was said to have cut.

218–19. *true fire ... train*] a good match to a false line of gunpowder (for exploding a mine, etc.); hence true love to a false trap.

Sworn to the shame of women, 'gainst a woman
Born to their honours: I'll attend your Lordship.
Tam. No, I will write (for I shall never more
Speak with the fugitive), where I will defy him,
Were he ten times the brother of my King. *Exeunt.*

[IV. ii]

Music: and TAMYRA *enters with her* Maid, *bearing a letter.*

Tam. Away, deliver it: O may my lines *Exit* PERO.
(Fill'd with the poison of a woman's hate
When he shall open them) shrink up his eyes
With torturous darkness, such as stands in hell

222. I'll attend your Lordship] *A;* but I will to him *B.* 224. Speak] *A;* Meet *B.*
225.] *A; B adds:*

To him my Lord, and ile to cursing him.

IV. ii. 0.1. *Tamyra*] *she A.* 1. *Exit Pero.*] *not in A.*
0.1–11.] *A; B reads:*

Enter D'Ambois and Frier.
D'Amb. I am suspitious my most honour'd Father,
By some of Monsieurs cunning passages,
That his still ranging and contentious nosethrils,
To scent the haunts of mischiefe, have so us'd
The vicious vertue of his busie sence,
That he trails hotly of him, and will rowze him,
Driving him all enrag'd, and foming on us,
And therefore have entreated your deepe skill,

222–225a.] B's changes make Pero offer to go alone, and Tamyra suggest Montsurry should go too; whereas in A Pero assumes that Montsurry is going and offers to go with him as a witness, which Tamyra rejects in favour of writing a letter herself.

IV. ii. 0.1.] The musical interlude within an act (while Tamyra writes her letter) is unusual, and I assume that B's addition was to do away with it, the direction for music being retained by corrector's error. B's 'Pero *and* her maid' is no doubt an error by conflation of prompt-book 'Pero' with A 'her maid'.

3.] Parrott suggested B's addition assumed 'open them' as two syllables: if so, the change probably derives from an actor.

4. *torturous*] full of torture.

Stuck full of inward horrors, never lighted;
With which are all things to be fear'd, affrighted;
Father?

BUSSY *ascends with* COMOLET.

Buss. How is it with my honour'd mistress?
Tam. O servant help, and save me from the gripes
Of shame and infamy.

In the command of good aeriall spirits,
To assume these Magick rites, and call up one
To know if any have reveal'd unto him
Any thing touching my deare Love and me.
Frier. Good sonne you have amaz'd me but to make
The least doubt of it, it concernes so neerely
The faith and reverence of my name and order.
Yet will I justifie upon my soule
All I have done, if any spirit i'th earth or aire
Can give you the resolve, doe not despaire.

Musick: and Tamira enters with Pero and her maid, bearing a Letter.

Tam. Away, deliver it: O may my lines *Exit Pero.*
(Fill'd with the poyson of a womans hate
When he shall open them) shrink up his curst eyes
With torturous darknesse, such as stands in hell,
Stuck full of inward horrors, never lighted;
With which are all things to be fear'd, affrighted.
D'Amb. How is it with my honour'd Mistresse?
Tam. O servant help, and save me from the gripes
Of shame and infamy. Our love is knowne,
Your Monsieur hath a paper where is writ
Some secret tokens that decipher it.
D'Amb. What cold dull Northern brain, what foole but he,
Durst take into his Epimethean breast

7. *Bussy ascends*] *Ascendit Bussy A.*

---

6. *to be fear'd*] Boas and Parrott gloss 'capable of fear', but I suggest 'which one normally fears': i.e., even terrifying creatures are themselves terrified by this darkness. (Cf. construction in IV. i. 182–3.)

9a–b.] B's lines belong with oa–r: it may be that the undercurrents of IV. i were judged too obscure; but these explanations seem to me (as to Ure) clumsily laboured, and the paper described cannot be identified with any in A (see IV. i. 123).

9–10.] B's change here is partly consequential on the others, but Parrott justly notes its quality: the same point is made again in quite different terms, which may indicate Chapman's authorship.

Buss. What insensate stock,
Or rude inanimate vapour without fashion,
Durst take into his Epimethean breast
A box of such plagues as the danger yields,
Incurr'd in this discovery? He had better
Ventur'd his breast in the consuming reach
Of the hot surfeits cast out of the clouds,
Or stood the bullets that (to wreak the sky)
The Cyclops ram in Jove's artillery.

Com. We soon will take the darkness from his face
That did that deed of darkness; we will know
What now the Monsieur and your husband do;
What is contain'd within the secret paper
Offer'd by Monsieur, and your love's events:
To which ends, honour'd daughter, at your motion,
I have put on these exorcising Rites,
And, by my power of learned holiness
Vouchsaf'd me from above, I will command
Our resolution of a raised spirit.

Tam. Good Father raise him in some beauteous form,
That with least terror I may brook his sight.

---

9. *insensate*] without senses: cf. 'inanimate' in l. 10.

stock] tree-trunk, block of wood, as type of lifelessness (as in phrase 'stock and stone').

10. *rude*] in sense 'unfinished', used of craft-work.

fashion] form.

11. *Epimethean*] Epimetheus ('afterthought') lacked the forethought of his brother Prometheus, and so accepted Pandora's box from which issued all the plagues of humanity.

15. *hot surfeits*] evidently lightning: presumably understood to derive from surplus heat or energy.

16. *bullets*] i.e., thunderbolts.

wreak] revenge.

the sky] Uranus, personifying the heavens; he was deposed by his son Cronos, and avenged by Cronos' son Zeus (Jove).

17.] The Cyclops were one-eyed giants who forged Zeus' thunderbolts. Cf. *Hymnus in Noctem*, ll. 21–2, and *Caesar and Pompey*, II. v. 4, which is identical with this line.

22. *events*] outcomes.

26–7. *I . . . spirit*] i.e., I will raise a spirit (devil) and command him to resolve our doubts.

Com. Stand sure together then, whate'er ye see,
And stir not, as ye tender all our lives. *He puts on his robes.*

Occidentalium legionum spiritalium imperator (magnus ille Behemoth) veni, veni, comitatus cum Astaroth locotenente invicto. Adjuro te per stygis inscrutabilia arcana, per ipsos irremeabiles anfractus averni: adesto o Behemoth, tu cui pervia sunt Magnatum scrinia; veni, per Noctis et tenebrarum abdita profundissima; *Thunder.* per labentia sidera; per ipsos motus horarum furtivos, Hecatesque altum silentium: Appare in forma spiritali, lucente splendida et amabili.

[BEHEMOTH] *ascends* [*with* CARTOPHYLAX *and other* Devils, *carrying torches*].

Beh. What would the holy Friar?
Com. I would see
What now the Monsieur and Montsurry do;
And see the secret paper that the Monsieur
Offer'd to Count Montsurry, longing much
To know on what events the secret loves
Of these two honour'd persons shall arrive.
Beh. Why call'dst thou me to this accursed light
To these light purposes? I am Emperor

30. ye] *A;* you *B.* 31. *He puts on his robes.*] *B; not in A.* 32. spiritalium] *A; spiritualium B.* 37. *Thunder.*] *A; not in B.* 40.1–2.] *Ascendit. A; Thunder. Ascendit. B.*

---

30. *sure*] surely, in the sense of 'steadfastly'.

31. *tender*] value.

32–40.] Commander of the western legions of spirits, O mighty Behemoth, come—come—attended by Astaroth, unconquerable lieutenant. I adjure you by the inscrutable mysteries of Styx, by the windings of the infernal regions through which there is no return: help O Behemoth, you to whom the secret papers of Great Ones are available; come, through the deepest secret places of night and darkness; through the gliding stars; through the stealthy motions of the hours, and the deep silence of Hecate: become visible in the form of a spirit, shining, splendid, and lovely.

40.1. *Cartophylax*] 'a post-classical Greek term for "guardian of papers"' (Boas).

47–8. *light . . . light*] playing between 'sunlight' and 'trivial'.

Of that inscrutable darkness, where are hid
All deepest truths, and secrets never seen,
All which I know, and command Legions
Of knowing spirits that can do more than these:
Any of this my guard that circle me
In these blue fires, and out of whose dim fumes
Vast murmurs use to break, and from their sounds
Articulate voices, can do ten parts more
Than open such slight truths, as you require.

Com. From the last night's black depth, I call'd up one
Of the inferior ablest ministers,
And he could not resolve me; send one then
Out of thine own command, to fetch the paper
That Monsieur hath to shew to Count Montsurry.

Beh. I will: Cartophylax, thou that properly
Hast in thy power all papers so inscrib'd,
Glide through all bars to it and fetch that paper.

Cart. I will. *A torch removes.*

Com. Till he returns, great Prince of darkness,
Tell me, if Monsieur and the Count Montsurry
Are yet encounter'd.

Beh. Both them and the Guise
Are now together.

Com. Shew us all their persons,
And represent the place, with all their actions.

Beh. The spirit will straight return: and then I'll shew thee:

[*Enter* CARTOPHYLAX.]

See he is come; why brought'st thou not the paper?

Cart. He hath prevented me, and got a spirit

54–6.] an explanation of the physical nature of raised spirits.
54. *blue fires*] presumably achieved by burning liquid spirits.
55. *use to*] do regularly.
58. *one*] Boas and Parrott state that B reads 'on': in fact, parts of the 'e' are visible in most copies; it was evidently a piece of damaged type.
59. *inferior*] (1) of the lower regions; (2) lower in rank.
66. A torch removes] i.e., exit Cartophylax (see l. 40.1).
73. *prevented*] anticipated.

Rais'd by another, great in our command,
To take the guard of it before I came.
Beh. This is your slackness, not t' invoke our powers
When first your acts set forth to their effects;
Yet shall you see it, and themselves: behold
They come here and the Earl now holds the paper.

Enter MONSIEUR, GUISE, MONTSURRY *with a paper.*

Buss. May we not hear them?
Com. No, be still and see.
Buss. I will go fetch the paper.
Com. Do not stir:
There's too much distance and too many locks
'Twixt you and them (how near soe'er they seem)
For any man to interrupt their secrets.
Tam. O honour'd spirit: fly into the fancy
Of my offended Lord: and do not let him
Believe what there the wicked man hath written.
Beh. Persuasion hath already enter'd him
Beyond reflection; peace till their departure.

79.1. *with a paper*] *B; not in A.* 80. *Com.*] *Fri. Phelps, Bo, P; Mons. A, B; Beh. D.* 88. *Beh.*] *D, Bo, P; Pre. A, B (catchword Per. A).*

---

74. *great in our command*] either 'powerful in exercising command over us' (Boas); or, qualifying 'spirit', 'great in our host' (Parrott). The latter understands 'command' in the same sense as in l. 61; the former seems more likely here.

79.1.] Boas suggested an inner stage, Parrott thought on the balcony, and compared Greene's *Friar Bacon and Friar Bungay*, II. iii and IV. iii, though that seems to be equally uncertain. One or the other does seem probable: perhaps a discovery by drawing back curtains from an inner stage?

80. Com.] Dilke's *Beh.* is possible, A and B *Mons.* seems impossible.

85. *fancy*] in Renaissance psychology, the faculty of apprehending objects of perception.

87.] Tamyra again assumes that Monsieur wrote the paper, and does not suggest forgery; the assumption that the paper is evidence, not just accusation, is natural, and I am not sure Chapman had a very clear notion what this paper exactly was.

88. Beh.] '*Pre.*' in A (and B) may derive from a misreading of '*Be*'.

89. *reflection*] turning back. *O.E.D.* (s.v., 4b) cites this line for a special-

Mons. There is a glass of ink wherein you see
How to make ready black-fac'd Tragedy:
You now discern, I hope, through all her paintings
Her gasping wrinkles, and fame's sepulchres.
Gui. Think you he feigns my Lord? what hold you now?
Do we malign your wife: or honour you?
Mons. What stricken dumb? nay fie, Lord be not daunted:
Your case is common: were it ne'er so rare
Bear it as rarely: now to laugh were manly:
A worthy man should imitate the weather
That sings in tempests: and being clear is silent.
Gui. Go home my Lord, and force your wife to write
Such loving stuff to D'Ambois as she us'd
When she desir'd his presence.
Mons. Do my Lord,
And make her name her conceal'd messenger,
That close and most inennarable Pandar
That passeth all our studies to exquire:
By whom convey the letter to her love:
And so you shall be sure to have him come
Within the thirsty reach of your revenge;
Before which, lodge an ambush in her chamber
Behind the arras, of your stoutest men
All close and soundly arm'd: and let them share
A spirit amongst them, that would serve a thousand.

90. wherein you] *A;* where you may *B.* 102. stuff] *A;* lines *B.*

---

ized sense 'turning back from a state of anger or resentment'; this is hardly necessary, though possible.

90. *glass of ink*] written image.

93. *gasping*] ? gaping: the words derive from the same root, but *O.E.D.* does not give them as alternative forms.

fame's sepulchres] i.e., the wrinkles are graves for her reputation.

98. *rarely*] unusually well.

105. *inennarable*] indescribable (see *Iliads*, II. 422; *Homer's Hymns*, Hercules, 8).

106. *passeth*] surpasses (cf. *Common Prayer*, Blessing, 'The peace of God, which passeth all understanding').

exquire] find out by searching (see *Odysses*, IV. 520).

112. *close*] hidden.

Enter PERO *with a letter.*

Gui. Yet stay a little: see she sends for you.
Mons. Poor, loving Lady, she'll make all good yet,
Think you not so my Lord? *Exit* MONTSURRY *and stabs* PERO.
Gui. Alas poor soul.
Mons. This was ill done i'faith.
Pero. 'Twas nobly done.
And I forgive his Lordship from my soul.
Mons. Then much good do 't thee Pero: hast a letter?
Pero. I hope it be, at least, if not a volume
Of worthy curses for your perjury.
Mons. Now out upon her.
Gui. Let me see my Lord.
Mons. You shall presently: how fares my Pero?

Enter Servant.

Who's there? take in this maid, sh' has caught a clap:
And fetch my surgeon to her; come my Lord,
We'll now peruse our letter. *Exeunt* MONSIEUR, GUISE.
Pero. Furies rise
Out of the black lines, and torment his soul.
[Servant] *lead*[*s*] *her out.*

113.1.] *B; not in A.* 116. *Exit Montsurry and stabs Pero.*] *B; not in A.*
117. ill] *A;* cruelly *B.* i'faith.] *B;* y'faith. *Exit Mont. A.*
120–2.] *A; B reads:*

Per. I hope it rather be a bitter volume 120
Of worthy curses for your perjury. 121
Guise. To you my Lord. 121a
Mons. To me? Now out upon her.
Gui. Let me see my Lord. 122

123.1.] *B; not in A.* 127.1.] *after 126 A, B.*

113.1. letter] the one Tamyra wrote between IV. i and IV. ii.

116. S.D.] There is no significance in the changed position of the exit: Montsurry evidently stabs Pero on his way out.

120–2.] B's changes are evidently to clarify: especially that the letter is *addressed* to Monsieur, although Guise takes it first.

124. *caught a clap*] punning between violence and venereal disease.

127.1. lead[s] her out] Parrott conjectured that these words might be a

Tam. Hath my Lord slain my woman?
Beh. No, she lives.
Com. What shall become of us?
Beh. All I can say
Being call'd thus late, is brief, and darkly this:
If D'Ambois' mistress stain not her white hand
With his forc'd blood, he shall remain untouch'd:
So Father, shall yourself, but by yourself:
To make this Augury plainer, when the voice
Of D'Ambois shall invoke me I will rise,
Shining in greater light: and shew him all
That will betide ye all; meantime be wise,
And let him curb his rage, with policy.
He descends with his [Devils].
Buss. Will he appear to me, when I invoke him?
Com. He will: be sure.
Buss. It must be shortly then:
For his dark words have tied my thoughts on knots
Till he dissolve, and free them.
Tam. In meantime
Dear servant, till your powerful voice revoke him,

131. mistress stain] *P conj.;* mistresse, stay *A;* Mistresse die *B.* 132. With] *A;* In *B.* his] *A, B;* her *D, Bo.*
138.] *A; B reads:*
And curb his valour, with your policies.
138.1.] *Descendit cum suis: A, B.* 143. revoke] *A, B;* invoke *D.*

---

cancelled conclusion to Monsieur's speech; but the imperative S.D. is not so very strange.

130. *darkly*] obscurely.

131–2.] Parrott's conjecture that A's 'stay' was an error for 'stayne' is convincing; thus, B's revisions in both lines look most like editorial emendation, grasping the intended sense, but not the actual word. Dilke's 'her' for 'his' is quite unnecessary, since in v. iii. 171 ff. Tamyra clearly regards her hand as guilty of Bussy's death, and so stained with his blood as well as (more literally) her own.

138.] Parrott and Ure assume that B's feeble changes were to produce a rhyming couplet.

141. *on*] in.

142. *dissolve*] disintegrate, undo.

143. *revoke*] recall.

Be sure to use the policy he advis'd:
Lest fury in your too quick knowledge taken
Of our abuse, and your defence of me
Accuse me more than any enemy:
And Father, you must on my Lord impose
Your holiest charges, and the Church's power
To temper his hot spirit: and disperse
The cruelty and the blood I know his hand
Will shower upon our heads, if you put not
Your finger to the storm, and hold it up,
As my dear servant here must do with Monsieur.

Buss. I'll soothe his plots: and strew my hate with smiles
Till all at once the close mines of my heart
Rise at full date, and rush into his blood:
I'll bind his arm in silk, and rub his flesh
To make the vein swell, that his soul may gush
Into some kennel, where it longs to lie,
And policy shall be flank'd with policy.
Yet shall the feeling centre where we meet
Groan with the weight of my approaching feet:

145–6.] I suspect the awkward construction may derive from an imperfectly achieved portmanteau use in 'quick knowledge' = (1) sudden information, (2) lively awareness. The latter sense of 'too quick' is then understood with 'your defence'. 'our abuse' = abuse (injury) of us.

152–3. *if . . . storm*] The phrase sounds traditional, but I cannot find close analogues in the Bible or elsewhere.

155. *soothe*] humour, flatter.

156. *mines*] same sense as in military breaching of walled towns: an excavated gallery filled with gunpowder fired by a slow match acting like a time fuse.

157. *at full date*] at the end of the appointed term.

160. *kennel*] gutter.

longs] (1) wants; (2) belongs.

161. *flank'd*] *O.E.D.* has only 'attacked on the flank', but the obvious sense is Parrott's 'outflanked'; there may also be a more literal one, 'laid side by side', i.e. 'met'.

162. *feeling centre*] 'centre', as Boas noted, is used of the Earth (as centre of the Ptolemaic universe): cf. l. 171. 'feeling' is used to personify centre (cf. 'the groaning earth'), to suggest the sublunar world of sense, and simultaneously the whole phrase indicates 'the centre of feeling', the passionate core of the tragedy.

I'll make th' inspired threshals of his Court
Sweat with the weather of my horrid steps
Before I enter: yet will I appear
Like calm security, before a ruin;
A politician, must like lightning melt
The very marrow, and not print the skin:
His ways must not be seen: the superficies
Of the green centre must not taste his feet,
When hell is plough'd up with his wounding tracts:
And all his harvest reap'd, from hellish facts. *Exeunt.*

169. print] Print *A;* taint *B.* 173. reap'd, from] *A;* reap't by *B.* *Exeunt.*] *Exeunt. / Finis Actus quarti. B; Finis Actus Quarti. A.*

164–5.] Parrott suggested a reference to *Odyssey*, xx. 351–4, when walls run blood; but there is no close resemblance, and none at all to Chapman's translation (ll. 533–5).

164. *inspired*] breathing, i.e., conscious (cf. 'feeling' in l. 162); another sense, 'blown on', seems to suggest 'weather' in l. 165.

threshals] thresholds (the plural is not usual, and so is presumably used deliberately to heighten terror, indicating at all doors at once).

165. *weather*] used for bad weather (*O.E.D.*, s.v., 1g and h): Brooke and Paradise suggest the clammy air before a storm, which makes the walls sweat.

167.] obviously related to 'calm before a storm': but 'ruin' does not seem to have been used specifically of storms, so that I suppose 'security' and 'ruin' are used to connect the storm with the general figurative sense of the passage, and the house image in particular.

168–9. *melt / The very marrow*] Passions were supposed to melt by their excessive heat the marrow which is the core of all animal life.

169. *print*] A's capital P is strange, and may indicate a misreading of 'taint' (B). But 'print' is the stronger word here: it was used for 'merely marking the surface' (*O.E.D.*, s.v., 2a), and connects with 'steps' above, 'feet' and 'tracts' below.

170–1. *superficies / Of the green centre*] i.e., the green (fields, etc.) of the Earth's surface. 'superficies' contrasts with hell, which is at the centre of the Earth.

172–3. *tracts . . . facts*] same rhyme, with the same meanings for words, as in I. i. 39–40.

Act V

[v. i]

[Enter] MONTSURRY *bare, unbraced, pulling* TAMYRA *in by the hair,* COMOLET, One *bearing light, a standish and paper, which sets a table.*

Com. My Lord remember that your soul must seek
Her peace, as well as your revengeful blood:
You ever, to this hour have prov'd yourself
A noble, zealous, and obedient son
T' our holy mother: be not an apostate:
Your wife's offence serves not (were it the worst
You can imagine, without greater proofs)
To sever your eternal bonds, and hearts;
Much less to touch her with a bloody hand:

Act V] Actus Quinti Scena Prima. *A, B.* 0.1. *by the hair*] *B; not in A.*
1.] *A; B adds:*

Tamy. O Help me Father.
Frier. Impious Earle forbeare. 0a
Take violent hand from her, or by mine order b
The King shall force thee.
Monts. Tis not violent; come you not willingly? c
Tamy. Yes good my Lord. d

7. imagine, . . . proofs)] *A, B;* imagine) . . . proofs, *Bo, P.*

0.1. bare] bare-headed.

unbraced] dress unfastened.

by the hair] likely enough stage practice, though it is closely linked to B's added dialogue.

0.2. standish] portable writing desk.

0a–d.] Parrott and Ure note the theatrical effectiveness of these lines: I would rate higher still the irony of the last line and a half.

2. *blood*] passion: the connection with 'seek' is loose, implying 'satisfaction'.

7. *without greater proofs*] i.e., to say nothing of proof of something greater.

Nor is it manly (much less husbandly)
To expiate any frailty in your wife,
With churlish strokes, or beastly odds of strength:
The stony birth of clouds will touch no laurel,
Nor any sleeper; your wife is your laurel
And sweetest sleeper; do not touch her then:
Be not more rude than the wild seed of vapour,
To her that is more gentle than it rude;
In whom kind Nature suffer'd one offence
But to set off her other excellence.

Mont. Good Father leave us: interrupt no more
The course I must run for mine honour sake.
Rely on my love to her, which her fault
Cannot extinguish; will she but disclose
Who was the hateful minister of her love,
And through what maze he serv'd it, we are friends.

Com. It is a damn'd work to pursue those secrets
That would ope more sin, and prove springs of slaughter;
Nor is 't a path for Christian feet to touch;
But out of all way to the health of souls,
A sin impossible to be forgiven:

17. it] *A;* that *B.* 24. hateful] *A;* secret *B.* 28. touch] *A;* tread *B.*

---

12. *beastly*] brutal; but also literally, contrasting with 'manly' in l. 10.

13. *stony birth of clouds*] thunderbolts: lightning was thought of as very hot solid objects which did the damage when they struck; they cooled as stones. 'birth' here means offspring, as in *Odysses*, VIII. 337, 'To banquet with your Wife and Birth at home'.

laurel] said to be impervious to 'lightninges flasshe, and thunderboltes' in G. Whitney, *A Choice of Emblemes*, p. 67; and see Pliny, *Hist. Nat.*, XV. xl. 134–5.

14. *sleeper*] Lightning was supposed not to touch men while asleep. Parrott cites Pierre Matthieu, *Histoire de France* (1605), II. 145v, marginal comment on a speech of Biron: 'Les hommes en dormant ne sont jamais frappez du foudre'. The coincidence is curious, but the superstition was widespread, so this cannot be taken as evidence for dating *Bussy*.

16. *the wild seed of vapour*] i.e., thunderbolts, issuing from clouds.

25. *maze*] winding path; fig. for deception (commonly so in Middle English).

Which he that dares commit—
Mont. Good Father cease:
Tempt not a man distracted; I am apt
To outrages that I shall ever rue:
I will not pass the verge that bounds a Christian,
Nor break the limits of a man nor husband.
Com. Then God inspire ye both with thoughts and deeds
Worthy his high respect, and your own souls. *Exit.*
Mont. Who shall remove the mountain from my heart,
Ope the seventimes-heat furnace of my thoughts,
And set fit outcries for a soul in hell?

MONTSURRY *turns a key.*

O now it nothing fits my cares to speak,
But thunder, or to take into my throat
The trump of Heaven; with whose determinate blasts
The winds shall burst, and the enraged seas
Be drunk up in his sounds; that my hot woes
(Vented enough) I might convert to vapour,
Ascending from my infamy unseen;

31. cease:] *A;* cease: your terrors *B;* cease your terrors. *D, Bo, P.* 36. God] *A, P;* heaven *B.* ye] *A;* you *B.*
37. *Exit.*–39.] *A; B reads:*
Tamy. Father. *Frier.* I warrant thee my dearest daughter 37a
He will not touch thee, think'st thou him a Pagan; b
His honor and his soule lies for thy safety. *Exit.* c
Mont. Who shall remove the mountaine from my brest, 38
Stand the opening furnace of my thoughts, 39
39.] *A; as B P; as B, but* Or stand . . . *D; as B, but* Stand in the . . . *Bo.* 41. O] *A;* For *B.* cares] *A;* woes *B.* 44. enraged] *A;* devouring *B.*

31.] B's extra-metrical addition is odd: Parrott thought it belonged before the colon; I wonder if it is a fragment from a fuller revision which the corrector failed to complete?

36. *God*] B's 'heaven' is presumably due to the 'Blasphemy' Act.

37a–c.] I agree with Ure in thinking this addition bad: Parrott suggested that it strengthened the Friar's reasons for going; if so, the strength is so absurd it looks more like weakness.

43. *determinate*] establishing the end, i.e. of the world (the last trump).

45. *his*] its.

46. *Vented*] given free course; (of vapours, etc.) forced out.

Shorten the world, preventing the last breath
That kills the living, and regenerates death.
Tam. My Lord, my fault (as you may censure it
With too strong arguments) is past your pardon:
But how the circumstances may excuse me
God knows, and your more temperate mind hereafter
May let my penitent miseries make you know.
Mont. Hereafter? 'Tis a suppos'd infinite,
That from this point will rise eternally:
Fame grows in going; in the 'scapes of Virtue
Excuses damn her: they be fires in cities
Enrag'd with those winds that less lights extinguish.
Come Siren, sing, and dash against my rocks
Thy ruffi'n Galley, laden for thy lust:
Sing, and put all the nets into thy voice,
With which thou drew'st into thy strumpet's lap

53. God] *A, P;* Heaven *B.* 61. laden for thy] *A;* rig'd with quench for *B.*

---

48. *preventing*] (1) anticipating; (2) precluding.
breath] both the breathing of a living man, and the breath that blows the last trump.
49.] i.e., the living shall die, the dead come back to life.
55–6.] Montsurry plays on 'hereafter'=life after death.
57. *Fame . . . going*] The common proverb is in *Aeneid*, IV. 173–5: it implies growth in motion, like a snowball.
57–8. *in . . . her*] The stress is on *Virtue*: for her to have 'scapes is monstrous, and what would excuse lesser beings, damns her. Hence the image that follows.
61.] B's 'rig'd with quench for lust' may suggest a connection with *Revenge of Bussy*, I. i. 27–9: 'This blood that cockatrice-like thus thou brood'st / Too dry is to breed any quench to thine. / And therefore now (if only for thy lust . . .)'. Parrott supposed this to be an echo of the revised *Bussy* (as three lines later comes a clearer repetition of III. ii. 399) and so dated the revision before the *Revenge*. But: (1) the relationship could be either way round; (2) the verbal similarity is not very close, except for the rare sb. 'quench'. B's line is certainly striking; I am not sure it is an improvement.
ruffi'n Galley] i.e., Bussy.
62. *nets*] fig. snares (and see l. 64). The association of 'nets' with 'spawn of Venus' suggests the adultery of Mars and Venus, who were caught in a net (cf. *Teares of Peace*, l. 6).
63. *lap*] genitals (see IV. i. 180).

The spawn of Venus; and in which ye danc'd;
That, in thy lap's stead, I may dig his tomb,
And quit his manhood with a woman's sleight,
Who never is deceiv'd in her deceit.
Sing (that is, write), and then take from mine eyes
The mists that hide the most inscrutable Pandar
That ever lapp'd up an adulterous vomit:
That I may see the devil, and survive
To be a devil, and then learn to wive:
That I may hang him, and then cut him down,
Then cut him up, and with my soul's beams search
The cranks and caverns of his brain, and study
The errant wilderness of a woman's face;
Where men cannot get out, for all the Comets

---

64. *The spawn of Venus*] (1) Venus' child, i.e. Bussy; (2) *spawn* evidently suggests seminal fluid. (Aeneas was Venus' son: Ferguson thought this was suggested by reminiscence of Virgil in l. 57.)

in which ye danc'd] taking 'net' in another sense, from the proverb 'You dance in a net and think nobody sees you' (Tilley, N130).

65–6.] Montsurry's sex-driven rhetoric breeds double meanings, which strain the syntax. Bussy is seen as (ac)quitting his manhood (proving his masculinity) in Tamyra's lap, but now (in . . . stead) quitting his manhood (leaving his life) in a tomb; and the phrase has a third sense: Montsurry will (re)quit(e) Bussy's manhood (adultery) by deceiving and killing him.

66–7. *a woman's . . . deceit*] I suppose 'a woman's sleight' is the trick by which she invites her lover whilst seeming not to—a deceit which must *not* deceive the lover. This is the essence of Comolet's couplets in II. ii. 225–30.

70.] that ever took a voyeur's pleasure in the copulation he had engineered. Montsurry's jealousy drives his righteous indignation to a vileness of imagination the opposite of righteous; a condition familiar to modern psychology, as to Shakespeare in *Othello* and *The Winter's Tale*.

71–2.] i.e., 'that I may see the devil and nevertheless survive to become a devil myself, and so learn how to manage a wife'.

75. *cranks*] winding paths; crevices.

76.] This image governs the rest of the speech: the wilderness in which men may wander despite the adders and basilisks, despite its savage amorality, despite the density which prevents either escape or penetration to the heart.

errant] (1) arrant; (2) erring, wandering (morally and physically).

77–8.] Comets may be the errant phenomena rising from this source, preventing men escaping ('for' = because of); or they may be the warnings of poets, etc., against women, in spite of which men cannot escape ('for' = in spite of).

That have been lighted at it; though they know
That Adders lie a-sunning in their smiles,
That Basilisks drink their poison from their eyes,
And no way there to coast out to their hearts;
Yet still they wander there, and are not stay'd
Till they be fetter'd, nor secure before
All cares distract them; nor in human state
Till they embrace within their wives' two breasts
All Pelion and Cythæron with their beasts.
Why write you not?

Tam. O good my Lord forbear
In wreak of great sins, to engender greater,
And make my love's corruption generate murder.

Mont. It follows needfully as child and parent;
The chain-shot of thy lust is yet aloft,
And it must murder; 'tis thine own dear twin:
No man can add height to a woman's sin.
Vice never doth her just hate so provoke,
As when she rageth under Virtue's cloak.
Write: for it must be; by this ruthless steel,

84.] *A; B reads:*
All cares devoure them, nor in humane Consort
88. sins] *A;* faults *B.*

---

79. *their*] i.e., women's.

80. *Basilisks*] fabulous reptiles (cf. cockatrices) whose look (and breath) was said to be poisonous.

81. *coast out*] a paradoxical phrase: 'coast' implies keeping close to, hence it cannot normally be combined with 'out'. Here it contrasts the opaque wilderness of the face with the close connection that *ought* to be between it and the heart.

84. *in human state*] The stress is on 'human' as opposed to 'animal': Montsurry's savage irony comments on one of the play's central themes, the necessity of 'animal' passion to 'human' nature.

86. *Pelion and Cythæron*] two mountains in Greece, notorious for wild animals, symbolizing lust. For Pelion, see IV. i. 176; for Cythæron, see *Hymnus in Cynthiam*, gloss 7.

91. *chain-shot*] two balls joined by chain, used to destroy masts, rigging, etc.

94. *her . . . hate*] i.e., hatred of her.

96–7. *steel . . . torture*] Presumably the knife and rack are already in evidence.

By this impartial torture, and the death
Thy tyrannies have invented in my entrails,
To quicken life in dying, and hold up
The spirits in fainting, teaching to preserve
Torments in ashes, that will ever last.
Speak: will you write?

Tam. Sweet Lord enjoin my sin
Some other penance than what makes it worse:
Hide in some gloomy dungeon my loath'd face,
And let condemned murderers let me down
(Stopping their noses) my abhorred food.
Hang me in chains, and let me eat these arms
That have offended: bind me face to face
To some dead woman, taken from the cart
Of execution, till death and time
In grains of dust dissolve me; I'll endure:
Or any torture that your wrath's invention
Can fright all pity from the world withal:
But to betray a friend with shew of friendship,
That is too common for the rare revenge
Your rage affecteth; here then are my breasts,
Last night your pillows; here my wretched arms,
As late the wished confines of your life:
Now break them as you please, and all the bounds
Of manhood, noblesse, and religion.

Mont. Where all these have been broken, they are kept
In doing their justice there: thine arms have lost
Their privilege in lust, and in their torture

122.] *A; B reads:*
In doing their justice there with any shew 122
Of the like cruell cruelty: Thine armes have lost 122a

122a. cruell] *not in P.*

---

98. *tyrannies*] outrages.

100. *to*] how to.

112–13. *that . . . withal*] i.e., with which.

121–2. *Where . . . there*] i.e., manhood, etc., are preserved by executing justice there where they have been broken. B's addition emphasizes but hardly clarifies the crude revenge impulse.

Thus they must pay it. *Stabs her.*
Tam. O Lord.
Mont. Till thou writ'st
I'll write in wounds (my wrongs' fit characters)
Thy right of sufferance. Write.
Tam. O kill me, kill me:
Dear husband be not crueller than death;
You have beheld some Gorgon: feel, O feel
How you are turn'd to stone; with my heart blood
Dissolve yourself again, or you will grow
Into the image of all Tyranny.
Mont. As thou art of Adultery, I will still
Prove thee my like in ill, being most a monster:
Thus I express thee yet. *Stabs her again.*
Tam. And yet I live.
Mont. Ay, for thy monstrous idol is not done yet:
This tool hath wrought enough: now Torture use

Enter Servants [*and place* TAMYRA *on the rack*].

This other engine on th' habituate powers
Of her thrice damn'd and whorish fortitude.

124. *Stabs her.*] *B; not in A.* 125. wrongs'] *D;* wrongs *A, B;* wrong's *P.* 132. still] *A;* ever *B.* 133. like in ill] *A;* parallel *B.* 134. *Stabs her again.*] *B; not in A.* 136.1.] *B; not in A.* *and place Tamyra on the rack*] *P, D subs.*

---

125. *characters*] letters, emblems.

128. *Gorgon*] Medusa, whose hideous head turned to stone any man that saw it; she was killed by Perseus (using mirrors), but her head retained its power, and in Homer is used as a device on shields to frighten the enemy.

131. *image*] i.e., stone emblem; see 'idol' (l. 135).

134. *express*] (1) press out (her blood); (2) portray, represent emblematically.

135. *thy . . . done*] Montsurry is making a physical emblem of adultery out of Tamyra, not yet finished.

136.1. rack] The machine of torture is not named: l. 149 indicates something on which Tamyra is bound, and l. 148 'wrack' may be a kind of pun.

137. *engine*] tool or machine.

habituate] established by habit.

Use the most madding pains in her that ever
Thy venoms soak'd through, making most of death;
That she may weigh her wrongs with them, and then
Stand Vengeance on thy steepest rock, a victor.

Tam. O who is turn'd into my Lord and husband?
Husband? My Lord? None but my Lord and husband.
Heaven, I ask thee remission of my sins,
Not of my pains: husband, O help me husband.

COMOLET *ascends.*

Com. What rape of honour and religion?
O wrack of nature. *Falls and dies.*

Tam. Poor man: O my Father,
Father? look up; O let me down my Lord,
And I will write.

Mont. Author of prodigies!
What new flame breaks out of the firmament,
That turns up counsels never known before?
Now is it true, earth moves, and heaven stands still;
Even Heaven itself must see and suffer ill:

146.1.] *Ascendit Comolet. A; Ascendit Frier with a sword drawne. B.* 148. *Falls and dies.*] *B; not in A.* 149. Father?] *A;* Farher, *B.*

139–40.] The subject is still torture; the image of saturating poison is confusing when machinery is actually being used. I take 'making most of death' to mean 'making her life as near death as possible without killing her' rather than 'draw out her death as long as possible', since Montsurry clearly intends her to live. Ferguson suggests that the 'venoms' derive from the shirt of Nessus which Dejanira put on Hercules: see Appendix B, p. 150.

142. *Stand . . . rock*] Vengeance as a vulture seems an obvious emblem, though I can find no analogues.

145. *remission of*] (1) forgiveness for (sins); (2) release from (pains).

146.1.] B's 'with a sword drawne' probably reflects stage practice, but seems to imply death by suicide, or fighting, whereas in fact Comolet dies of shock alone: see l. 170, and v. ii. 58–9.

150. *prodigies*] marvels, usually ominous; hence comets, etc.

152. *counsels*] plans; hence secrets.

153.] a traditional image of the reversal of all order, sharpened by reference to Copernicus. But the image in the next ten lines is simply of Earth turning over, not continually revolving.

The too huge bias of the World hath sway'd
Her back-part upwards, and with that she braves
This Hemisphere, that long her mouth hath mock'd:
The gravity of her religious face
(Now grown too weighty with her sacrilege
And here discern'd sophisticate enough)
Turns to th' Antipodes: and all the forms
That her illusions have impress'd in her,
Have eaten through her back: and now all see,
How she is riveted with hypocrisy:
Was this the way? was he the mean betwixt you?

Tam. He was, he was, kind innocent man he was.

Mont. Write, write a word or two.

Tam. I will, I will.
I'll write, but in my blood that he may see,
These lines come from my wounds and not from me. *Writes.*

Mont. Well might he die for thought: methinks the frame
And shaken joints of the whole world should crack
To see her parts so disproportionate;
And that his general beauty cannot stand
Without these stains in the particular man.
Why wander I so far? here here was she
That was a whole world without spot to me:

166. innocent] *A;* worthy *B.* 168. in] *A;* with *B.* 169. *Writes.*] *B; not in A.*

---

155. *bias*] weighting of a sphere, as in bowls, upsetting its motion.
156. *braves*] challenges, insults (i.e., with her anal 'mouth').
157. *Hemisphere*] astronomical: see 'Antipodes' in l. 161.
158. *gravity*] (1) solemnity; (2) physical weight.
religious face] because it looked towards heaven.
160. *sophisticate*] mixed with foreign matter, adulterated.
162. *illusions*] mockeries; deceptions (*O.E.D.*, s.v., 1 and 2).
164. *riveted*] joined firmly to; or, perhaps, hypocrisy is the rivet, driven right through her?
165. *mean*] go-between.
170. *thought*] reflection; perhaps conscience (i.e., shock).
172. *disproportionate*] See IV. i. 96 and V. iii. 9.
173. *his*] i.e., mankind's.
176. *a whole world*] a common image in Donne (e.g., *The Good-Morrow*,

Though now a world of spots; O what a lightning
Is man's delight in women! what a bubble,
He builds his state, fame, life on, when he marries!
Since all earth's pleasures are so short and small,
The way t' enjoy it, is t' abjure it all:
Enough: I must be messenger myself,
Disguis'd like this strange creature: in, I'll after,
To see what guilty light gives this cave eyes,
And to the world sing new impieties.

Exeunt: He puts the Friar [COMOLET] *in the vault and follows, she wraps herself in the Arras.* [*Curtains closed.*]

185.1–2.] *B; not in A.*

v. ii.] *B inserts:*

[v. iia.] *Enter Monsieur and Guise.*

[*as V. iii. 1–56*]

Enter Montsurry disguis'd with the murtherers.

[*Mons.*] Away my Lord, you are perfectly disguis'd,
Leave us to lodge your ambush.
Monts. Speed me vengeance. *Exit.*
Mons. Resolve my Masters, you shall meet with one
Will try what proofes your privy coats are made on:
When he is entred, and you heare us stamp,
Approach, and make all sure.
Murth. We vvill my Lord. *Exeunt.*

---

st. 2), combining the geometric symbol of a sphere as perfection, with the idea of satisfied love as enclosing all human experience.

180–1.] The Stoic asceticism is here clearly placed as a complement of jealous nausea. Cf. *The Revenge of Bussy* and *Caesar and Pompey*, where it is the endorsed attitude of Clermont and Cato respectively.

185.1–2.] Evidently Tamyra covers her naked breasts with some drapery at the back of the stage; this direction (B only) obviously goes with v. iii. 56.1–2 where Tamyra is 'discovered' wrapped (A only) in a 'Canopy'. It is clear that Arras and Canopy are identical, and additional to the curtains which close the recess (see I. ii. 0.1–2). W. A. Armstrong ('"Canopy" in Elizabethan Theatrical Terminology', *N. & Q.*, 1957, pp. 433–4) assumes that both directions refer to a curtained recess: this seems to take too little notice of 'wraps'. For arras as wall hangings, see III. ii. 193 and IV. ii. 111.

v. iia.] For discussion of B's reorganization and additions, see Introduction, pp. lxix–lxx, and commentary on v. iii. 0–56.

[v. ii]

[*Enter* BUSSY] D'AMBOIS *with two* Pages *with tapers.*

Buss. Sit up to-night, and watch, I'll speak with none
But the old Friar, who bring to me.
Page. We will sir. *Exeunt* [Pages].
Buss. What violent heat is this? methinks the fire
Of twenty lives doth on a sudden flash
Through all my faculties: the air goes high
In this close chamber, and the frighted earth *Thunder.*
Trembles, and shrinks beneath me: the whole house
Cracks with his shaken burden; bless me, heaven.

Enter COMOLET'S Ghost.

Ghost. Note what I want, my son, and be forewarn'd:
O there are bloody deeds past and to come,
I cannot stay: a fate doth ravish me:
I'll meet thee in the chamber of thy love. *Exit.*
Buss. What dismal change is here? the good old Friar
Is murder'd; being made known to serve my love;
Note what he wants? he wants his utmost weed,
He wants his life, and body: which of these
Should be the want he means, and may supply me

0.1. *with tapers*] *B; not in A.* 2. *Exeunt*] *B; Exit A.* 6. *Thunder.*] *B; not in A.* 8. Cracks] *A;* Nods *B.* 8.1.] *Enter Vmb. Comol. A; Enter Umb. Frier. B.* 9. my] *A;* deare *B.*
14.] *A; B adds:*
And now his restlesse spirit would fore-warne me
Of some plot dangerous, and imminent.
15. utmost] *A;* upper *B.*

---

v. ii. 5. *air goes high*] Presumably the ceiling seems to rise, as the floor to sink in l. 7.
9. *want*] lack.
11. *ravish*] carry away; remove from earth (*O.E.D.*, s.v., 3).
14a–b.] Ure described B's addition as ill-advised or unlike Chapman. It is of a piece with B's general stress on plotting in Act v.
15. *utmost*] exterior (of garments—*O.E.D.*, s.v., 1b). B's 'upper' may have been modernization.
weed] garment.

With any fit forewarning? this strange vision
(Together with the dark prediction
Us'd by the Prince of darkness that was rais'd
By this embodied shadow) stir my thoughts
With reminiscion of the Spirit's promise;
Who told me, that by any invocation
I should have power to raise him; though it wanted
The powerful words, and decent rites of art;
Never had my set brain such need of spirit
T' instruct and cheer it; now then, I will claim
Performance of his free and gentle vow,
T' appear in greater light; and make more plain
His rugged oracle: I long to know
How my dear mistress fares; and be inform'd
What hand she now holds on the troubled blood
Of her incensed Lord: methought the Spirit
(When he had utter'd his perplex'd presage),
Threw his chang'd countenance headlong into clouds;
His forehead bent, as it would hide his face;
He knock'd his chin against his darken'd breast,
And struck a churlish silence through his pow'rs—
Terror of darkness: O thou King of flames,
That with thy music-footed horse dost strike

19–25.] See IV. ii. 129–37.

21. *this embodied shadow*] Comolet when still alive.

22. *reminiscion*] remembering.

23. *any*] as distinct from the correct one.

25. *decent*] suitable (*O.E.D.*, s.v., 1).

26. *set*] fixed, resolute.

spirit] courage generally, with a specific reference to Behemoth.

30. *rugged*] austere, harsh.

32. *hand*] presumably as in horsemanship: the hand controls the reins, and so the horse (*O.E.D.*, s.v., 6).

34. *perplex'd*] involved; hence obscure.

39–51.] Bussy's invocation to alternative spirits seems strange, and Dilke's emendation in l. 45 is tempting, although 'Oh' is not a usual form in A. Boas assumes ll. 39–44 to be addressed to the sun-god, the rest to Behemoth. Line 39 is ambiguous: 'Terror of darkness'—either terror *to*, or terror *from*; 'King of flames' suggests Hell as well as the sun.

40. *music-footed horse*] The sun-god Apollo was also the god of music;

The clear light out of crystal, on dark earth;
And hurl'st instructive fire about the world:
Wake, wake the drowsy and enchanted night,
That sleeps with dead eyes in this heavy riddle:
Or thou great Prince of shades where never sun
Sticks his far-darted beams (whose eyes are made
To see in darkness: and see ever best
Where sense is blindest) open now the heart
Of thy abashed oracle, that for fear
Of some ill it includes would fain lie hid,
And rise thou with it in thy greater light.

Thunders. The Spirit [BEHEMOTH] *springs up with his* [Devils].

Beh. Thus to observe my vow of apparition
In greater light, and explicate thy fate,
I come; and tell thee that if thou obey
The summons that thy mistress next will send thee,
Her hand shall be thy death.

Buss. When will she send?

Beh. Soon as I set again, where late I rose.

45. Or] *A, B;* Oh *D.* 47. see in] *A;* shine in *B.* 48. sense is] *A;* men are *B.* 51.1. *Thunders.*] *B; not in A.* *The Spirit springs up with his* Devils] *Surgit Spiritus cum suis A, B.*

Jacquot thinks the horse is Pegasus, who produced the Muses' fountain by a stamp of his hoof. *Byron's Conspiracy*, I. ii. 45–9, seems to combine both ideas:

They follow all my steps with music
As if my feet were numerous, and trod sounds
Out of the centre with Apollo's virtue,
That out of every thing his each part touch'd
Struck musical accents.

44. *riddle*] mystery: the 'enchanted' night obscures what Bussy would understand. The image has more rhetorical power than clarity.

47. *see in*] B is presumably avoiding the repetition of 'see', but not effectively.

48. *sense*] Behemoth's vision is, of course, supersensory.

49. *abashed*] *O.E.D.* does not have exactly this sense: what follows indicates 'checked by fear of ill'.

52. *apparition*] appearing.

53. *explicate*] unfold in words.

Buss. Is the old Friar slain?
Beh. No, and yet lives not.
Buss. Died he a natural death?
Beh. He did.
Buss. Who then,
Will my dear mistress send?
Beh. I must not tell thee.
Buss. Who lets thee?
Beh. Fate.
Buss. Who are Fate's ministers?
Beh. The Guise and Monsieur.
Buss. A fit pair of shears
To cut the threads of Kings, and kingly spirits,
And consorts fit to sound forth harmony,
Set to the falls of Kingdoms: shall the hand
Of my kind mistress kill me?
Beh. If thou yield *Thunders.*
To her next summons; y' are fair warn'd: farewell.
Exit [*with* Devils.]
Buss. I must fare well, how ever: though I die,
My death consenting with his augury;
Should not my powers obey when she commands,
My motion must be rebel to my will:
My will, to life: if when I have obey'd,
Her hand should so reward me, they must arm it,
Bind me and force it: or I lay my soul
She rather would convert it many times

66. *Thunders.*] *B; not in A.* 68. well, how ever:] *A, B;* well, how ever, *Bo;* well, however, *P.* 70. obey when she commands,] *B;* obay, when she commands *A.* 72. My will, to life: if] My will: to life, If *A;* My will to life, if *B.* 73. me,] me: *A, B.* 74. and] *A;* or *B.* soul] *A;* life *B.*

---

61. *lets*] prevents.

61–3.] See note on the Fates, III. ii. 404–5.

63. *of . . . kingly spirits*] e.g., his own: see III. ii. 95–7, etc.

64. *consorts*] (1) partners; (2) musicians (or instruments) playing together.

69. *consenting with*] being in accordance with.

On her own bosom, even to many deaths:
But were there danger of such violence,
I know 'tis far from her intent to send:
And who she should send, is as far from thought
Since he is dead, whose only mean she us'd. *Knocks.*
Who's there? look to the door: and let him in,
Though politic Monsieur, or the violent Guise.

Enter MONTSURRY *like the Friar, with a letter written in blood.*

Mont. Hail to my worthy son.
Buss. O lying Spirit: welcome loved Father,
How fares my dearest mistress?
Mont. Well, as ever,
Being well as ever thought on by her Lord:
Whereof she sends this witness in her hand
And prays, for urgent cause, your speediest presence.

80. *Knocks.*] *B; not in A.* 82.1. *with . . . blood*] *B; not in A.*
83–8.] *A; B reads:*
Mont. Haile to my worthy sonne.
D'Amb. O lying Spirit! 83–4
To say the Frier was dead; Ile now beleeve 84a
Nothing of all his forg'd predictions. b
My kinde and honour'd Father, well reviv'd, c
I have beene frighted with your death, and mine, d
And told my Mistresse hand should be my death e
If I obeyed this summons. f
Monts. I beleev'd / your love had bin much clearer, then to give 85a
Any such doubt a thought, for she is cleare, b
And having freed her husbands jealousie, 86
(Of which her much abus'd hand here is witnesse) 87
She prayes for urgent cause your instant presence. 88
D'Amb. Why then your prince of spirits may be call'd 88a
The prince of lyers.
Monts. Holy writ so calls him. b

---

82. *politic Monsieur . . . violent Guise*] This states clearly their difference of character, which corresponds to the difference of philosophic attitude defined in v. iii. 1–56.

84. *O lying Spirit*] Behemoth, because Bussy thinks he sees Comolet alive. B's addition, as Parrott noted, is to clarify Bussy's consequent neglect of Behemoth's warning: it seems to me both clumsy and unnecessary, making a good dramatic point seem, because laboured, a possible weakness in the plot.

Buss. What? writ in blood?
Mont. Ay, 'tis the ink of lovers.
Buss. O 'tis a sacred witness of her love.
So much elixir of her blood as this
Dropp'd in the lightest dame, would make her firm
As heat to fire: and like to all the signs,
Commands the life confin'd in all my veins;
O how it multiplies my blood with spirit,
And makes me apt t' encounter death and hell:
But, come kind Father; you fetch me to heaven,
And to that end your holy weed was given. *Exeunt.*

[v. iii]

Enter MONSIEUR, GUISE, *above.*

Mons. Now shall we see, that Nature hath no end

98. *Exeunt*] *B; Exit A.*

v. iii. 0.1–56.] *A; after V. i, B.* 0.1. *above*] *A; not in B.*

---

91. *elixir*] alchemical preparation for turning base metal to gold, so here for making a prostitute faithful.

93. *signs*] portents, astrological indications; perhaps specifically, 'signs of the Zodiac'.

95. *multiplies . . . spirit*] (1) physiological: the elixir distilled in his blood adds spirit; (2) psychological: adds spirit to his passion.

98.] i.e., that is your function as a friar.

v. iii. 0–56.] B transfers this dialogue to before v. ii, and by omitting '*above*' in S.D. presumably implies that it was there brought on to the main stage (see Introduction, p. lxix). The number of variants is unusually high, but apparently composed of the usual mixture of deliberate and accidental changes. Ll. 18–25 become, through several errors, unintelligible; before l. 26 the prefix is, unusually, expanded: these facts suggest that (because of the earlier placing) MS. copy was here used for printing B (Introduction, p. lxii). The large cut in ll. 7–12 is (because of a consequential new half-line) clearly deliberate: Parrott suggested a wish to reduce anti-Roman venom, but the point of the lines is retained; Ure found the result a successful verbal clarification, and that may have been its sole intention. The revision of l. 46 results in an impressive half-line which may well be deliberate too (if it is not the result of careless revision); if so, it would probably be Chapman's, though it is slightly strange that the new phrase 'whole man' is picked up from l. 34, where B substitutes 'full man'. I there-

In her great works, responsive to their worths,
That she who makes so many eyes, and souls,
To see and foresee, is stark blind herself:
And as illiterate men say Latin prayers
By rote of heart, and daily iteration;
In whose hot zeal, a man would think they knew
What they ran so away with, and were sure
To have rewards proportion'd to their labours;
Yet may implore their own confusions
For anything they know, which oftentimes
It falls out they incur: so Nature lays
A mass of stuff together, and by use,
Or by the mere necessity of matter,
Ends such a work, fills it, or leaves it empty
Of strength, or virtue, error or clear truth;
Not knowing what she does; but usually

3. who] *A;* that *B.*
7–12.] *A, T; B reads:*
Not knowing what they say; so Nature layes
13. mass] *A;* deale *B.*

---

fore wonder whether even here the change may be due to a copyist-reviser allowing his memory very free play?

2. *responsive*] correspondent (cf. 'answering' now).

4. *stark blind*] identifying Nature with Fortune, always 'blind' because without any end 'in view'.

6. *By rote of heart*] by heart; as a mere routine (*O.E.D.*, s.v. *rote*, has 'by rote' = 'by heart', but not this full form).

iteration] repetition (*O.E.D.*, s.v., 1: commonly associated with sacraments; hence its use here with 'prayers').

9. *proportion'd*] See IV. i. 96 and V. i. 172; 'proportion' is a basic word for Chapman's sense of order.

13. *stuff*] matter, as opposed to spirit (cf. German 'Stoff'; *O.E.D.*, s.v., 6, has this sense only in nonce-uses).

use] habit, as opposed to deliberate action. Nature can inform matter, but her action is not purposive.

14.] The obstinacy of matter imposes limitations on the forming power of Nature (see Spenser, *An Hymne in honour of Beautie*, ll. 141–7).

17–20.] This implies something perverse rather than merely casual: a man is ruined by his very merits (as, ll. 21–5, the powder carried to guard a ship blows it up). The notion does not arise logically out of the doctrine of blind Fortune; but asserts an idea of the tragic hero as possessed of virtù

Gives that which we call merit to a man
(And believe should arrive him on huge riches,
Honour, and happiness), that effects his ruin;
Right as in ships of war, whole lasts of powder
Are laid (men think) to make them last, and guard them:
When a disorder'd spark that powder taking,
Blows up with sudden violence and horror
Ships that kept empty, had sail'd long with terror.
Gui. He that observes, but like a worldly man,
That which doth oft succeed, and by th' events
Values the worth of things; will think it true,
That Nature works at random, just with you:
But with as much decorum she may make
A thing that from the feet up to the throat
Hath all the wondrous fabric man should have,

18. we call] *A, Bo, P;* she calls *B, Baskervill etc.* 19. believe should] *A, P;* beliefe must *B, Baskervill etc.;* believes must *T.* 21. Right] *A, P;* Even *B, Baskervill etc.* 22. men think] *A, P;* me thinks *B, Baskervill etc.* guard them:] gard them; *A, Bo, P;* guard, *B, Baskervill etc.;* guards *Pearson.* 26. *Gui.*] *A; Guise. B.* 30. decorum] *A;* proportion *B.*

---

alien to the mediocrity of the natural order, so that what elevates must itself ultimately destroy him—thus rendering his apparent elevation worthless. The relevance of this to Bussy is obvious, and he himself echoes the idea in his dying speech (ll. 188–93), judging his own achievements by their futile end. This initial statement coming from Monsieur limits the acceptance given to the idea, and Comolet will ultimately reject it altogether (ll. 268–74).

18–22.] See Introduction, p. lxii.

19. *arrive him*] (of ships) bring to port, or land (*O.E.D.*, s.v., 1, citing Chapman's *Homer's Hymn to Apollo*, ll. 684–5). *O.E.D.* (s.v., 4) cites this line for a much rarer general sense, but the subsequent ship image shows Chapman's awareness of the specific association.

21. *lasts*] measures of weight in ships' cargoes; of gunpowder, 1 last = 24 barrels (2,400 lb.).

23.] The clumsy syntax may derive from the fact that 'taking' = 'catching fire' is normally intransitive. 'that' is presumably demonstrative.

25. *terror*] quality of causing terror (*O.E.D.*, s.v., 2).

26. Gui.] See note on ll. 0–56.

29. *just with*] exactly as (*O.E.D.*, s.v. *just*, 1, only in phrase 'just as').

30. *decorum*] B supplies Chapman's favourite 'proportion', but it may come from memory.

And leave it headless for an absolute man,
As give a whole man valour, virtue, learning,
Without an end more excellent than those
On whom she no such worthy part bestows.

Mons. Why you shall see it here, here will be one
Young, learned, valiant, virtuous, and full mann'd;
One on whom Nature spent so rich a hand,
That, with an ominous eye, she wept to see
So much consum'd her virtuous treasury;
Yet, as the winds sing through a hollow tree,
And (since it lets them pass through) let it stand;
But a tree solid, since it gives no way
To their wild rages, they rend up by th' root:
So this full creature now shall reel and fall,
Before the frantic puffs of purblind Chance
That pipes through empty men, and makes them dance:
Not so the sea raves on the Lybian sands,
Tumbling her billows in each other's neck—
Not so the surges of the Euxine sea

33. an absolute] *A;* a perfect *B.* 34. whole] *A;* full *B.* 35. those] *B;* those, *A.* 37. Why you shall] *A;* Yet shall you *B.* 43. let] *A;* let's *B.* 45. rages] *A;* rage *B.* th' root] *A;* the root *B.*
46.] *A; B reads:*

So this whole man 46
(That will not wind with every crooked way, 46a
Trod by the servile world) shall reele and fall b

47. purblind] *A;* blind borne *B.* 51. Euxine] *A, P;* Euxian *B.*

33.] i.e., pass it off as a complete man, although without a head.

34. *learning*] See Introduction, pp. xxiii–xxiv.

38. *full mann'd*] (1) fig., equipped with men (of a ship); (2) lit., invested with manly quantities: cf. *Odysses*, IX. 688–9, 'Of one Ulysses; who I thought was mand / With great and goodly personage' (cited in *O.E.D.*, s.v. *manned*, 8).

41. *virtuous*] of virtue. As this appears to be a nonce-use, it may derive from a play with 'potent—sometimes magical' (*O.E.D.*, s.v., 5, 6).

47. *purblind*] totally blind.

49–56.] from Seneca's *Agamemnon*, possibly via Comes: see Appendix B, p. 153.

49. *Lybian sands*] Lybia was all North Africa west of Egypt through to the Atlantic coast. Seneca referred to notorious sandbanks.

51. *Euxine*] the Black Sea (see I. i. 113–14).

(Near to the frosty Pole, where free Boötes
From those dark-deep waves turns his radiant Team)
Swell being enrag'd, even from their inmost drop—
As Fortune swings about the restless state
Of Virtue, now thrown into all men's hate.

Thunder. COMOLET'S Ghost *enters, and discovers* TAMYRA, *wrapped in a Canopy.*

Ghost. Revive those stupid thoughts, and sit not thus,

53. dark-deep] *A;* dark deep *B.* 54. Swell being . . . drop—] Swell being . . . drop, *A, P subs.;* Swell (being . . . drop) *B.* 56.1. *Thunder.*] *B; not in A.* 56.1–2. *Comolet's . . . Canopy*] *Intrat vmbra, Comolet to the Countesse, / wrapt in a Canapie A; Intrat Vmbra Frier, and discovers Tamyra B.* 57. *Ghost.*] *not in A.*
57–75.] *A; B reads:*

Frier. Up with these stupid thoughts, still loved daughter,
And strike away this heartlesse trance of anguish,
Be like the Sunne, and labour in eclipses,
Look to the end of woes: oh can you sit

---

52. *Boötes*] a northern constellation, represented as a man with a club in one hand, and two dogs leashed in the other.

54.] B's repunctuation may be deliberate, and right.

inmost drop] supposing the waves to be an effusion from the bottom of the sea; alternatively, it may mean that every drop swells, even the inmost one.

56.1–2.] 'wrapped in a Canopy', from A, presumably looks back to the end of v. i, where B has a similar phrase.

57–75.] B's version differs very considerably: the changes of form in prefixes to ll. 64 and 69, and in l. 74.1, suggest the use of MS. copy, though the reviser continues to be fussy about prefixes for some pages here. Parrott described the revision of ll. 57–60 as plainly superior in dramatic force, and Ure cited ll. 57b–c as obviously Chapman's. Of this I am not convinced, if Field is considered as a possible alternative. The deletion of l. 59 removes an effective reproof to Tamyra. On the other hand Ure, and even Parrott (with hesitation), suspected another hand in ll. 69a–f, replacing the characteristic ll. 71–4: Tamyra's new question calls attention to a weakness in the plot, which the Friar's reply does nothing to redeem. It is the more curious that the deleted lines express a Stoic doctrine on which Chapman laid increasing stress in his later work. Since B brings Monsieur and Guise on 'above' here, I assume that in A they remain there for the rest of the play in impressive silence (see Introduction, p. l).

57. *Revive*] restore from depression (*O.E.D.*, s.v., 7).

stupid] adj. from stupor; perhaps coloured by usual sense.

Gathering the horrors of your servant's slaughter
(So urg'd by your hand, and so imminent)
Into an idle fancy; but devise
How to prevent it; watch when he shall rise,
And with a sudden outcry of his murder,
Blow his retreat before he be engag'd.

Tam. O Father, have my dumb woes wak'd your death?
When will our human griefs be at their height?
Man is a tree, that hath no top in cares;
No root in comforts; all his power to live
Is given to no end, but t' have power to grieve.

Ghost. 'Tis the just curse of our abus'd creation,
Which we must suffer here, and 'scape hereafter:
He hath the great mind that submits to all
He sees inevitable; he the small

Mustering the horrors of your servants slaughter 58
Before your contemplation, and not study 60
How to prevent it? watch when he shall rise, 61
And with a suddaine out-crie of his murther, 62
Blow his retreat before he be revenged. 63

Tamyra. O Father, have my dumb woes wak'd your death? 64
When will our humane griefes be at their height? 65
Man is a tree, that hath no top in cares; 66
No root in comforts; all his power to live 67
Is given to no end, but have power to grieve. 68

Frier. It is the misery of our creation. Your true friend, 69
Led by your husband, shadowed in my weed, 69a
Now enters the dark vault.

Tamyr. But my dearest Father, b
Why will not you appeare to him your selfe, c
And see that none of these deceits annoy him. d

Frier. My power is limited, alas I cannot, e
All that I can doe—See the Cave opens. *Exit.* f

D'Amboys at the gulfe.

Tamyr. Away (my Love) away, thou wilt be murther'd. 75

Enter Monsieur and Guise above.

---

60. *idle fancy*] hallucination.
devise] consider.
63. *Blow . . . retreat*] i.e., like a bugle call.
engag'd] B's 'revenged' may be a slip of memory.
69. *abus'd*] misused, perverted.

That carps at earth, and her foundation-shaker,
And rather than himself, will mend his maker. *Exit.*

[BUSSY] D'AMBOIS [*appears*] *at the gulf.*

Tam. Away, my love, away, thou wilt be murder'd.
Buss. Murder'd? I know not what that Hebrew means:
That word had ne'er been nam'd had all been D'Ambois.
Murder'd? By heaven he is my murderer
That shews me not a murderer; what such bug
Abhorreth not the very sleep of D'Ambois?
Murder'd? Who dares give all the room I see
To D'Ambois' reach? or look with any odds
His fight i' th' face, upon whose hand sits death;
Whose sword hath wings, and every feather pierceth?
Let in my politic visitants, let them in,
Though ent'ring like so many moving armours;
Fate is more strong than arms, and sly than treason,
And I at all parts buckled in my Fate:

74. *Exit.*] *not in A.*
84.] *A; B adds:*
If I scape Monsieurs Pothecarie Shops,
Foutir, for Guises Shambles, 'twas ill plotted
They should have mall'd me here,
When I was rising, I am up and ready.
84c–d.] *lines ending:* rising, / ready. *P.* 86. armours;] armours. *Bo, P;* armours, *A, B.*

---

73. *foundation-shaker*] God; the epithet suggests Homeric descriptions of Poseidon, responsible for storms and earthquakes: see *Odysses*, v. 554, 'the great Earth-shaker'.

76. *Hebrew*] i.e., unintelligible language (cf. 'Greek' nowadays; *O.E.D.* not before 1705).

77.] because of his open honesty.

79. *bug*] bugbear.

84a–d.] These lines, effective in themselves, do not have any distinct 'theatrical purpose', and so might readily be accepted as Chapman's. Some doubt is cast by their proximity to so much reviser's work, and by their reference to Monsieur and Guise as vulgar plotters, where in A they are already silent presences moving from chorus-figures towards apotheoses as Death and Destiny (see Introduction, pp. xlix–l).

85. *politic*] i.e., murderers, as opposed to open killers.

88. *buckled*] as in armour.

Dare they not come?

Enter Murderers [*at one door*], *with* Friar [COMOLET'S Ghost] *at the other door.*

Tam. They come.
Murd. 1. Come all at once.
Ghost. Back coward murderers, back.
All. Defend us heaven.
Exeunt all but the first.
Murd. 1. Come ye not on?
Buss. No, slave, nor goest thou off.
Stand you so firm? Will it not enter here?
You have a face yet: so in thy life's flame
I burn the first rites to my mistress' fame. [*Kills him.*]
Ghost. Breathe thee brave son against the other charge.
Buss. O is it true then that my sense first told me?
Is my kind Father dead?
Tam. He is my love.
'Twas the Earl my husband in his weed that brought thee.
Buss. That was a speeding sleight, and well resembled.
Where is that angry Earl my Lord? Come forth
And shew your own face in your own affair;
Take not into your noble veins the blood
Of these base villains, nor the light reports

89. Dare they not come?] *A; B reads:*
Mons. Guise. Why enter not the coward villains?
D'Amb. Dare they not come?
89.1–2.] *B; not in A.* 90. *All.*] *Omn. A, B.* 90.1. *all but the first*] *B; not in A.* 100. Earl my Lord?] *A, B;* Earle? My lord! *Bo;* Earl? My lord, *P.*

89.1–2.] Line 90 implies that the ghost confronts the murderers head on, which seems the natural interpretation of 'at the other door', assuming a door on either side of the stage.
92. *Will . . . here*] Presumably the murderer is wearing armour.
95. *Breathe*] take breath, rest.
96. *sense*] used of any particular sense, here hearing.
99. *speeding*] effective.
well resembled] The resemblance was well made.

Of blister'd tongues, for clear and weighty truth:
But me against the world, in pure defence
Of your rare Lady, to whose spotless name
I stand here as a bulwark; and project
A life to her renown, that ever yet
Hath been untainted even in Envy's eye,
And where it would protect, a sanctuary.
Brave Earl come forth, and keep your scandal in:
'Tis not our fault if you enforce the spot,
Nor the wreak yours if you perform it not.

Enter MONTSURRY *with all the* Murderers.

Mont. Cowards, a fiend or spirit beat ye off?
They are your own faint spirits that have forg'd
The fearful shadows that your eyes deluded:
The fiend was in you; cast him out then thus—

[*He attacks;* BUSSY] D'AMBOIS *hath* MONTSURRY *down.*

Tam. Favour my Lord, my love, O favour him.
Buss. I will not touch him: take your life, my Lord,
And be appeas'd: *Pistols shot within.*
O then the coward Fates

113.1. *all the Murderers*] *B; others A.* 117.1.] *B; not in A.* 118. Favour my Lord, my love,] *Bo, P;* Fauour (my Lord) my loue, *A, B.* 120. *Pistols shot within.*] *B after 118; not in A.*

104. *blister'd tongues*] a common phrase for the slanderous.
107. *project*] (1) cause to jut out (like a bulwark); (2) throw away.
110. *it*] i.e., her renown.
112. *spot*] moral stain.
114. *spirit*] ghost; but commonly an evil spirit: see Marlowe's *Dr. Faustus*, 1616, l. 96: '*Enter the Angell and Spirit*' for 1604 '*Enter the good Angell and the evill Angell*' (ed. W. W. Greg, Oxford, 1950).
118.] Tamyra is obviously addressing Bussy: A's brackets (indicating vocative) were presumably misprinted and inadvertently copied in B.
Favour] spare.
120. Pistols shot within] presumably a marginal prompter's note, hence B's misplacing. D'Urfey has Monsieur and Guise shoot Bussy themselves, which may have been suggested to him by this note, plus a literal reading of ll. 124–5. That cannot have been Jacobean stage practice, even after the revision, I think.

Have maim'd themselves, and ever lost their honour.
Ghost. What have ye done slaves? irreligious Lord!
Buss. Forbear them, Father; 'tis enough for me
That Guise and Monsieur, Death and Destiny
Come behind D'Ambois: is my body then
But penetrable flesh? And must my mind
Follow my blood? Can my divine part add
No aid to th' earthly in extremity?
Then these divines are but for form, not fact:
Man is of two sweet courtly friends compact;
A mistress and a servant: let my death
Define life nothing but a Courtier's breath.
Nothing is made of nought, of all things made;
Their abstract being a dream but of a shade.
I'll not complain to earth yet, but to heaven,
And (like a man) look upwards even in death.
[And if Vespasian thought in majesty
An Emperor might die standing, why not I?
She offers to help him.
Nay without help, in which I will exceed him;
For he died splinted with his chamber-grooms.]
Prop me, true sword, as thou hast ever done:
The equal thought I bear of life and death,

137–40.] *B; not in A.* 138.1.] *B, at 141–2.*

129.] 'divines' means primarily 'souls' giving form to bodies, but not ensuring achievement ('fact' = deed). There seems also to be a satiric reference to 'divines' = priests. Bussy's despair echoes Monsieur's cynicism.

131. *A mistress and a servant*] passion and reason, or body and soul; in either case stressing the servility of the second term.

131–4. *let my death . . . shade*] echoing I. i. 18–19; see Appendix B, p. 154.

133.] 'of all things made' qualifies 'Nothing', and governs the next line. All things are assumed to be created from nothing; Bussy asserts that they equally come to nothing: the idea therefore that something substantial is achieved is only an illusion—a dream but of a shade.

134. *abstract*] epitome.

136. *like a man*] Man's upright posture was commonly interpreted emblematically as a unique ability to look up to heaven.

137–40.] It is hard to exclude lines of such obvious (and characteristic) quality. Their only weakness is that they duplicate the image in ll. 143–4.

140. *splinted*] supported, as if with splints.

Shall make me faint on no side; I am up
Here like a Roman statue; I will stand
Till death hath made me marble: O my fame
Live in despite of murder: take thy wings
And haste thee where the gray-ey'd Morn perfines
Her rosy chariot with Sabæan spices;
Fly, where the Evening from th' Iberian vales
Takes on her swarthy shoulders Hecate
Crown'd with a grove of oaks; fly where men feel
The burning axletree, and those that suffer
Beneath the chariot of the Snowy Bear:
And tell them all that D'Ambois now is hasting
To the eternal dwellers; that a thunder
Of all their sighs together (for their frailties
Beheld in me) may quit my worthless fall

143–4. up . . . statue;] *A, B;* up. . . . statue, *Bo, P subs.* 147. perfines] perfines, *A;* perfumes *B.*

143–4.] Boas's repunctuation seems unjustified; but no punctuation will indicate, what the rhythm suggests, that 'Here . . . statue' governs *both* 'I am up' *and* 'I will stand'.

147–55.] adapted from Seneca: see Appendix B, p. 150.

147. *perfines*] not in *O.E.D.*; it may be a coinage from medieval Latin *perfinio*=to finish absolutely, i.e. perfect (*O.E.D.* has *perfinish* in this sense in 1523). By analogy with 'finery', the intention here might be 'completes the adornment' (there is nothing analogous in Seneca). On the other hand, B's 'perfumes' makes obvious sense, and the words look alike; but it is difficult to see why the compositor of A should invent so unusual a word, whereas B may have been normalizing.

148. *Sabæan*] from the Yemen, celebrated for myrrh, aloes, cassia, etc.

150. *Hecate*] goddess of night, hell, witchcraft, etc.

151. *Crown'd . . . oaks*] I presume this to have been a common representation of Hecate, but have found no confirmation.

152. *burning axletree*] The astronomical 'axle' brings the sun nearest to the tropics.

153.] The Pole Star is in the constellation Little Bear: the Great Bear is more usually described as a chariot.

155–6. *thunder . . . together*] suggests Dante's entrance to Limbo in *Inferno*, IV. But see also Appendix B, p. 151.

157. *quit*] requite, balance.

worthless] (1) without value or significance; (2) not corresponding to my worth.

With a fit volley for my funeral.
Ghost. Forgive thy murderers.
Buss. I forgive them all;
And you my Lord, their fautor; for true sign
Of which unfeign'd remission, take my sword;
Take it, and only give it motion,
And it shall find the way to victory
By his own brightness, and th' inherent valour
My fight hath still'd into 't, with charms of spirit.
And let me pray you, that my weighty blood
Laid in one scale of your impartial spleen
May sway the forfeit of my worthy love
Weigh'd in the other: and be reconcil'd
With all forgiveness to your matchless wife.
Tam. Forgive thou me dear servant, and this hand
That led thy life to this unworthy end,
Forgive it, for the blood with which 'tis stain'd
In which I writ the summons of thy death:
The forced summons, by this bleeding wound,
By this here in my bosom: and by this

166. And] *Bus.* And *A;* Now *B.*

---

158. *fit volley*] i.e., military salute for a hero.

160. *fautor*] patron.

165. *fight*] fighting.

still'd] distilled (hence 'spirit').

166.] A has an unnecessary prefix '*Bus.*' here. There is no evidence of an omission between the two parts of Bussy's speech, and it seems more likely that the rest of the speech was an afterthought, to make Bussy beg Montsurry to forgive Tamyra, which he could scarcely do later. Line 171 could follow l. 165, when 'me' would get a natural and effective stress, whereas in the text Tamyra is required to stress 'thou', which is awkward.

weighty] by virtue of its worth.

167. *spleen*] various properties supposed to depend on the physical organ: here evidently courage, resolution, etc.

168. *forfeit*] penalty for crime.

171. *this hand*] i.e., which wrote her last invitation to Bussy (v. i. 169; and see IV. ii. 131–2).

175–8.] Tamyra, half-naked, holding up her bleeding hands, forms an emblem of the fallen woman, as Bussy sees it in l. 181.

That makes me hold up both my hands imbru'd
For thy dear pardon.
Buss. O, my heart is broken.
Fate, nor these murderers, Monsieur, nor the Guise,
Have any glory in my death, but this:
This killing spectacle: this prodigy:
My sun is turn'd to blood 'gainst whose red beams
Pindus and Ossa (hid in endless snow),
Laid on my heart and liver, from their veins
Melt like two hungry torrents: eating rocks
Into the Ocean of all human life,
And make it bitter, only with my blood:
O frail condition of strength, valour, virtue,
In me like warning fire upon the top
Of some steep beacon, on a steeper hill;

182. 'gainst] *A;* in *B.* 183–4. (hid . . . snow), . . . liver, from their veins] *this ed.;* (hid . . . snow . . . liuer; from their vains) *A, B;* (hid . . . snow . . . liver), from their veines *Bo, P subs.* 183. endless] *A;* drifts of *B.* 188. valour,] *D, Bo, P;* valure; *A, B.* virtue,] *A, P;* vertue *B.* 189–91. like . . . hill; . . . it] *this ed.;* (like . . . hill) . . . it: *A, B.*

---

177. *imbru'd*] stained with blood.

179.] either a catalogue of four distinct items, or else Bussy identifies Monsieur and Guise as *both* Fate *and* murderers.

180. *glory*] triumph; cause to boast (*O.E.D.*, s.v., 3).

181–91.] Jacquot quotes from the destruction of the world in *Revelations*, viii. 8–11, where a burning mountain falls into the sea and makes it bloody, and a falling star makes the sea bitter, poisoning mankind. It certainly looks as though reminiscence of this had coagulated with Seneca to make this passage. See Introduction, pp. xxxii–xxxiii, and Appendix B, p. 151.

183–4.] My punctuation derives from the possibility that the bracket in A after l. 184 was accidentally transferred from l. 183.

183. *Pindus and Ossa*] Pindus is a range of mountains in central Greece: but Seneca refers to it as a peak more than once in *Hercules Oetaeus*, along with Athos, Pelion, and Ossa; the Titans were buried under them all.

185–6. *eating . . . / Into*] perhaps comparable with 'eat in' = take into the mouth and consume (*O.E.D.*, s.v. *eat*, 15). This strong sense retains A's punctuation, and seems preferable to reading 'Melt . . . (eating rocks) / Into . . .'

189–93.] The mountain image is finally transposed, from a contrast of good or evil eminence, into one of achievement or mere futility.

189. *warning fire*] i.e., on the beacon: Bussy himself is now an emblem.

Made to express it like a falling star
Silently glanc'd—that like a thunderbolt
Look'd to have stuck, and shook the firmament. *He dies.*
Ghost. Son of the earth, whom my unrested soul
Rues t' have begotten in the faith of heaven
(Since thy revengeful Spirit hath rejected
The charity it commands, and the remission,
To serve and worship the blind rage of blood):
Assay to gratulate and pacify
The soul fled from this worthy by performing
The Christian reconcilement he besought

193. stuck,] stucke *A, B;* struck, *Bo.* *He dies.*] *Moritur. B; not in A.*
193.] *A; B adds from 268–74:*
Vmb. Frier. Farewell brave reliques of a compleat man. 193a(268)
Look up and see thy spirit made a starre, b(269)
Jove flames with her rules, and when thou set'st c(270)
Thy radiant forehead in the firmament, d(271)
Make the vast chrystall crack with thy receipt: e(272)
Spread to a world of fire, and the aged skie f(273)
Cheere with new sparks of old humanity. g(274)
193a.] *Pearson, Shepherd, Phelps, T, Spencer, insert 265–7; other eds. as B.*
193c.] *as B D.* 194. *Ghost.*] *Vmb. A; Frier. B.* 196–8.] *A; not in B.*
197. remission,] remission *A.* 198. worship] worship, *A.*

191–3.] perhaps from Euripides, via Plutarch: see Appendix B, p. 158.
191. *express*] represent emblematically.
192. *glanc'd*] (of weapons) glided off without sticking.
193. *stuck*] Parrott glossed 'pierced', citing 'Sticks' in v. ii. 46; but Ferguson (p. 18) showed that Chapman used the word for 'stop' or 'stay', so that here it refers to the permanent, as opposed to shooting, stars. See *Byron's Tragedy*, v. iii. 67, 'And lightning sticks 'twixt heaven and earth amaz'd'; also *Chabot*, I. ii. 153, *Caesar and Pompey*, III. i. 60. The sense is not far from that in II. i. 83, and Boas's emendation is quite unnecessary.
193a–g.] B inserts Comolet's epitaph here, without its prelude (ll. 265–7) which in A sums up the Montsurry-Tamyra dialogue before Comolet reverses Bussy's judgement of himself. Parrott's note 'these lines . . . constitute the closing speech in A' has misled some readers into supposing that ll. 194–264 were an addition in B. The misprints in l. 193c must derive from misread MS.; printed copy was resumed in l. 194 where the reviser altered instead of cancelling the prefix. See Introduction, p. lxii.
194. *Son of the earth*] stressing the base element which yields the humour 'blood' of l. 198.
195. *begotten*] as spiritual father.
199. *Assay*] attempt.
gratulate] recompense; please.

Betwixt thee and thy Lady, let her wounds
Manlessly digg'd in her, be eas'd and cur'd
With balm of thine own tears: or be assur'd
Never to rest free from my haunt and horror.
Mont. See how she merits this: still sitting by
And mourning his fall, more than her own fault.
Ghost. Remove, dear daughter, and content thy husband:
So piety wills thee, and thy servant's peace.
Tam. O wretched Piety, that art so distract
In thine own constancy; and in thy right
Must be unrighteous: if I right my friend
I wrong my husband: if his wrong I shun,
The duty of my friend I leave undone;
Ill plays on both sides; here and there, it riseth;
No place, no good so good, but ill compriseth;
My soul more scruple breeds, than my blood, sin,
Virtue imposeth more than any stepdame:
O had I never marry'd but for form,
Never vow'd faith but purpos'd to deceive:
Never made conscience of any sin,
But cloak'd it privately and made it common:
Nor never honour'd been, in blood, or mind;
Happy had I been then, as others are
Of the like licence; I had then been honour'd:

206. sitting] *A;* kneeling *B.* 216. place,] *Bo, P;* place: *A, B.* 217–18.] *A; not in B.*

---

203. *Manlessly*] inhumanly (apparently Chapman's word: he used the adj. in *Iliads*, IX. 164, 'manlesse crueltie').

206. *sitting*] B's 'kneeling' suggests a theatre change.

209.] Parrott conjectured that in the revised version the Friar should exit here: B has no direction.

210–15.] adapted from Seneca: see Appendix B, p. 151.

210. *distract*] pulling in different directions, divided; esp. of thoughts (*O.E.D.*, s.v., 1 and 3).

214. *duty*] due.

217–18.] There is no obvious reason for B's omission, except the rhythmic weakness of l. 218.

223. *honour'd*] (1) noble; (2) honourable.

225. *honour'd*] respected.

Liv'd without envy: custom had benumb'd
All sense of scruple, and all note of frailty:
My fame had been untouch'd, my heart unbroken:
But (shunning all) I strike on all offence—
O husband? dear friend? O my conscience!

Mont. I must not yield to pity nor to love
So servile and so traitorous: cease my blood
To wrestle with my honour, fame and judgement:
Away, forsake my house, forbear complaints
Where thou hast bred them: here 're all things full
Of their own shame and sorrow, leave my house.

Tam. Sweet Lord forgive me, and I will be gone,
And till these wounds, that never balm shall close
Till death hath enter'd at them (so I love them,
Being open'd by your hands) by death be cur'd,
I never more will grieve you with my sight:
Never endure that any roof shall part
Mine eyes and heaven: but to the open deserts
(Like to hunted tigers) I will fly:
Eating my heart, shunning the steps of men,

230. husband?] *A, B;* husband! *D, Bo, P.* friend?] *A, B;* friend! *D, Bo, P.* conscience!] *B;* conscience? *A.*
230.] *A; B adds:*

Mons. Come let's away, my sences are not proofe 230a
Against those plaints.— *Exeunt Guise, Mons.* b
D'Ambois is borne off.

235. here 're all things full] *P conj.;* heere all things full, *A;* here all things full, *B;* here [are] all things *P;* here all things [are] full *D, Bo.* 244. hunted tigers] *Shepherd;* hunted Tygres *A;* a hunted Tygres *B;* a hunted tigress *P.*

230a–b.] B's addition indicates how fully Monsieur and Guise have been brought into the action, and also confirms the deliberate intention to leave the end of the play to Montsurry and Tamyra, perhaps to link the play to its successor.

235–6. *here 're . . . house*] i.e., Tamyra must not intrude her shame and sorrow where there is already too much.

244. *Like to hunted tigers*] *O.E.D.* has 'tygres' as a common form of 'tigers' but never for 'tigress', so I take B's version to be a sophistication. For the construction, cf. *Teares of Peace*, l. 674, 'like to Spirits raisde . . .'.

245. *Eating my heart*] suffering from silent grief.

And look on no side till I be arriv'd.
Mont. I do forgive thee, and upon my knees
(With hands held up to heaven) wish that mine honour
Would suffer reconcilement to my love:
But since it will not, Honour, never serve
My Love with flourishing object till it starve:
And as this Taper, though it upwards look,
Downwards must needs consume, so let our love;
As having lost his honey, the sweet taste
Runs into savour, and will needs retain
A spice of his first parents, till (like life)
It sees and dies; so let our love: and lastly,
As when the flame is suffer'd to look up
It keeps his lustre: but, being thus turn'd down
(His natural course of useful light inverted)
His own stuff puts it out: so let our love

248. (With hands held up to heaven)] *Bo*, *P subs.;* With hands (held vp to heauen) *A*, *B*. 251. starve] sterue *A*, *B*. 261. love] *B;* love, *A;* love! *Bo*, *P*.

---

246. *be arriv'd*] be brought into port, i.e., death (see l. 19).

251. *starve*] die, not necessarily of hunger.

254–7.] another case where it is easier to grasp the total effect than define the modulating images. Boas and Parrott note that the candle image underlies all this—its wax, deriving from bees, retaining some savour of honey until it gives a final flare and goes out. But the particular choice of words directs attention on to the declining series of sweetness (first of love, then of all life), honey—taste—savour—spice (i.e., slight trace of smell, etc.); and finally the phrase 'first parents' (for the bees) also indicates Adam and Eve as the image ends in a generalized reference—'like life'—to the values of their story, and to original sin from which the escape is a final clarity of vision in the moment of death (hence the use of 'sees' for the shining of the candle). This idea of a moment of sight which is death may be implicit in Tamyra's l. 246. Cf. the association of the true Florimel in *The Faerie Queene*, III. i. 15–16, with a blazing star which 'importunes death and dolefull drerihed'.

261. *His ... out*] Parrott relates this to Grimestone's account of the death of Biron and D'Auvergne, where the same image occurs; since neither Grimestone nor his French source was in print when Chapman wrote *Bussy*, this must be coincidence.

so let our love] Boas's punctuation is more logical; but the rhetorical movement makes the text quite possible. Rhythmically, 'so let our love' is felt

Now turn from me, as here I turn from thee,
And may both points of heaven's straight axletree
Conjoin in one, before thyself and me.

Exeunt [MONTSURRY *and* TAMYRA] *severally.*

Ghost. My terrors are struck inward, and no more
My penance will allow they shall enforce
Earthly afflictions but upon myself:
Farewell brave relicts of a complete man:
Look up and see thy spirit made a star,
Join flames with Hercules: and when thou set'st
Thy radiant forehead in the firmament,
Make the vast continent, crack'd with thy receipt,

264. *Exeunt severally.*] *B; not in A.* 265–7.] *A; not in B.* 268–74.] *A; B at 193a–g.* 272. continent, crack'd] *this ed.;* continent, cracke *A;* chrystall crack *B.*

---

as going both with the line before *and* the one after. Boas makes 'Now turn from me' an imperative to Tamyra, which seems to me rhythmically awkward, divorced from the previous movement.

264. severally] i.e., through doors on opposite sides of the stage.

265–74.] See note on ll. 193a–g for B's placing of this speech.

265. *terrors*] acts causing terror.

268. *relicts*] remains.

complete] of persons, fully endowed, perfect (*O.E.D.*, s.v., 5). Cf. 'great men' in I. i. 6, etc.

269–74.] Hercules was burnt to death and became a star: for possible connections with Seneca, see Appendix B, pp. 152–2.

272. *continent*] (1) what contains (which is 'crack'd'); (2) what is contained (which 'spreads'); (3) the modern sense, latent in the progression 'continent'—'world'. B's 'chrystall' (of which the spheres were made) fits the reading 'cracke', and may derive from the reviser's puzzlement at the word 'continent': I suppose Chapman is thinking of the sphere of the moon, the outer bound of the corrupted elements since the Fall; Bussy's 'native noblesse' returning to man's pre-lapsarian communication with the heavens; hence ll. 273–4.

crack'd] A's 'cracke' following a comma is unintelligible; B's solution was to delete the comma, but I cannot see why the compositor should have introduced it in such an unlikely place; it is much easier to suppose that he misread 'crackd' as 'cracke', since final -e and -d are almost indistinguishable in early 17th-century handwritings. The consequences of my emendation are (a) that sense (2) of 'continent' becomes relevant; (b) that 'continent' and not Bussy becomes the subject of 'Spread', which seems more likely. The significance which Comolet attaches to Bussy's death is

Spread to a world of fire: and th' aged sky,
Cheer with new sparks of old humanity. [*Exit.*]

274.] *A, B add: Finis Actus Quinti & vltimi.*

---

not just that one man goes to heaven, but that in his example all mankind may see a—remote—hope of escape from the fallen world.

receipt] reception.

274. Exit] accompanying Bussy's body, presumably carried by attendants (perhaps the murderers, since no exit is provided for them). It is possible that Bussy lies on the inner stage, and curtains close at the end; but it is difficult to imagine all his last speeches delivered from there.

APPENDIX A

Prologue and Epilogue from the 1641 text

No one has ever suggested that these verses were Chapman's work. They are concerned to defend, rather apologetically, a revival of the play by the King's Men, presumably in the 1630's (and perhaps for the Court performance of 7 April 1634). Their significance for stage history, and the identity of the actors referred to, are discussed in Section 3 of the Introduction.

Prologue.

Not out of confidence that none but wee
Are able to present this Tragedie,
Nor out of envie at the grace of late
It did receive, nor yet to derogate
From their deserts, who give out boldly, that
They move with equall feet on the same flat;
Neither for all, nor any of such ends,
Wee offer it, gracious and noble friends,
To your review, wee farre from emulation
(And charitably judge from imitation)
With this work entertaine you, a peece knowne
And still beleev'd in Court to be our owne,
To quit our claime, doubting our right or merit,
Would argue in us poverty of spirit
Which we must not subscribe to: Field *is gone*
Whose Action first did give it name, and one
Who came the neerest to him, is denide
By his gray beard to shew the height and pride
Of D'Ambois *youth and braverie; yet to hold*
Our title still a foot, and not grow cold
By giving it o're, a third man with his best
Of care and paines defends our interest;
As Richard *he was lik'd, nor doe wee feare,*
In personating D'Ambois, *hee'le appeare*
To faint, or goe lesse, so your free consent
As heretofore give him encouragement.

Epilogue.

With many hands you have seene D'Ambois *slaine,*
Yet by your grace he may revive againe,
And every day grow stronger in his skill
To please, as we presume he is in will.
The best deserving Actors of the time
Had their ascents; and by degrees did clime
To their full height, a place to studie due
To make him tread in their path lies in you;
Hee'le not forget his Makers; but still prove
His thankfulnesse as you encrease your love.

FINIS.

APPENDIX B

Latin passages contributing to *Bussy D'Ambois*

(*a*) Seneca: *Hercules Oetaeus*; (*b*) Seneca: *Agamemnon*; (*c*) Virgil: *Aeneid*; (*d*) Virgil: *Georgics*; (*e*) Erasmus: *Adagia*; (*f*) Plutarch (Xylander): *Moralia*

Boas and Parrott noted the most striking passages which Chapman adapted; some others were added by Ferguson; but a far greater number were assembled by Schoell, who tried (unsuccessfully) to demonstrate that Chapman's poetry was a palimpsest of plagiaries. Recently a few more have been added by Jacquot, and I have myself re-examined Seneca's *Hercules Oetaeus*. Close verbal identity with any source is rare, and I have not found by any means all suggested parallels worth reproducing. Two works clearly were much in his mind when Chapman wrote *Bussy*: *Hercules Oetaeus* and Plutarch's *Moralia*. Parrott quoted Seneca in the Elizabethan translation, but it is immediately obvious that Chapman did not use this. Schoell tried to determine which Renaissance source Chapman was following for Plutarch, but they are all so dependent on each other that identification is doubtful. Thus Schoell ascribes several passages to both Erasmus and Plutarch; and his claim that the Plutarch came from Xylander's Latin version has been challenged by D. J. Gordon in 'Chapman's use of Cartari in the Fifth Sestiad of "Hero and Leander"' (*M.L.R.* XXXIX, 1944, 280–5). No alternative has yet been suggested for the passages in *Bussy*, so I have followed Schoell's quotations.

My translations make no pretence at elegance: they are designed to be as close a guide as possible to the Latin words whilst remaining (I hope) intelligible. Line-divisions can only be approximate.

(*a*) Seneca: *Hercules Oetaeus*

III. ii. 286–9. *H.Oe.*, ll. 233–6:

O quam cruentus feminas stimulat furor,
cum patuit una paelici et nuptae domus!

Scylla et Charybdis Sicula contorquens freta
minus timendae, nulla non melior fera est.

O how bloody a fury arouses women
when one home has been opened to a mistress as well as a wife!
Scylla and Charybdis whirling the Sicilian straits
are less terrifying, no wild beasts are not better.

[Chapman has greatly elaborated the imagery, and transferred the situation to the contrast of calm and passion in a woman who has her lover in her husband's home.]

v. i. 139–42. Ferguson suggests a coalescence of the shirt of Nessus with Dejanira's wish to be broken from a rock in *H.Oe.*, ll. 861–5. The connection is remote, but Tamyra's guilt is (oddly) apt to suggest Dejanira's, especially in her self-punishment in v. iii. 237–46, and the language is overall Senecan.

v. iii. 147–55. *H.Oe.*, ll. 1518–27:

O decus mundi, radiate Titan,
cuius ad primos Hecate vapores
lassa nocturnae levat ora bigae,
dic sub Aurora positis Sabaeis,
dic sub occasu positis Hiberis,
quique sub plaustro patiuntur ursae
quique ferventi quatiuntur axe,
dic sub aeternos properare manes
Herculem et regnum canis inquieti,
unde non umquam remeabit ille.

O glory of the universe, shining Titan [i.e. the sun],
at whose first warm airs Hecate
eases the tired mouths of her nocturnal horses,
tell the Sabaeans placed under Aurora [i.e. the dawn, or the east],
tell the Hiberians placed under the sunset [i.e. the west],
and those who suffer under the chariot of the bear [the great bear, i.e. the arctic],
and those who are harassed by the burning axletree [i.e. the tropics],
tell them that Hercules hastens down to the eternal spirits
and to the kingdom of the unresting dog,
whence he will never return.

[Unusually close, but far from literal translation. Chapman's 'dwellers' may derive from associating 'manes' (1525) with 'maneo'.]

v. iii. 155–6. *H.Oe.*, ll. 1544–5:

> . . . quem parem tellus genuit Tonanti.
> planctus immensas resonet per urbes . . .

> . . . he whom the earth brought forward as the equal of the thunderer [i.e. Jupiter].
> Let sighs resound through the immense cities . . .

[At most a distant recollection, associating 'thunder' with the resounding sighs.]

v. iii. 181 ff. *H.Oe.*, ll. 1308–10:

> emitte Siculo vertice ardentes, pater,
> Titanas in me, qui manu Pindon ferant
> Ossamque, qui me monte proiecto opprimant.

> send forth from the Sicilian peak, O father,
> the burning Titans on me, to seize Pindus in a hand
> and Ossa, to crush me by hurling a mountain.

[This passage shows why Chapman refers to Pindus instead of the more familiar Pelion; ll. 1152–4 also mention Pindus along with Athos, Pelion, and Ossa.]

v. iii. 210–15. *H.Oe.*, ll. 1027–30:

> o misera pietas! si mori matrem vetas,
> patri es scelestus; si mori pateris, tamen
> in matre peccas. urget hinc illinc scelus.
> inhibenda tamen est, verum ut eripiam scelus.

> O wretched loyalty ['filial piety']! if you forbid your mother to die
> you are criminal to your father; if you allow her to die, still
> you sin against your mother. Crime presses on both sides.
> But she must be checked, only so that I may tear her guilt from her.

[Chapman's adaptation of Hyllus' comments on Dejanira tends to confirm Ferguson's suggestion that Tamyra is related in his mind to Dejanira. 'O wretched Piety' is an interesting case of added meaning derived from pseudo-literal translation.]

v. iii. 269. *H.Oe.*, l. 1564:

> Sed locum virtus habet inter astra

> But virtue has a place among the stars

H.Oe., l. 1971:

virtus in astra tendit, in mortem timor.

Virtue tends towards the stars, fear towards death.

H.Oe., ll. 1570–1:

Quis erit recepto
tutus Alcide locus inter astra?

Which place among the stars will be safe
when Alcides has been received?

[The first two are only of general relevance; for the last, Jacquot suggests that 'recepto' may have suggested 'receipt' in l. 272; the lines are ambiguous, but if Chapman took them to imply aggression against the stars, that would certainly suggest 'crack'd' as well.]

v. iii. 270–4. *H.Oe.*, ll. 1707–10:

nube discussa diem
pande, ut deorum voltus ardentem Herculem
spectet; licet tu sidera et mundum neges,
ultro, pater, cogere . . .

the cloud dispersed, spread out the day,
that the eyes [countenances, foreheads] of the gods may see
the burning Hercules;
you may deny [me] the stars and the heavenly world,
but you will even be compelled [to accept me] . . .

[The connection is remote: but these lines from Hercules' final claim to be a star may, I think, have been re-created in Chapman's mind, perhaps unconsciously since the words have been regrouped without regard to Seneca's grammatical connections. Chapman's 'continent' could derive from the obstructive clouds which are 'cracked' to let the gods see Hercules; 'voltus' and 'ardentem' by position suggest 'radiant forehead' (which Chapman, like Seneca, uses for eyes); similarly 'sidera et mundum' could turn into 'world of fire'; the most literal rendering of 'pande' is 'spread'; and the defiant 'cogere' suggests the force of 'Make . . .' in l. 272. This may be far-fetched: I offer it as a possible instance of radical recreation at the opposite extreme from the close translation in v. iii. 147–55. (This implies no reflection on Chapman's Latinity.)]

(*b*) Seneca: *Agamemnon*

V. iii. 49–56. *Agam.*, ll. 64–72:

According to Schoell, in his early poems Chapman drew freely from Comes, *Mythologiae*; it therefore seems likely that, for this single passage from the *Agamemnon*, he used the extract which Comes prints, Lib. IV, Cap. ix:

Non sic Libycis Syrtibus aequor
Furit alternos volvere fluctus,
Non Euxini turget ab imis
Commota vadis unda, nivali
Vicina [polo],[1] ubi caeruleis
Immunis aquis lucida versat
Plaustra Bootes.
Ut praecipites Regum casus
Fortuna rotat!

Not so the sea on the Lybian Syrtes [sandbanks]
Rages to tumble its waves one after another,
Not so, excited from its deepest waters,
Swells the wave of the Euxine sea,
Near to the snowy pole, where free
From the dark-blue waters[2] Boötes turns
His shining wagons—
As Fortune swings about
The headlong lots of kings.

[Chapman seems to misunderstand the point about Boötes, and so gives 'free' a moral force, which combines with his substitution of 'Virtue' for 'kings' to make a characteristic allegorical stress.]

(*c*) Virgil: *Aeneid*

II. i. 94–101. *Aeneid*, II. 626–31:

Ac veluti summis antiquam in montibus ornum
Cum ferro accisam crebrisque bipennibus instant
Eruere agricolae certatim: illa usque minatur
Et tremefacta comam concusso vertice nutat,
Volneribus donec paulatim evicta supremum
Congemuit traxitque iugis avolsa ruinam.

And just as on the high mountains the foresters
Press emulously on to root up an ancient ash

[1] The edition of Comes I have used omits *polo*, presumably a printer's error.

[2] i.e., Boötes never goes below the horizon, into the sea.

Cut with the iron, and by repeated axe-blows; for a long time it stands menacingly upright
And trembling, its head violently shaken, it nods to and fro its locks [foliage]
Until, little by little overcome by its wounds, it has groaned
Its last and, torn away from the ridge, it has come crashing down.

[Some verbal suggestions seem to lie here; but the simile is common; it is used with an oak in *Aeneid*, IV. 441–6, and also in Seneca, *Hercules Oetaeus*, ll. 1623–30, but neither offers any detailed similarity.]

(*d*) Virgil: *Georgics*

IV. i. 109. *Georgics*, II. 325:

Tum pater omnipotens fecundis imbribus Aether . . .

Then Aether, almighty father, with his fruitful rains . . .

[Virgil's line is closely imitated from Lucretius, I. 220, and Chapman may derive from either.]

(*e*) Erasmus: *Adagia*

I. i. 18–19, V. iii. 131–4. *Adagia*, II. iii. 48:

Homo Bulla

Pindarus vicit etiam Homericam similitudinem: ut qui hominem non frondes, sed umbrae somnium vocarit. Locus est in Pythiis hymno 8 . . . id est, Diurni, Quid autem aliquis ? Quid autem nullus ? Umbrae somnium homo. Nihil inanius umbra. . . Sophocles item in Aiace: . . . id est, Nil aliud ab umbra atque flatus est homo . . .

Man a Bubble

Pindar outdoes also the Homeric similitude: where he called man not leaves, but of a shadow, a dream. The context is in the Pythian Ode 8 . . . that is, creatures of a day, What is anybody ? What on the other hand is nobody ? A dream of a shadow is man. There is nothing emptier than a shadow. . . Sophocles likewise in the *Ajax*: . . . that is, Nothing but shadow and winds is man . . .

[Erasmus gets this from Plutarch, and Schoell gives both; I have chosen Erasmus because 'sed umbrae' may have suggested 'but of a shadow', and 'breath' in V. iii. 132 may come from 'flatus'.]

I. i. 33. *Adagia*, I. v. 76:

In Portu Impingere

Est apud Quintilianum in Institutionibus: In Portu impingere.

To wreck in Port

This is in Quintilian, in the *Institutions*: to wreck [his boat] in Port.

[No other detail is verbally relevant.]

(*f*) Plutarch: *Moralia*

I. i. I. 97C: *De Fortuna*

Vitam regit fortuna, non sapientia.

Of Fortune

Fortune, not wisdom, rules life.

[This comes from Chaeremon, via Cicero, *Tusc. Disp.*, V. 25, which may be Chapman's source.]

I. i. 6–17. 779F: *Ad Principem ineruditem*

Sed plerique principum atque regum ob amentiam imitantur imperitos statuarios, qui putant magnos ac validos visum iri colossos, si eos admodum divaricatis cruribus, distentosque & hiantes fingant. Sic enim & ipsi vocis gravitate, & vultus torvitate, morumque importunitate, & aversatione convictus videntur maiestatem imperij prae se ferre: nihil omnino differentes a colossicis istis, statuis, quae foris heroica aut divina ornatae forma, intus terra, lapidibus, & plumbo sunt repleti [*sic*].

To an uneducated Ruler

But most rulers and kings because of folly imitate unskilful sculptors [statuaries], who think their colossi will seem to be great and powerful, if they form them with widely spread out legs, and muscles straining, and mouths agape. For thus they fancy that they, with gravity of voice, with grimness of countenance, and with insolence of manners, and hostility to friendship, display the dignity of sovereignty: not in any way different from those colossic statues, which are furnished externally with a heroic and divine form, within are filled with earth, stones, and lead.

[Exceptionally close translation.]

I. i. 59–81. 1128B, 1129B, C:

An recte dictum sit, Latenter esse vivendum

Ego autem

"Odi sapientem, qui ipsus non sapit sibi."

Philoxenum Eryxidis F. & Gnathonem Siculum obsoniorum nimia cupiditate impulsos, narium sordes emungere in patinas solitos ferunt, ut aliis ab edendo deterritis ipsi soli implerentur propositis cibis. Atque sic etiam isti nimio gloriae studio repleti, gloriam apud alios traducunt tanquam rivales suos, ut ipsi ea absque certamine potiri possint. . .

Cur vivens ignorari velit? . . . Si Themistocles Atheniensibus ignotus fuisset, non repulissent Graeci Xerxem: si Camillus Romanis, periisset Roma: si Dioni Plato, non fuisset liberata Sicilia. Nimirum sic sentio: sicut lumen non manifestos tantum nos, sed & utiles invicem facit: ita noticia non gloriam modo, sed & agendi materiam virtutibus parari. Epaminondas quidem ad quadragesimum usque annum obscurus, nihil profuit Thebanis: postmodo cognitus & rebus praefectus, patriam pessum euntem servavit, Graeciamque servitute liberavit, in fama tanquam luce virtutem apto tempore efficacem praebens.

> Namque aeris instar quod longo post tempore
> Usu refulget attritum, virtus viri
> Comperta splendet actionibus probis.

ut est apud Sophoclem.

Whether it was rightly said, one ought to live in obscurity

But for myself

"I hate the man of wisdom who isn't wise for his own good."

They say Philoxenus son of Eryxis and Gnatho the Sicilian, impelled by excessive greed for delicacies, were accustomed to wipe out the dirt from their noses on to the dishes, so that others should be deterred from eating and they alone could fill up with the foods provided. And so also with those filled with too great a devotion to glory, they traduce the glory of others as if [they were] their rivals, so that they themselves can possess it without competition. . .

Why should a living man wish to be unknown? . . . If Themistocles had been unknown to the Athenians, the Greeks would not have repulsed Xerxes: if Camillus to the Romans, Rome would have been destroyed: if Plato to Dion, Sicily would not have been liberated. Thus, without doubt, do I feel: just as light not only makes us visible, but also useful in turn: so being known not only makes for glory, but also provides our virtues with the matter for action. Epaminondas indeed, obscure right up to his fortieth year, profited nothing to the Thebans: afterwards when he was well-known and a governor, he saved his country when it faced disaster, and freed Greece from slavery, in fame, as if in limelight, exhibiting his virtue, powerful at the proper time.

> For like bronze which has been worn in use a long
> time

shines; so the known virtue of man
shines in honourable deeds—

as Sophocles has it.

[Chapman omits Plutarch's original moral, gives only a brief summary of the first paragraph, and joins it to a fuller and closer rendering of the rest, adding a sentence from the life of Camillus, omitting Plato and Dion, and transferring 'sicut lumen . . . virtutibus parari' to combine it with the gist of Sophocles' image at the end.]

I. i. 132–3. 801C:

Praecepta gerendae reipublicae

Neque tamen propterea ita negligenda est orationis elegentia ac facultas, ut omnia virtuti adscribantur, sed ut non opificem persuasionis censeamus esse rhetoricam, adiutricem tamen sentiamus, corrigamusque illud Menandri,

Mores movent dicentis, haud oratio.

Precepts of Statecraft

However, the elegance and capability of eloquence should not therefore be so far neglected, that everything is ascribed to virtue, but so far as for us to hold rhetoric to be not the creator of persuasion, but rather to judge it to be its assistant, and to correct this saying of Menander:

The speaker's morals move in speaking, not his eloquence.

III. i. 50–2. 75F:

Quomodo quis suos in virtute paranda sentire possit profectus

Enimvero recte dictum est,

Applicandus lapis amussi, non ad lapidem amussis est.

At Stoici non sua rebus accomodatantes decreta sed res ad decreta sua, cum quibus consentire eas natura non sinit, detorquentes, multis difficultatibus philosophiam impleverunt.

How a man may become aware of his progress in Virtue

Certainly it has been rightly said,

The stone must be laid to the line, not the line to the stone.

But the Stoics, not accommodating their principles to facts, but twisting facts to their principles, with which Nature does not suffer them to fit, have filled philosophy with many difficulties.

[Erasmus quotes this proverb from Plutarch with his own comment; but Ferguson traces it back to Aristotle, *Ethics*, v. 10, where the Latin version includes 'naturae rerum', perhaps more likely to suggest 'th' whole work of Nature' (l. 47) than either Plutarch or Erasmus.]

III. i. 92–3. 655A: *Symposiacon*, liber III

Porro autem Homerus neminem heroum vel cum uxore vel cum pellice concumbentem fecit: Paridem duntaxat a pugna profugum in gremium se abducere Helenae scribit: non mariti, sed adulteri rabiosi diurnum coitum ostendens esse.

Symposium, book III

But furthermore Homer depicts no hero lying either with his wife or his concubine [by day]: except that he writes of Paris fleeing from the fight and hiding himself away in Helen's embrace: thus showing that coitus in the daytime is not with a husband but with a violent lover [adulterer].

[Homer (*Iliad*, III. 383 ff.) makes Helen object to Paris' cowardice, not to daytime coitus, which may be why Xylander omits Plutarch's 'by day' in the first sentence; Schoell reads 'diuturnum coitum' (lasting union), but later editions of Xylander which I have seen read (correctly) 'diurnum'. Plutarch seems to be the origin of this quaint notion, and the Greek is quite unambiguous in its objection to any coition in daytime.]

V. iii. 191–3. 1090C:

Non posse suaviter vivi secundum Epicteti decreta

Est enim, inquit Hippocrates, ad summum progressa corporis bona affectio periculosa. Et Euripides ille,

Modo qui vigebat carne coelitus vel ut
Delapsa stella exstinctus est.

That it is not possible to live pleasurably by following the precepts of Epictetus

For, said Hippocrates, the good condition of the body when it has reached its peak is precarious. And Euripides has,

He who was flourishing in the flesh just now, just like
A star fallen from heaven, is extinguished.

[Plutarch has Euripides' lines also in 416D, but Hippocrates' saying suggests 'O frail condition of strength', etc.]

APPENDIX C

Printer's Corrections in the Quartos

I have collated all copies that I know of in the British Isles; there are, however, several copies of both quartos in the U.S.A. which I have not seen.

A 1607–8: copies collated:

British Museum	C.34.c.12 (1607)
	Ashley 375 (1607)
	644.d.41 (1608)
Victoria and Albert Museum	Dyce 2034 (1608) [autographed Lew: Theobald]
Bodleian Library, Oxford	Mal.240(8) [title page below 'at Paules' missing; head titles cropped throughout; last sheet defective; otherwise text complete]
	Mal.Add.787 (1607) [sheet G wrongly folded, yielding the sequence: G2, G2v, G1, G1v, G4, G4v, G3, G3v]
Worcester College, Oxford	Plays 4.31 (1608)

Although there are a few consistent variants of replaced type, etc., there is no evidence of proof-correction during printing; either proof sheets were run off before printing began, or no correction was undertaken.

B 1641: copies collated:

Pepys Library, Magdalene College, Cambridge		(1641)
British Museum	C.12.g.5	(1641)
	644.d.42	(1641)
	644.d.43	(1646)
	644.d.44	(1657)
Gonville and Caius College, Cambridge		(1641)
Victoria and Albert Museum	Dyce 2035	(1641)
	Forster 1528	(1657) [A4 missing]

Bodleian Library, Oxford	Mal.Q.1(9)	(1641)
	Mal.163(7)	(1641) [C1 & K2 cropped]
Trinity College, Cambridge		(1641) [K4 missing]
Eton College		(1641) [several sheets cropped]
Worcester College, Oxford	Plays 3.6(A)	(1641)
National Library of Scotland	Bute 81	(1641) [acquired 1956; a copy recorded in *Wing* was stolen in the 1880's]

Clear evidence of correction appears on approximately half of the formes. Uncorrected readings usually show dependence on 1607–8; the corrector clearly used intelligence at times, but I cannot be sure he ever consulted copy.

Index to Annotations

An asterisk before a word indicates information which supplements or corrects that given in *O.E.D.*